MARK TWAIN: CRITICAL STUDY

Encyclopaedia of World Great Novelists Series

MARK TWAIN

A Critical Study

Edited by

Robert Hudson

Edwin Arnold

ANMOL PUBLICATIONS PVT. LTD.

NEW DELHI - 110 002 (INDIA)

ANMOL PUBLICATIONS PVT. LTD.
4374/4B, Ansari Road, Daryaganj
New Delhi - 110 002
Ph.: 23261597, 23278000
Visit us at: www.anmolpublications.com

Mark Twain: A Critical Study

First Published, 2005

ISBN 81-261-2062-2

PRINTED IN INDIA

Published by J.L. Kumar for Anmol Publications Pvt. Ltd., New Delhi - 110 002 and Printed at Mehra Offset Press, Delhi.

Contents

Preface

Samuel Clemens, more commonly known as Mark Twain was born in Florida, Missouri on Nov. 30, 1835. He held many different jobs during his lifetime. Among them, a reporter, a publisher, and a riverboat pilot. In 1862 Sam began writing for many magazines and newspapers under the pen name of Mark Twain, a name taken from a riverboat term. Twain was a great writer, his three best books *were Roughing It, The Adventures of Tom Sawyer,* and *The Adventures of Huckleberry Finn.* His books sold many copies. One of his books, *A Tramp Abroad* sold 25,000 copies. The year he was born, Halley's Comet passed over. Twain vowed that he would not die until he saw the famous comet.

Mark Twain was great even during his lifetime. He had many jobs that gave him a good education and varied experiences with many kinds of people. Something else that helped him achieve greatness in the world was that he was determined. He set goals to write his books and set many goals to write magazine articles, newspaper articles and other types of articles. A third thing that helped him achieve greatness was that he had perseverance. That quality helped him write books because he kept on trying to think of varied ways to write his stories and articles. Finally, Mark Twain learned from his experiences. He learned early on that his readers liked different writing styles. He didn't disappoint them when he wrote his humor, satire, and adventure. If his books got bad ratings, he would know not to try something different. Some of his characteristics were integrity, sense-of-humor, and initiative. Mark Twain's personality was funny, out-going, and cooperative. His humorous and insightful remarks were often quoted around the world, both then and now. Mark Twain will be remembered and quoted for a long time.

"A lie can travel halfway around the world while the truth is still putting on its shoes."

This book gives a vivid account of his life events and critique of his literary works by various commentators on him. Certainly this will be useful and informative for students, researchers and teachers besides the general readers.

—Editors

1

Mark Twain: An Overview

Mark Twain remains to this day America's most picturesque literary figure. He still keeps his hold on the public mind, a hold so secure that few are the days when one does not somewhere see his name in print, or hear someone remark, "As Mark Twain said," even if it be but to repeat that apocryphal comment on the weather. Perhaps a part of his appeal to the mass-imagination lies in the fact that he himself was the embodiment of what many cherish as "the American dream": from commonplace beginnings he had struggled up to a towering, dazzling fame, to stand, as he himself once said of Daniel Webster, "for a single, splendid moment on the Alps of fame, outlined against the sun."

Although the splendid moment of his fame is still prolonged and extends immeasurably far into the future, that fame was only a small part of his power. There was something about him that moved people who knew nothing of his renown, who did not even know who he was. Mark Twain's personality was of a sort that compelled those about him so strongly that wherever he went, as his biographer Albert Bigelow Paine said, he seemed a being from another planet, a visitant from some remote star.

It was a matter of pride to him that he was born when Halley's comet hung in the night sky. He "came in with it," he said, and he confidently expected to "go out with it." And he did, although he did not know, as he lay on his deathbed, that it was again shining in the heavens. Life was always marking him out for unusual adventures which occurred at moments of dramatic effect. He was dynamic, irrepressible, unpredictable; and he was irrefutably a genius.

What Manner of Man was Mark Twain?

Born in Florida, Missouri, on November 30, 1835, "Little Sam" was "a wild-headed, impetuous child of sudden ecstasies," who was constantly running away in the direction of the river and, as he later wrote, was "drowned nine times in Bear Creek and was suspected of being a cat in disguise"; a vividly imaginative child, who loved the companionship of the good-natured slaves and visited the Negro quarters beyond the orchard as a place of ineffable enchantment; a child whose sympathy included all inanimate things; a child who, Paine said, "pitied the dead leaf and the murmuring dried weed of November" because for them the summer was over forever; a child who, Van Wyck Brooks remarked, was "to retain through life that exquisite sensibility of which so many have spoken."

At the age of nine Sam Clemens "grew up" and became the leader of his boy companions, roving the hills and woods around Hannibal and yielding unreservedly to the fascinations of the Mississippi. He had a thatch of light, sandy hair, which he vainly tried to keep from curling, keen blue-gray eyes, a delicate complexion, and a winning smile. His slow, measured way of speaking — "Sammy's long talk," his mother called it-had an arresting quality even then; Paine tells us that, although Sam's mental attainments were not highly regarded and he did not talk much, "for some reason, whenever he did speak every playmate in hearing stopped and listened."

As a young man he was slender and loose-limbed, with a great tangle of hair which had deepened from sandy into the rich, mahogany tone called auburn. He could drum on piano or guitar, singing songs in a pleasant tenor voice; and his frank nature and the jokes he told in his slow, quaint fashion made him a general favorite. By the time he was twenty-one, some unusual quality of his mind or heart was making itself felt: when Horace Bixby took him on to "learn the river," the last thing Bixby wanted at that time was a "cub pilot." But he yielded to something in young Sam Clemens.

At twenty-three, a full-fledged pilot on the *City of Memphis*, "the largest boat in the trade," Sam dressed in dandified fashion in blue serge, white duck, fancy shirts, and patent leathers. He wrote to his older brother Orion about feasting at a French restaurant in New Orleans, "dissipating on a ten-dollar dinner-breathe it not to Ma!" He confessed to Orion that he derived "a *living* pleasure" and "a stern joy" from showing off a bit before the young pilots, then unemployed, who had once told him patronizingly that he could never "learn the river." But, employed and unemployed, the pilots of St. Louis and New Orleans regularly gathered around him when he began spinning his yarns and telling the droll tales which convulsed his hearers while his own face remained perfectly sober.

Three years later he accompanied Orion Clemens west when Orion was appointed territorial secretary of Nevada. They arrived in Carson City in August, 1861, and Sam Clemens soon became a conspicuous figure on the Carson streets. No longer a dandy, he was then fashionable in the Western mode; clad in old slouch hat, flannel shirt, and rough trousers half in and half out of heavy cowhide boots, he had become, in Paine's phrase, a paragon of disarray. His bushy head of auburn hair, his piercing eyes, and his lounging gait drew the instant attention of strangers and made them turn for a second look, followed by quick inquiries about his identity. Carson City citizens who saw him leaning for hours at a time against a corner awning, smoking a clay pipe and watching the human motley of the Plaza, did not prophesy much for his future; but at night those same citizens clustered about the stove in Orion's office to hear him tell river yarns in his inimitable drawl.

When he had temporarily abandoned the study of human nature to succumb to the Western mining mania, he once sought diversion from the discomforts of a winter cabin and the disappointments of a miner's life by attending a dance in the mining camp of Aurora. His behavior there, recorded by an onlooker, shows his characteristic ability to lose himself in the present moment. "In changing partners, whenever he saw a hand raised he would grasp it with great pleasure and sail off into another set, oblivious to his surroundings. Sometimes he would act as though there was no use in trying to go right or to dance like other people, and with his eyes closed he would do a hoedown or a double-shuffle all alone, talking to himself and saying that he never dreamed there was so much pleasure to be obtained at a ball. It was all as natural as a child's play. By the second set, all the ladies were falling over themselves to get him for a partner, and most of the crowd, too full of mirth to dance, were standing or sitting around, dying with laughter."[1] He was an innate actor, of course. Although his natural personality had a magnetic quality, he frequently reinforced nature with art, and by his manner and voice secured the effects he desired to make on others.

In August, 1862, the disgruntled seeker after gold abandoned mining to become a reporter and feature writer on the *Territorial Enterprise*, the leading newspaper of

Virginia City, Nevada. Early in 1863 Joseph Goodman, editor of the *Enterprise*, sent Sam Clemens up to Carson City to report the doings of the territorial legislature. With this added dignity, he once more became a fashion plate, arraying himself in a long broadcloth coat, a starched shirt, and polished boots. His biographer described him during the period of his newspaper work on the Comstock as "high-strung and neurotic," with a highly organized nervous system that made him an easy prey to the tortures of noisemakers and practical jokers. Many were the jokes played on him in the Far West, mostly designed to draw forth an exhibition of his profanity; but, then and throughout his life, he was never able to appreciate fully a joke played on himself.

His performance in profanity seems to have been billed as a stellar attraction first in the West. When he was blowing off steam by swearing, it was his custom to begin a slow, circular walk, a habit earlier acquired within the confines of the pilothouse, and then his "rotary denunciations" were something both to hear and to see. An eyewitness, W.H. Rideing, described the spectacle thus: "When anger moved him, you could see his lean figure contract and his eyes ominously screw themselves into their sockets. Every fibre in him quivered, and for the moment his voice became acid and sibilant and out of tune-almost a whine. Then he would let himself out in a break like that of a dam unable to hold the flood, in language as candid and unshrinking as the vernacular of the Elizabethans." The change in voice became less noticeable with the years; finally he seems to have conducted these profane interludes in the same beautiful speaking voice that was his by nature. Upon his remarkable gift of phrase he had overlaid refinements gathered first from the printing office, later from the river, and finally from the mining camp. According to Paine, "To hear him denounce a thing was to experience the fierce, searching delight of galvanic waves . . . And somehow his profanity was seldom an offense. His selection of epithet was always dignified and stately, from whatever source -and it might be from the Bible or the gutter . . . Mark Twain's profanity . . . seemed, in fact, the safety-valve of his high-pressure intellectual engine. When he had blown off he was always calm, gentle, forgiving, and even tender." Katy Leary, a servant in his home for thirty years, insisted that his swearing "never seemed really bad" to her: "It was . . . a part of him, somehow. Sort of amusing it was and gay — not like real swearing, 'cause he swore like an angel." And Katy related that when Baby Jean, Mark Twain's youngest daughter, was shocked at hearing a man swear in the street and was reminded that she had often heard her father swear, she replied gravely: "Oh, no Katy! You're mistaken. That wasn't swearing. That was only one of papa's *jokes!*" The deliberate quality of his profanity was accented by Miss Elizabeth Wallace, who had occasionally heard him holding forth in the privacy of the billiard room: "Gently, slowly, with no profane inflexion of voice, but irresistibly as though they had the head-waters of the Mississippi for their source, came this stream of unholy adjectives and choice expletives." Howells underscored the lofty effect of Mark Twain's swearing by calling it his "pious profanity."

His eyes, his splendid head, his hands, his voice, and his walk were the features that most impressed his acquaintances. Bret Harte described him as he was upon their first meeting in San Francisco: "His head was striking. He had . . . the aquiline nose, and even the aquiline *eye*-an eye so eagle-like that a second lid would not have surprised me-of an unusual and dominant nature."

Leaving Nevada and the *Enterprise* in May, 1864, Mark Twain had gone to San Francisco to do newspaper work. From March to July, 1866, he was in the Sandwich (Hawaiian) Islands, and upon his return he launched himself in a new profession, one which displayed him in some of the most brilliant aspects of his career. In October, 1866, he delivered in San Francisco his first public lecture, "The Sandwich Islands", beginning a series in California and Nevada; and in May, 1867, he gave his first lecture in New York City. He was chary of appearing before strangers, but he found that the Eastern audience responded as eagerly to his odd, quaint style as had his old friends in the West. He loved to sway his hearers by his oral art; and forty years later, recalling how that New York audience had laughed and shouted, he remembered, "For an hour and fifteen minutes I was in paradise." His personal power he had carried with him from the West to the East.

On June 8, 1867, he sailed on the *Quaker City* on the excursion which resulted in *The Innocents Abroad*. On board, he was described by Mrs. A. W. Fairbanks, one of his first literary critics, who wrote: ". . . all eyes are turned toward Mark Twain. . . . Sitting lazily at the table, scarcely genteel in his appearance, there is something, I know not what, that interests and attracts." That this quality was present in him even in those early days is attested more forcibly still by a curious fact. When the *Quaker City* lay in the harbor of Yalta, the Emperor of Russia decided to pay a visit to the American ship. There was a perfect furor of preparation on board. A committee was appointed to draft an address of welcome to the Emperor; and from the ministers, educators, and prominent people among the passengers, Mark Twain was elected chairman and commissioned to write the entire address. That the important task of welcoming the Czar of all the Russias was entrusted to one recently known to fame as "The Wild Humorist of the Pacific Slope" is significant. Significant, too, is the fact that Mark Twain accepted the task without qualms and without apparent self-consciousness.

Among the *Quaker City* passengers was Dr. W.F. Church, an orthodox deacon who thought Mark Twain irreverent, profane, and therefore sinful. Years later, Church paradoxically summed up his impressions, formed at this time: "He was the worst man I ever knew. And the *best*." Mark Twain, it appears, attracted ministers particularly. They seemed to love him, though they did not always approve of him. He once wrote characteristically to his mother that he was "as thick as thieves" with various ministers and added: "I am running on preachers now altogether, and I find them gay." Henry Ward Beecher sought his acquaintance, and the Reverend Joseph Twichell of Hartford was his closest friend for forty years and more.

When the travelers had returned from the Holy Land, Elisha Bliss of the American Publishing Company wrote to Mark Twain suggesting a book to be compiled from the *Quaker City* letters. Mark Twain went to Hartford for an interview with the publisher. Bliss, who had been eager to meet him, was disappointed in what he saw. Mark Twain's traveling clothes, says Paine, were "neither new nor neat, and he was smoking steadily a pipe of power." But when this strange visitor began to talk, Bliss fell a victim to his charm, invited him to stay at the Bliss home, and decided that personally Mark Twain was even greater than the sought-after letters.

Certainly, when Mark Twain first settled in the East, he was heretical towards most of the conventions of the polite society of that day. This heresy was no more noticeable in his clothes than in his speech, which was frequently brilliant and occasionally startling. The latter quality is illustrated by the remark he made in the sedate offices of the *Atlantic Monthly* at his first meeting with William Dean Howells. Howells had written a review praising *The Innocents Abroad*, and Mark Twain called and delivered his thanks in these words: "When I read that review of yours, I felt like the woman who was so glad that her baby had come white."

From that first meeting dated a friendship that lasted more than forty years. Howells was always his closest friend, next to the clergyman Joe Twichell. The Westernisms of the frontier still clung to him in those early years. When Thomas Bailey Aldrich took Mark Twain home with him one evening, Mrs. Aldrich did not invite the visitor to dinner because she thought him drunk; he "showed marked inability to stand perpendicular, . . . swayed from side to side, and had also difficulty with his speech; he did not stammer exactly, but after each word he placed a period." This was Mark Twain's natural manner, which he never lost; some of his rough edges, however, were polished away in a process of attrition against Eastern customs. In commenting on Mark Twain's "sealskin coat, with the fur out," worn then to gratify his love of strong effect, Howells said that in spite of Mark Twain's own warmth in it, it "sent the cold chills through me when I once accompanied it down Broadway, and shared the immense publicity it won him." His down-tilted hat and up-tilted cigar were a common sight on the streets, where, no doubt, he came and went on a wave of lifted eyebrows. But even in those days he was conventionally attired for his evening lectures and had already carried his art on the platform to the point where it was probably, as Paine called it, "the purest exemplification of the platform entertainer's art which this country has ever seen. It was the art that makes you forget the artisanship." In later years Howells declared, "He was the most consummate public performer I ever saw, and it was an incomparable pleasure to hear him lecture." When H.R. Haweis went to hear him, not knowing what to expect, he was rather disappointed; yet Haweis himself gave testimony to Mark Twain's spell by relating his surprise when his watch told him he had sat listening for an hour. It had seemed no more than ten minutes, at most.

In 1872, Mark Twain paid his first visit to England, and the intellectual aristocracy of that country took him to their hearts at once. He was "shy as a girl" at first, when he found the great of London ready to pay him homage. Van Wyck Brooks remarked that he was not gulled in England as Joaquin Miller had been, "because the beautiful force of his natural personality would have commanded attention anywhere." In England, said Howells, "rank, fashion, and culture rejoiced in him . . . and his bold genius captivated the favor of periodicals which spurned the rest of our nation." England could turn out cultured humorists aplenty, but not Mark Twains. He returned there in 1873 to lecture to the Londoners on "Our Fellow Savages of the Sandwich Islands" and was greeted with high enthusiasm.

After his emphatic success in England, the fastidious and "refined" of America were more ready to welcome him. Now his fame was so wide that when travelers first arrived in this country, they often expressed a desire to see two things: Niagara Falls and Mark Twain. By the time he was forty, his name was familiar everywhere, in every sort of environment. Countless Mark Twain anecdotes were being passed around the clubs, many of them illustrating his penchant for what Howells termed "the Southwestern, the Lincolnian, the Elizabethan breadth of parlance." In the luxurious home in Hartford where he lived with his wife and three daughters and elaborately entertained his guests, it was his custom to rise from the dinner table between courses and walk up and down the room, waving his napkin and talking the marvelous talk that for him was just a way of killing time. Sometimes he complained that his expenses in the Hartford house were "ghastly"; he spent money lavishly and then had thrifty intervals marked by small economies. In one of these seizures, after a long evening spent with pencil and paper, he announced that he could find but two items on which a saving was possible: the family must cancel its subscription to *Harper's Magazine* and buy a cheaper brand of toilet paper.

Mrs. J.T. Fields, wife of the editor of the *Atlantic Monthly*, described Mark Twain at forty years of age: "His eyes are grey and piercing, yet soft, and his whole face expresses great sensitiveness. He is exquisitely neat also, but careless, and his hands are small, not without delicacy. He is a small man, but his mass of hair seems the one rugged-looking thing about him." A decade later he was described by his thirteen-year-old daughter Susy as having "beautiful curly grey hair, . . . kind blue eyes, and . . . a wonderfully shaped head and profile . . . He . . . has got a temper, but we all of us have in this family. He is the loveliest man I ever saw, or ever hope to see, and oh so absent-minded!" Mark Twain once essayed a description of himself: "Twenty-four years ago, I was strangely handsome . . . so handsome that . . . even inanimate things stopped to look-like locomotives, and district messenger boys . . . In San Francisco, in the rainy season I was often mistaken for fair weather." Howells' carefully done portrait dates from the same period as Susy's: "Clemens was then hard upon fifty, and he had kept, as he did to the end, the slender figure of his youth, but the ashes of the burnt-out years were beginning to gray the fires of that splendid shock of red hair which he held to the height of a stature apparently greater than it was, and tilted from side to side in his undulating walk. He glimmered at you from the narrow slits of fine blue-greenish eyes, under branching brows which with age grew more and more like a sort of plumage, and he was apt to smile into your face with a subtle but amiable perception, and yet with a sort of remote absence; you were all there for him, but he was not all there for you." Hamlin Garland, too, found in Mark Twain a curious aloofness of glance, as though he spoke through a mask.

Kipling, who pictured himself "smoking reverently" through their meeting "as befits one in the presence of his superior," presented the Mark Twain of fifty-four as "a man with eyes, a mane of grizzled hair, a brown mustache . . . a strong, square hand shaking mine, and the slowest, calmest, levelest voice in all the world. . . . The thing that struck me first was that he was an elderly man; yet . . . in five minutes, the eyes looking at me, I saw that the gray hair was an accident of the most trivial. He was quite young."

Kipling, on a round-the-world tour, insisted that he had traveled fourteen thousand miles to meet Mark Twain. A few years earlier, however, a visiting Britisher had harbored no such eagerness. When Matthew Arnold came to Boston, he called upon Howells and was told that Howells was at Hartford, visiting Mark Twain. Surprised, he said, "Oh, but he doesn't like *that* sort of thing, does he?" Howells recorded what happened later at a reception in Hartford, where Arnold had gone to lecture: "While his hand laxly held mine in greeting I saw his eyes fixed intensely on the other side of the room. 'Who-who in the world is that?' I looked and said, 'Oh, that is Mark Twain.' I do not remember just how their instant encounter was contrived by Arnold's wish, but I have the impression that they were not parted for long during the evening, and the next night Arnold, as if still under the glamour of that potent presence, was at Clemens's house." On the night of Arnold's visit, Mark Twain was at his best and kept going a string of comment and anecdote of a kind which Joe Twichell declared the world had never seen before and Howells maintained it would never see again. " Arnold seemed dazed by it," wrote Paine. On his way home Arnold "repeated some of the things Mark Twain had said; thoughtfully, as if trying to analyze their magic."

In this way Mark Twain impressed, even dazzled, almost everyone who came into contact with him. Most of those Easterners who had first looked askance at him yielded in time, as Bernard DeVoto says, "to the personality that seems to have been the most glamorous of our literature." That his personality did not need to be strengthened by his reputation is shown in an incident related by George Bernard Shaw. When Mark Twain visited him at Adelphi Terrace, Shaw's parlor maid "did not know him from Adam, yet she admitted him without question and unannounced."[2]

People were most impressed, apparently, by his eyes and his voice. W.H. Rideing tried to describe the latter: "It was not a laughing voice, or a light-hearted voice, but deep and earnest like that of one of the graver musical instruments, rich and solemn, and in emotion vibrant and swelling with its own passionate feeling." Mark Twain told Rideing he had discovered that the Jumping Frog story was two thousand years old. "Two thousand years never seemed so long to me, nor could they have seemed longer to anybody than they did in his enunciation of them which seemed to make visible and tangible all the mystery, all the remoteness . . . of that chilling stretch of time. His way of uttering them and his application of them often gave the simplest words which he habitually used a pictorial vividness, a richness of suggestion, a fullness of meaning with which genius alone could endow them." He did not keep this art of his merely for parading in public. Talking at home, for instance, he once mentioned a word "that perfectly disgusts me" — the word was *optimist* — and as he spoke his voice and his features seemed to materialize the disgust he felt.

He still accompanied himself at the piano and sang occasionally. In the West his one song had been "I Had an Old Horse Whose Name Was Methusalem," but in the Hartford house in the evenings he would sit at the piano and sing the old Negro songs, spirituals and jubilees, that he had loved in his childhood. In memorable words his servant Katy Leary tells of a summer evening, a lovely night with a full moon, when the Warners had entertained friends at dinner. Afterwards the company assembled in the music room, with no lights inside the house, and sat looking out upon the moonlight. "And suddenly Mr. Clemens got right up without any warning and begun to sing one of them negro Spirituals . . . he just stood up with both his eyes shut and begun to sing kind of soft like — a faint sound, just as if there was wind in the trees . . . kind o' low and sweet, and it was beautiful and made your heart ache somehow. And he kept on singin' and singin' and became kind of lost in it, and . . . when he got through, he put his two hands up to his head, just as though all the sorrow of them negroes was upon him; and then he begun to sing, 'Nobody Knows the Trouble I Got, Nobody Knows but Jesus' . . . and when he come to the end, to the Glory Halleluiah, he gave a great shout-just like the negroes do . . . They said it was wonderful and none of them would forget it as long as they lived."

Here he is portrayed in a mood of sadness, but his moods were myriad. He never got too old for clowning, and one of his letters tells how he "caught it" from Olivia Clemens, his wife, for impersonating a drunken colonel in the Howells home. He boyishly teased the exquisite Olivia as he had earlier teased his mother. Howells remembered seeing him "come into his drawing-room at Hartford in a pair of white cowskin slippers, with the hair out, and do a crippled colored uncle to the joy of all beholders." Say, rather, to the joy of most beholders; for Howells remembered, too, "the dismay of Mrs. Clemens, and her low, despairing cry of 'Oh, Youth!' " She called him "Youth" throughout their thirty-four years of married life, recognizing thus the youthful strain that was always in him, although he was ten years older than she; and he called her "Livy" as her family had done. She was physically frail, and Mark Twain followed her about with a chair. Their friends found his love for her one of his most moving qualities. As a father he was fun for his children, often playing with them as unrestrainedly as a frolicsome boy. In her biography of him, his little daughter Susy wrote, "The difference between papa and mama is, that mama loves morals and papa loves cats." Mark Twain belongs with Richelieu and Dr. Johnson, among the great cat-lovers of all time.

In 1877 his personal imp of the burlesque betrayed him into his greatest fiasco-the Whittier birthday-dinner speech in which he burlesqued Longfellow, Emerson, and Holmes with those gentlemen present, to the horror and consternation of all reverent Bostonians. Later, he sent humble apologies to the august trinity concerned and wrote in penitence to Howells: "My sense of disgrace does not abate. It grows." But he was freely forgiven by the authors themselves; and the resiliency of his spirit was such that, before many days passed, he wrote again to Howells: "I haven't done a stroke of work since the *Atlantic* dinner. But I'm going to try tomorrow. How could I ever — Ah, well, I am a great and sublime fool. But then I am God's fool, and all His works must be contemplated with respect."

Restless in temperament, he roamed about the world. He lived in Europe for one continuous period of nine years and for several shorter periods. He crossed the Atlantic fourteen times in three and one-half years and at various times resided in London, Vienna, Paris, Berlin, and Florence, with summers in Switzerland and Sweden. During these intervals he was sought after by the wealth, nobility, and even royalty of Europe. The family spent the winter of 189192 in Berlin, where Mark Twain was invited to dine with Emperor William II. Little Jean, awed by such royal favor, declared, "Why, papa, if it keeps on like this, pretty soon there won't be anybody left for you to get acquainted with but God" — a statement whose complimentary value her father questioned. When Mark Twain settled down in Vienna for the winter of 1897,

Paine says, his apartments were "like a court, where with those of social rank assembled the foremost authors, journalists, diplomats, painters, philosophers, scientists, of Europe . . . Mark Twain's daily movements were chronicled as if he had been some visiting potentate." During the second winter in Vienna, the Clemens drawing room became known as "the Second Embassy."

Mark Twain had no head for business. He lost the fortune which he had sunk in the Paige typesetting machine, that marvelous piece of machinery, that "cunning devil" of steel that could all but think; it proved impracticable because of its extreme delicacy and its high cost of manufacture. When his publishing company, managed by others, ran into difficulties during a business depression and declared bankruptcy, Mark Twain wrote: "The law recognizes no mortgage on a man's brain, and a merchant who has given up all he has may take advantage of the laws of insolvency and start free again for himself. But I am not a business man, and honor is a harder master than the law. It cannot compromise for less than 100 cents on the dollar, and its debts never outlaw." Resolving that his creditors should lose nothing, he determined to "go platforming around the world" to pay his debts, and he set off, accompanied by his wife and his daughter Clara. He was nearing sixty when he assumed this stupendous task, a task that would have tried the courage of a far younger man. While they were away, tragedy struck back home in the death of the eldest daughter, Susy, the one who seemed most of all to have inherited her father's genius. Mark Twain's daughter Clara tells how, with a father's natural feeling that if Susy's parents had only been there, her death might somehow have been averted, he walked the floor in grief and cried out in bitterness against the way God runs this world:

> Do you remember, Livy, the hellish struggle it was to settle on making that lecture trip . . . ? To pay

> debts that were not even of my making . . . But once the idea of that infernal trip struck us we couldn't shake it. Oh, no! for it was packed with sense of honor-honor-honor . . . plenty of honor, plenty of ethical glory. And as a reward for our selfcastigation and faithfulness to ideals of nobility we were robbed of our greatest treasure, our lovely Susy.

Financially, however, the undertaking was a success, and by 1898, Mark Twain had completed the payment of his debts.

When he returned to America after following the equator around the world, the public hailed him with renewed affection. "He had behaved like Walter Scott," said Howells, "as millions rejoiced to know who had not known how Walter Scott behaved till they knew it was like Clemens." His opinion was sought on everything under the sun, and he was unfailing copy for reporters. But when a plan was under way for forming a Mark Twain Association and having a Mark Twain Day at the St. Louis World's Fair, he would have none of it, refusing on the ground that "such compliments are not proper for the living; they are proper and safe for the dead only." There was always the chance, he said, that "while I am still alive . . . I might . . . do something which would cause its members to regret having done me that honor . . . I shall be a doubtful quantity, like the rest of our race."

Despite the honors heaped upon him, he always retained a certain modesty, a sort of humility even. At seventy he served as pallbearer for his former coachman, taking his place along with his own gardener and some neighbor coachmen. A few days later, addressing a group of young men, he gave them the characteristics of the dead coachman, Patrick McAleer, as his idea of an ideal gentleman. "It was the sort of thing that no one but Mark

Twain has quite been able to do," commented his biographer, "and it was the recognized quality behind it that had made crowds jam the street and stampede the entrance to be in his presence-to see him and to hear his voice."

In 1904 the death of his wife left him, as he said, "washing about on a forlorn sea of banquets," and there was a period when he felt little interest in what the world could offer. But when Oxford University requested the honor of conferring upon him the degree of Doctor of Literature, he eagerly accepted the proposal, saying, "Although I wouldn't cross an ocean again for the price of the ship that carried me, I am glad to do it for an Oxford degree." When his ship stopped at Tilbury, the stevedores stood on the dock and gave him athroughU round of cheers, a welcome which he said "went to the marrow of me."

This was the beginning of an unprecedented demonstration on the part of the English people, an ovation which continued +00AD out the four weeks of his stay. His London hotel became not only a royal court but also, perforce, a post office; Paine said that two skilled men were required, working from sixteen to twenty hours a day, to receive callers and reduce the pile of correspondence. Acquiring Oxford degrees along with Mark Twain were Rudyard Kipling, Auguste Rodin, Saint-Saëns, Sidney Lee, and others; but, according to Sidney Lee, the crowd centered its attention chiefly on Mark Twain, and the Oxford pageant held on the following day was called "Mark Twain's Pageant" by the London papers.[3] Upon his leavetaking the *London Tribune* declared: " Mark Twain has triumphed, and in his all-too-brief stay of a month has done more for the cause of the world's peace than will be accomplished by the Hague Conference." Perhaps it is true that, as Paine said, England had paid him "the greatest national tribute ever paid to a private citizen."

The rich scarlet of his Oxford gown did not lessen the value of the Oxford degree in his eyes. "I like the degree well enough," he said, "but I'm crazy about the clothes! . . . Think of the gloomy garb I have to walk the streets in at home, when my whole soul cries out for gold braid, yellow and scarlet sashes, jewels and a turban!" He had once likened to a garden the rainbow colors of women's dresses in an opera audience, with the men "clothed in odious black, scattered here and there like so many charred stumps." About the time of his seventy-first birthday he put off his dark suits in favor of white clothes for both winter and summer wear. Though he pined for a costume of silks and velvets resplendent with stunning dyes, he compromised on the white, a striking complement to his white hair.

He loved a spectacle always, particularly if he formed a part of it. He was not above making an entrance with studied theatrical effect, and he preferred the "Peacock Alley" corridor leading into a Washington hotel dining room to the quiet entrance-way Paine had recommended. His height was only medium, says Paine, but "with his head thrown up, and like a lion's, rather large for his body," he gave the impression of being tall. Dressed in his snowy flannels, he made an impressive figure striding up and down the stage of the world. On Sundays, he loved to mingle in the streets with the crowds; when Paine suggested that by going home a roundabout way he could avoid the throng, he replied quietly, "I like the throng."

Mark Twain liked women who were comely and attractive in appearance. He was superstitious beyond all telling. He was a perfect fury of energy, generating power like a dynamo. Two years before he was sixty, he wrote to Livy of attending a New York ball and reported: "By half past four I had danced all those people down — and yet was not tired." That was 1893, the year he first became known as "The Belle of New York." Apparently, he could do on much less sleep than the average person needs. Billiards was the game he loved best, and his love for it amounted to a passion. In his old age, he himself asserted that he walked ten miles a day around the billiard table, with a cue in his hand. He could play at "the science of angles" all night without tiring, another sign of his appalling energy, and he always took great delight in his conquests. But sometimes when his shots were bad, the air turned blue, temporarily. After such outbursts he would try to make amends to his opponent. Once, playing with Paine, he angrily seized the cue and literally mowed the balls across the table. Immediately afterward "he was very gentle and sweet, like the sun on the meadow after the storm has passed by"—as meek as a little child in his remorse.

But when that violent temper flared, profanity was likely to be accompanied by action, in or out of the billiard room. One Sunday morning he hurled out of the window all his shirts that he found with buttons off; and Katy Leary declared that "if he found a shirt that didn't have the proper cuff buttons in, he'd tear it up." Little things rent him completely apart, though he could be calm and courageous in the face of great trouble. His love of color, already mentioned, was but one of his many artistic traits. He had an abnormal sensitiveness to sound: the ticking clock, the gnawing mouse, the rustling paper, the barking dog, the cackling guinea hen-these things tortured him and led to outbreaks of temper. Unpleasant human voices made him suffer, but the liquid beauty in certain rare voices was compensation.

The intensity of his moods was remarkable. His sudden savage impulses might bring hardship, sometimes even injustice, to others; if he discovered the wrong, he could not rest until he had atoned for it. But he held an indignation that amounted to malevolence towards those he believed his enemies and wore himself out in the vehemence of his resentments. Of Paige, the inventor whose typesetter cost him a fortune, of Paige, the smooth talker who "could persuade a fish to come out and take a walk with him," Mark Twain wrote in his memoranda: "Paige and I always meet on effusively affectionate terms, and yet he knows perfectly well that if I had him in a steel trap I would shut out all human succor and watch that trap until he died." Howells said that Mark Twain went beyond Heine, who forgave his enemies when they were dead: "Clemens did not forgive his dead enemies; their death seemed to deepen their crimes, like a base evasion, or a cowardly attempt to escape." But he was more relentless to himself than to anyone else; he pyramided his shortcomings into mountains of crime and kept his conscience perpetually clothed in a hair shirt as penance for his sins.

He could be unexpectedly patient with those whom he considered underprivileged. Howells told how Mark Twain once inadvertently sat down upon a notebook a brakeman had left on a train seat; the brakeman was abusive to him and came back again and again to berate him. "The patience of Clemens . . . was so angelic that I saw fit to comment, 'I suppose you will report this fellow.' 'Yes,' he answered, slowly and sadly. 'That's what I should have done once. But now I remember that he gets twenty dollars a month.'" In philanthropy and charity he was extremely magnanimous. J.N. Larned of the Buffalo *Express* once characterized him with accuracy: "What one saw of him was always the actual Mark Twain, acting out of his own nature simply, frankly, without pretense, and almost without reserve. It was that simplicity and naturalness in the man which carried his greatest charm."[4]

Paine noted that "age and misfortune and illness had a tempering influence on Mark Twain's nature." Instead of becoming more harsh, more severe and bitter with the blows the passing years rained upon him, he grew "more gentle, more kindly." Nevertheless, he remained both trenchant and intrepid. He could still indulge, privately or semipublicly, his Southwestern or Elizabethan breadth of parlance. At seventy-two he attended a dinner given for Andrew Carnegie at the Engineer's Club and verbally cuffed Carnegie for his proposal to simplify spelling, protesting that "simplified spelling is all right enough, but, like chastity, you can carry it too far."

S.J. Woolf, the artist who painted him in 1906, described his appearance in his last years: "Instead of the weather-beaten face which I had expected, I saw one softer and calmer, but no less strong, while the delicacy and refinement of his features were most noticeable. His hair, too, which I had always thought wiry, was glossy and silken. Never have I seen a head where it seemed more an integral part — its ivory-like tones melting imperceptibly into the lighter hues of the skin so that the line of juncture was almost entirely lost. Even his hands betrayed a more actively nervous man than one would . . . imagine a former river-pilot could be."

His friends appreciated the innate fineness that was unknown to the world at large. Joseph Twichell, who accompanied him on the European tour which produced *A Tramp Abroad*, wrote in a letter home: "He has coarse spots in him. But I never knew a person so finely regardful of the feelings of others . . . He hates to pass another person walking, and will practise some subterfuge to take off what he feels is the discourtesy of it." Twichell told how their guide had wished to pass ahead of them, yet hesitated to do so. "Mark paused, went aside and busied himself a minute picking a flower. In the halt the guide got by and . . . Mark threw the flower away, saying, 'I didn't want that. I only wanted to give the old man a chance to go on without seeming to pass us.' " And Twichell summed him up: "A strange Mark he is, full of contradictions."

Howells admired his delicate, shapely hands, and noted that he "had the fine instinct of never putting his hands on you . . .; he did not paw you with them to show his affection." But perhaps the best record of his extreme sensitivity is preserved in the words of Helen Keller: "He knew with keen and sure intuition many things about me; how it felt to be blind and not to be able to keep up with the swift ones-things that others learned slowly or not at all. He never embarrassed me by saying how terrible it is not to see, or how dull life must be, lived always in the dark."

There was always, of course, another side to the picture. There were always those who did not like Mark Twain, who in fact disliked him intensely. Senator William H. Stewart of Nevada, whose Washington secretary Mark Twain had once been for a brief period distasteful to both men, described him as a disreputable looking person of sinister appearance, with an evil-smelling cigar butt protruding from the corner of his mouth. Robertson Nicoll was shocked at "his habitual, incessant, and disgusting profanity."[5] And Waldo Frank, who sat unresponsive through one of Mark Twain's humorous speeches at a benefit entertainment for the blind, objected to his humor and found his performance somehow shameful: "He stood there almost still . . . and dropped the ungainly humor from his mouth. And the audience before him snouted it, guzzled it, roared with delight." Mr. Frank is at some pains to make clear that he "hated this noble-looking fool."

Howells recognized that Mark Twain's effect on some persons was unpleasant: "His casual acquaintance might know him, perhaps, from his fierce intensity, his wild pleasure in shocking people with his ribaldries and profanities . . . as anything but exquisite, and yet that was what in the last analysis he was. They might come away loathing or hating him." Yet Howells maintained to the last that "Clemens's central and final personality was something exquisite."

Mark Twain liked to lie in his huge, carved bed in a room with deep red walls. He had acquired the habit of working in bed long before he grew old. He read there, he wrote there, and he frequently gave dictations to Paine from there; or sometimes he merely lay in his bed and talked what his friends considered the world's most remarkable entertainment. This talk of his was accompanied by incessant smoking, in bed or out. Missing him, Howells once wrote from England: "I would rather have you smoke in my face and talk for half a day than to go to the best house or club in London." A house where he had visited had to be aired from top to bottom, Howells said, for "he smoked all over it from breakfast to bedtime."

One spring morning when he was seventy, as he lay propped in bed, clad in his beautiful Persian silk dressing gown with his white hair spread against the pillows, a worshipful woman begged to be admitted to his presence for a moment. As she was leaving, she exclaimed reverently, "How God must love you!" Mark Twain answered softly, "I hope so"; but after she had gone he remarked in an odd, half-pathetic voice, "I guess she hasn't heard of our strained relations."

Sometimes in the dictations to Paine he went back to his earlier habit of walking up and down, resuming "the ceaseless slippered, shuffling walk" with its rocking, rolling movement. With that great mane of white hair, walking a regular measured beat in the habit acquired in the pilothouse, he must have resembled an aged lion, pacing up and down, just the length of his cage.

But he had, too, a lion's courage. In those last months, with all his immediate family dead except his daughter Clara, who had married the pianist Gabrilowitsch and gone abroad, Mark Twain was at best a somewhat pathetic figure. He retained to his last years, however, his faculty of living in the present. Howells recalled that on his last visit to Stormfield Mark Twain sang "Go Down, Daniel," in his quavering tenor and was up early in the mornings, swaying up and down the corridor in his long nightgown, "wagging his great white head like a boy that leaves his bed and comes out in the hope of frolic." Later, when the pain of the angina pectoris which killed him had kept him awake, he would remark, "Well, I had a picturesque night." But, nearing the end, he said once: "I am like a bird in a cage: always expecting to get out, and always beaten back by the wires." He got out on April 21, 1910, in his seventy-fifth year. His faithful servant Katy Leary insisted, "It was a terrible, cruel thing to have him die, really, because he was too young-that is, he felt young . . . and he could have said a good deal more." Attempting to explain why the world united in sorrow at his death, Paine suggested that it was "because he was so limitlessly human that every other human heart, in whatever sphere or circumstance, responded to his touch."

Howells, practiced writer though he was, admitted his failure at putting into words anything of the essence of Mark Twain: "It is in vain that I try to give a notion of the intensity with which he pierced to the heart of life." And Howells, who had known Emerson, Longfellow, Lowell, and Holmes — "I knew them all and all the rest of our sages, poets, seers, critics, humorists; they were like one another and like other literary men" — Howells pronounced Mark Twain's nature "rich and fertile beyond any I have known." In Howells' final judgment, "Clemens was sole, incomparable."

I have tried to set down here, in my turn, something of the man the world knew as Mark Twain, much that was good, some that was bad. I have emphasized his personality and the sway it held over others, using the testimony of those who knew him, those who heard him speak, and giving it mainly in their own words. But what of his writing, his literary work? His friends sometimes indicated that they felt it the lesser part of his career. John Macy wrote that it was "a pleasure to hear him in one of his coolly passionate tirades, speaking sentences amazingly finished and constructed, as if a prose style were as natural to him as breathing." Paine said that in the dictations Mark Twain delivered his sentences with a "measured accuracy" that seldom called for change; but in making his transcriptions, Paine found it hard to preserve "the bouquet, the subtleness of speech" of the original; "there is always lacking the wonder of his personality."

In fact, Paine went so far as to declare that he talked "in a strain and with a charm that he could never quite equal with his pen. It is the opinion of most people who knew Mark Twain personally that his impromptu utterances, delivered with that ineffable quality of speech, manifested the culmination of his genius." Sir Henry Irving told him that he would have made a greater actor than a writer. Apparently there was a tendency among his contemporaries to put the rare quality of the man himself above his literary work. Mr. Brooks, recalling that Howells had compared him with Cervantes and Swift and that Bernard Shaw had likened him to Voltaire, suggested that they gave the work more than its due because of the man: "Did they not, under the spell of that extraordinary personal presence of his, in the magnetism, the radiance of what might be called his temperamental will-to-satire mistake the wish for the deed?" A danger, it will be perceived, for those who were subjected to his charm. The danger has been recognized elsewhere. Edward Wagenknecht noted that "it was often his personality, rather than his art, by which his contemporaries were enthralled" and that he looms "more impressively in American literature as a personality than he does as a writer."

What great writer since his time has been able to capture the imagination of the public as he captured it and to hold it so long? Mr. Brooks prophesies that he will continue in the mass-mind for many generations as "a sort of arch type of the national character . . . By whom, however, with the exception of two or three of his books, is he read?" But with each generation that unique figure is farther removed from us, growing more dim and shadowy with time. Anecdotes lose their force with the passing of eyewitnesses. His voice was recorded in his seventieth-birthday speech, but the records, made of wax and stored by his secretary in a warm attic, were unfortunately ruined. One record of his voice still exists but is inaccessible to many people.[6] What remains to us? His books.

By his books he must be known to us, as to those who come after us. Mark Twain the man has too long overshadowed Mark Twain the writer. And he would have wished it otherwise. A year before he died, glancing retrospectively over the long way he had come, he wrote: "To me, the most important feature of my life is its literary feature." Let us, then, put the emphasis where it really belongs-upon his books, for better or for worse.

Mark Twain, perhaps, is the only Southwesterner to command a world audience, to attain world significance in the field of literature. In view of his eminence it is surprising that so little attention has been paid to his actual writing itself, surprising that no study of the aesthetic and technical aspects of his work has ever been made. Yet, beginning with 1920 when Van Wyck Brooks opened a new cycle of Mark Twain criticism, a new Mark Twain book has appeared every few years.

Mr. Brooks psychoanalyzed him and found that the humorist had frustrated the artist within him; Bernard DeVoto turned the spotlight on "Mark Twain's America, the sociological and economic background which produced him, studying his work in its broad effects, but not minutely; Edward Wagenknecht wrote on *Mark Twain: The Man and His Work*, but the emphasis throughout is on the man rather than the work; DeLancey Ferguson presented *Mark Twain: Man and Legend*, tracing the autobiographical material which appears in much of his work, but neither an autobiographical nor a documented biographical approach to that work can be fully adequate, for reasons which will later appear. An entire book has recently been devoted to Mark Twain's views on religion, another to Mark Twain as a businessman. Surely, it is time to examine Mark Twain as an author, as a professional writer, even as a literary artist.

The Critical Questions

If it be true, as is often said, that controversy over an author is an indication of his genius, then surely Mark Twain can claim the divine spark, for he has occasioned much disagreement among the critics. The battle first raged about various endeavors to "place" him, to determine his status and rank as a writer. There were those who saw him only as a frontier humorist and therefore, with elevated noses, relegated him to a seat below the salt. But Mark Twain, one of the most complex of literary personalities, refused to stay there; and now that criticism has accorded him a place nearer the head of the board, the critical effort has sought to "explain" him, to account for his being what he was and writing the sort of works he produced.

Critics have found it difficult to explain why Mark Twain — a man of genius, fame, wealth, happy domestic relations, and pleasant social environment — should have become a pessimist. He did not, in fact, become a pessimist, for pessimism flares out occasionally even in his early work. Surely, from an external view, life had brought him all that he could have hoped for. He had proved that a man might go just as far in America as his own talent and energy would take him. But he recoiled from the spiritual ugliness that grew up in the country in the years following the Civil War. Some of it escaped him, but what he had the vision to see he excoriated with force and power. His indictment of civilization is both explicit and implicit in his work. He was one of the first writers to sense what lay ahead of the United States in the course on which she was set. And, because to him America had long embodied the hope of the world, his fear and despair were for all the world. America as a democracy amid certain social conditions, under certain dominant factors of economics, politics, and religion, and the life he lived in such a setting -these elements make up the background. The foreground must remain his works themselves.

Critics have generally viewed him as an "unconscious artist," if the term may be admitted, explaining his faults of structural disharmony on the ground that he was merely the improvisator, the careless writer, unconcerned and working by impulse. In her book *American Humour*, Constance Rourke stated unequivocally: "He was never the conscious artist, always the improviser." Edward Wagenknecht agrees emphatically with Miss Rourke. Van Wyck Brooks charges Twain with habitual "indifference" and even "insolence" towards his own work, insisting that in all the endless pages of his writing "there is scarcely a hint of any concern with the technique, or indeed with any other aspect, of what was nothing else, surely, than his art." Seeming to agree with Mr. Brooks's comment that Mark Twain's interest was confined to the "purely or mainly verbal aspects" of writing, Bernard DeVoto asserts in *Mark Twain's America* that "it is unlikely that he ever analyzed, beyond its mere grammar, an effect of his own or anyone's else."

My personal interest in Mark Twain was, at first, an attempt to determine whether he was a "conscious" or an "unconscious" literary artist. Although the latter term seems an obvious contradiction within itself, since the word *artist* implies a selection and control of material, criticism has on occasion applied it to Mark Twain. But the evidence shows that, although he was never conscious of his art in the sense in which such self-conscious artists as Henry James and Joseph Conrad wrote, he was much more the conscious craftsman than is generally believed. To read his works is to sense the genius of the man and also to realize that many of his works fail to do justice to that genius. Having had that experience, I grew interested in a more inclusive question: Why was it that the combination of a native endowment that was remarkable and a literary craftsmanship that was by no means slight, working together in Mark Twain, still produced a number of works of mediocre quality and a good many others which fall short of complete artistic success? The attempt to answer this question satisfactorily has proved a fascinating study.

Aside from the question of his working consciously, other questions interested me: Was Mark Twain's boyhood in a raw Missouri frontier town warped and stunted, as Mr. Brooks holds, or was his boyhood environment beneficial for his development, as Miss Minnie M. Brashear holds? Did the Far West further stultify and thwart his artistic growth, as Mr. Brooks maintains, or did the West develop him, as Mr. DeVoto maintains? Was he really "imprisoned" in his boyhood, as both Brooks and DeVoto hold? Is Brooks right in believing that Mark Twain impaired his artistic and satiric talents by becoming a humorist, or is DeVoto right in believing that he fulfilled himself through the writing of humor? Was his native endowment for becoming a great writer really as fine as Mr. Brooks believes? or was there something lacking, something at the very core of his being, that frequently held him back from achieving the highest peak of mastery in literary work?

In the arena devoted to contests over Mark Twain, the two chief antagonists have been Van Wyck Brooks and Bernard DeVoto. In *The Ordeal of Mark Twain*, Mr. Brooks pictured his subject as an "artist born" who betrayed the artist within him to become a humorist — not only because the West demanded humor as a psychical defense against the frustrations inherent in frontier life, but also because humor was popular enough to bring him money; as a satirist for whom satire became impossible because he must, perforce, be one of the crowd; as a writer stunted first by the narrowness of his Southwestern frontier village and later by the raw and violent crudeness of the Far West; as a case of arrested development who remained always a child and who could write well only when producing books for boys. Yet, says Mr. Brooks, this pitiful figure was potentially one of the greatest of men, and his gifts, his "unbounded energy, his prodigal fertility, his large utterance, . . . his powers of feeling, the unique magnetism of his personality were the signs of an endowment, as one cannot but think, more extraordinary than that of any other American writer." In brief, Mr. Brooks finds the secret of Mark Twain's pessimism in the fact that he had betrayed the artist within him by writing humor; he holds that Mark Twain regarded his humorous writing "as something external to himself, as something other than artistic self-expression; and it was in consequence of pursuing it . . . that he was arrested in his moral and aesthetic development."

In *Mark Twain's America*, Mr. DeVoto admits that Mark Twain was a humorist but finds no indication of artistic unfulfillment implicit in that fact. In his introduction to *Mark Twain in Eruption*, he says that Mark Twain "had a coherent development up to *A Connecticut Yankee*," but was later crushed under an avalanche of personal calamities which so impaired his writing talent that for a long time it seemed to have been destroyed; and, when it was integrated again, "there is . .

. a new Mark Twain, the author of *What Is Man?* and *The Mysterious Stranger*." On this particular point Mr. Brooks had asserted, "Of the misfortunes of life he had neither more nor less than other men, and they affected him neither more nor less."

Mr. DeVoto insists that Mark Twain fulfilled himself abundantly as a writer, but grants that he had many faults as an artist — among them sporadic composition, painful disharmonies, failure to objectify his material enough to give it the discipline of form, negligence in revision, rambling improvisation, intrusion of burlesque into magnificent literary material, failure to subordinate impulse to plan, and, finally, lack of structure. And Mr. DeVoto finds the explanation of these weaknesses, as of many of Mark Twain's strengths, in the frontier that produced him.[7] In one passage DeVoto writes: "He left San Francisco at the end of 1866 and the frontier, having completed him, was done with him forever." That the frontier "completed" Mark Twain is a conception that cannot be granted.

Mr. Brooks sees Mark Twain's birth on the Southwestern frontier as the first step in life's betrayal of the artist he was destined to be. To Brooks, Hannibal was a desolate, barren place devoid of aesthetic possibilities, where the child Sam Clemens had only, on the one hand, the narrowness of his mother's iron-clad Presbyterianism and, on the other, the nerve-shattering voodoo tales of the Negro slaves. It is Miss Brashear who has done the most careful research for the purpose of bringing to life again Mark Twain's Missouri. She finds that Hannibal possessed "a more distinctly literary atmosphere than towns in Missouri have today." It had seven churches, an English and Classical School, a "female academy," five newspapers, three bookstores, and a public library which Sam Clemens's father had been instrumental in founding. At the time Sam left it at seventeen, it was the second city in the state in population. Miss Brashear maintains that the legend that Mark Twain sprang unaccountably from a western wilderness must be revised: "As a matter of fact, it is doubtful whether, anywhere in America, there could have been found in the forties and fifties a small section of country more favorable for his start in life than northeast Missouri."

The critics who look on Mark Twain's early environment as antagonistic to his artistic development make the old error of assuming that the content of his imagination was a more or less literal copy of his actual surroundings. Never completely true of any mind, the assumption is much less true in cases involving the artistic temperament. And for that matter, much of his actual environment was of a kind potentially rich in imaginative quality. By his boyhood village there flowed the Mississippi, "the majestic, the magnificent Mississippi, rolling its mile-wide tide along, shining in the sun"; and his literary treatment of the river testifies to the power which its beauty and its grandeur exerted over his imagination. As for the fact that he grew up among Negroes, that fact, too, is important for the artist; for, as Mr. DeVoto has said, much that is fruitful in his art springs from the slaves — from "the melancholy, the music, the laughter, the terror, and the magic of the slaves." Mr. Wagenknecht stated the case admirably when he wrote that to hear the marvelous ghost tales of the Negroes and "to thrill to them afterward, was probably the intensest form of emotional stimulation that young Sam Clemens ever received." The influence of the Negro on Mark Twain was not only deep; it was sustained throughout his life.

At first glance it would seem that Mr. Brooks and Mr. DeVoto are in opposite corners of the ring, that they are diametrically opposed in their views concerning Mark Twain. There are a few points, however, on which they appear to have agreed from the first. Mr. Brooks's belief that Mark Twain's interest in writing was confined to its verbal aspects and Mr. DeVoto's doubt that he ever analyzed any effect beyond its mere grammar have already been mentioned. In the next place, Brooks complains that Mark Twain is "still obsessed with the morbid fears of that old Western village of his"; and DeVoto has emphasized, in all his writings on Mark Twain, "the dread that was Hannibal" as the obverse side of the idyllic charm of that village. Further, Brooks pictures the child Sam Clemens as a high-strung, neurotic child of exquisite sensibilities and then shows him "abandoned to the fervid influences of the negro slaves," crouching in their cabins drinking in "wild, weird tales of blood-curdling African witchcraft," with the suggestion that this early subjection to such a fearful stimulus was a bad thing for his normal development; and here again DeVoto follows Brooks in part. He writes that the boy Sam Clemens entered wholly into the slave's world, a world which contained "abysses of horror"; he then amplifies that horror through fourteen pages and concludes that "it is not granted here that the nervous instability of Mark Twain requires explanation. But if it does . . . a nervous organism that has been racked from its beginning by the Negro's midnight magic need not depend on American contempt of art for its discords." And the two have agreed from the first in holding the frontier responsible for some of Mark Twain's literary defects. Brooks charges that the raw environment of the frontier stunted his artistic growth; and DeVoto, while maintaining that the frontier developed him as a writer, nevertheless seems to feel that his faults of structure and technique were largely derived from the characteristic practice of the tall tale and the frontier anecdote.[8]

Recently, these critics appear to have drawn closer together than they were a decade ago; and, surprisingly enough, it is Mr. DeVoto who has moved towards his opponent. Although in 1933 Mr. Brooks revised The Ordeal, following the appearance of DeVoto's *Mark Twain's America* in 1932, his central position remained the same: Mark Twain, halted in his artistic development by the stultifying conditions of life on the frontier, had sold his artist's birthright for a mess of materialistic success, had wasted himself on his milieu, had descended to the writing of humor when he had been intended for a great satirist. "The making of the humorist," asserts Mr. Brooks, "was the undoing of the artist."

The first of these more recent agreements concerns the question of sex in Mark Twain's work. Mr. Brooks contends that the frontiersmen lived a life which blocked their instincts on every side: "There were so few women among them . . . that their sexual lives were either starved or debased"; and he concludes that Mark Twain's verbal obscenities were the expression of that "vital sap," which, because of taboos, had been driven inward and left there to ferment -"the waste of a priceless psychic material." In 1932, Mr. DeVoto insisted that the sex expression of the frontiersmen had been free and natural, that among them there was no suppression of emotion, fear of passion, repression of instincts, or abstinence from joy; and he concluded his remarks on the sex life of the frontier with a reference to the social activities of young Sam Clemens in Hannibal, with the clear implication that in such respects Sam was not inhibited. But in his more recent book, *Mark Twain at Work*, he finds Twain "almost lustfully hypersensitive to sex in print," as a writer "rather more prudish than Howells," and guilty of timorous circumlocutions that are "astonishing." Quoting Mark Twain's statement that no girl in Hannibal was ever insulted or seduced, or even scandalously gossiped about, he observes finally: "Whatever the defect of experience or recognition that made him thus libel a full-blooded folk, that is how he remembered Eden." In hinting at some defect of experience or recognition, he implies that this "sexual queasiness" of Mark Twain's was somewhat abnormal; thus he approaches Mr. Brooks's diagnosis.

Whatever the source of the defect, most of Mark Twain's women characters float through his pages on pink-tinted clouds of sentimentality, with all the verve and zest and passion of bisque dolls. They are of charming purity, but they have no life. In the *Autobiography* he tells of meeting in Calcutta an acquaintance out of "the pathetic past, the beautiful past, the dear and lamented past," and his description of her is typical of his attitude toward Woman in general: "Mary Wilson . . . was dainty and sweet, peach-blooming and exquisite, gracious and lovely in character." He could draw with finality an old pioneer woman, or a middle-aged frontier woman, or a young slave woman; but in dealing with women who could be objects of desire, as Mr. DeVoto defines them, he could only sentimentalize the "virtuous" and ignore altogether their sisters of the opposite persuasion. In his young manhood he must have seen sex blatant and unveneered often enough. Tawdry queens of Natchez-under-the-Hill and broken-down beauties from the New Orleans dives undoubtedly traveled on the river boats, and the lights-o'-love of the western Gold Coast did not exactly hide their lights under bushels. Life must have shown him many a woman with a fascinating though irregular story, but one would never suspect it from reading his books; that is, with the single exception of *Pudd'nhead Wilson* and its courageous portrayal of Roxy, concubine and slave. The circumspect taste of his period cannot completely account for this tendency in Mark Twain, for his contemporary Henry James acknowledged in his novels the existence of sex and even his friend Howells, as Mr. DeVoto notes, was not so prudish in print as Mark Twain. It is both odd and significant that he practically excluded such material from his fiction, otherwise so amazingly full of the life of his times. There was a psychological block, apparently, which held him from the use of this material for literature.

Mr. Brooks further charges Mark Twain with spending a life in the leading-strings first of his mother and later of his wife, subjugating himself to feminine dominance in any available guise. Forgetting that he left home and mother at seventeen, that he did not marry until he was almost thirty-five years old, and that in the intervening years no one woman looms large in his life, Mr. Brooks asserts that he was the Eternal Child, devoted to the mother complex, afraid to stand alone. Add to this will-to-obey-Woman another ingredient which Mr. Brooks has emphasized — namely, the sex fear which he believes existed on the frontier — and we draw near the formula which Mr. DeVoto has recently suggested for solving "the dark, sensitive, and complex consciousness" which was Mark Twain's mind. In *Mark Twain at Work*, speaking of "the book that someone must eventually devote to the bases of Mark's mind," Mr. DeVoto prophesies that perhaps its central effort "will be to determine why death . . . colored his phantasy from childhood on," and that perhaps the answer, if it is found, "will show that the threat of death was twinned in his phantasy . . . with the fear of woman's sex." Mr. Brooks earlier believed that Mark Twain lived in subjugation to woman's sex; now Mr. DeVoto approaches him in the surmise that the fear of woman's sex was embedded in Mark Twain's mind.

Another charge of Mr. Brooks's was that Mark Twain was a case of arrested development, able to write well only when producing books about boys and for boys. In *Mark Twain at Work*, Mr. DeVoto comments: "If ever a writer was imprisoned in his boyhood, clearly Mark Twain was." It is possible to offer artistic and aesthetic reasons for Mark Twain's literary emphasis on Hannibal and for his repeated use of his two boy characters. These reasons will appear later; the significant thing at this point is that in Mr. DeVoto's choice of the word *imprisoned* he approaches the idea advanced earlier by Mr. Brooks. The difference in context shades the meaning in each case: for Brooks, Mark Twain was "imprisoned" in frustration, while for DeVoto he was "imprisoned" in imaginative faculty.

Nevertheless, despite the fact that Mr. DeVoto still views his own writing as "in part a refutation of Mr. Brooks's," it is apparent that he has recently made some admissions dangerous to his original position.

Mr. DeVoto appears pre-eminent as a source of Mark Twain criticism; but there remains — for me, at least — a residue of truth in the arguments of Mr. Brooks which his opponents have never quite been able to argue away. "One may agree with Mr. Brooks or one may disagree with him," says Edward Wagenknecht. "The only thing that one cannot do . . . is to ignore him. Nobody can write about Mrs. Clemens . . . as he might have written in 1919."[9] Although a good many years have gone by since *The Ordeal of Mark Twain* appeared in 1920, I would still agree with Mr. Wagenknecht that Mr. Brooks cannot be ignored; and I would add, "Nobody can write about Mr. Clemens as he might have written in 1919." Perhaps this is a good time to state my own position on two main points: I believe that Mr. Brooks was right in asserting that there was a strong internal conflict in Mark Twain; but I do not agree with him about the nature of that conflict. Again, I believe he was right in asserting that there was a certain amount of frustration in Mark Twain's literary work; but I do not agree with him about the nature of that frustration or the form it took. Mr. Brooks and Mr. DeVoto have each told part of the truth; each, however, has failed to consider certain evidence in Mark Twain's work.

As a reply to the joint charge of Messrs. Brooks and DeVoto that Mark Twain never analyzed any effect beyond its mere grammar, there exist his many letters to William Dean Howells, in which he discusses minute effects of dialect, characterization, and various other problems of writing technique. These references to technique are, I believe, valuable as an index to the conceptions he held concerning the nature and function of literature, since critics — from S.T. Coleridge to T.S. Eliot — have generally maintained that the writer's comment on the principles of his craft constitutes a fertile field for criticism.

In *Mark Twain at Work*, Mr. DeVoto describes certain unpublished manuscripts; he has there himself offered the most conclusive refutation of his own earlier doubt that Mark Twain "ever analyzed, beyond its mere grammar," an effect of his own or anyone else's. He presents a series of efforts made by Mark Twain to portray certain ideas in fiction. The two themes which then obsessed Mark Twain — and had long obsessed him — were man's helplessness in the grip of inexorable circumstance (or of the passionless, indifferent forces of the universe) and man's own pervading pettiness and cruelty. He was struggling to find the correct form for the embodiment of these ideas, ideas which Mr. DeVoto says are "repeated over and over in the various manuscripts, modulated, changed, adapted, blended, and in the end, harmonized." These ideas will be treated fully in connection with Mark Twain's fiction. Here it is noted merely that his struggle was an artist's attempt to objectify as art the innermost materials of his mind and heart, and that all this striving represents, surely, an effort on a much higher level than a mere preoccupation with grammar. Yet, in this same book, Mr. DeVoto indicates that when the drive of Mark Twain's genius and his impulse to write were "in circuit with the deeper levels of his phantasy things went well, but when the circuit was broken he could only improvise." In other words, when he was "right," he was wonderful; but he exerted no conscious control over his writing.

Aware of the importance of form in writing, Mark Twain says in the *Eruption* volume that there are "some books that refuse to be written . . . It isn't because the book is not there and worth being written — it is only because the right form for the story does not present itself. There is only one right form for a story." The passage does not exhibit a comprehensive grasp of writing discipline, but at least the concern with technique is there.

His light-handed attitude towards his own literary work, so much deplored by Mr. Brooks, must always be taken with a grain of salt, just as his disparagement of his own knowledge of books must be. Miss Brashear has made the pertinent comment that "it was a part of the legend he deliberately created about himself, either because it pleased his vanity to believe that what he had read had been of small value in his development, or because he knew that he was more interesting to his American public in the role of an original than as a man who had from boyhood extended his powers . . . by diligent reading. He was unacademic, but not unliterary." Speaking of his own assets as a novelist, he once wrote: "I surely have the equipment, a wide culture, and all of it real, none of it artificial, for I don't know anything about books." Again, he insisted that he did not know "enough to hurt" about books, "Only a few languages and a little history." Yet the compilations of his reading by Henry A. Pochmann, Miss Brashear, and Mr. Wagenknecht show that he had considerable familiarity with books. As Mrs. J.T. Fields recorded in her diary on April 6, 1876, after a visit from him, "he reads everything." Indeed, Miss Brashear goes so far as to declare that, leaving out of account all aspects of his training except the literary aspect, "Sam Clemens became a reader and critic of the best in literature by the time he was twenty-five years old."

Mr. Wagenknecht, whose book is devoted to the thesis that Mark Twain was not a conscious artist, states that "he did not take himself very seriously as a man of letters." Mr. Wagenknecht finds Mark Twain "abnormally sensitive, aesthetic, creative," although different from the general run of writing men. He follows Mr. DeVoto in his opinion of the frontier as the thing basically determinative in Mark Twain and perhaps goes beyond DeVoto when he declares:

"To say that Mark Twain was an 'improvisator,' a raconteur, is . . . virtually equivalent to saying that he was a talker and not a writer."

This, it seems to me, is going a bit too far. Of the element of orality in Mark Twain's work there can be no question. He could copy to the life the anecdotal technique of the frontier raconteur, reproducing carefully the vocal emphasis, the speech rhythms, the authentic idioms. But there can be no question, either, of his knowledge of the distinctions between talking and writing. He made distinctions even between the methods of handling frontier anecdotes which he intended for use on the platform and for printing in his books, because he knew, as he said in the *Eruption* book, that "written things are not for speech; their form is literary; . . . they have to be limbered up, broken up, colloquialized, and turned into the common forms of unpremeditated talk." He used as illustration the anecdote he called "Grandfather's Old Ram," which he revised night after night upon the lecture platform until its final form for oral delivery was quite different from the original version which he had printed for reading purposes in *Roughing* It. He remarked that if the reader will compare the two, he will notice how different the spoken version is from the reading version. He confessed himself unable to explain "why the one can be effectively recited . . . and the other can't; there is a reason but it is too subtle for adequate conveyance. . . . I sense it but cannot express it; it is as elusive as an odor, pungent, pervasive, but defying analysis."

Conversely, he held that spoken things are not for print. His reluctance to give interviews stemmed from his belief that what would sound satisfactory to reporters would not read well in print. The novelist Elinor Glyn once interviewed him, but he refused to let her publish her script, writing bluntly to her: "It . . . is a poor literary job . . . Approximations, synopsized speeches, translated poems, artificial flowers, and chromos all have a sort of value, but it is small." Edward W. Bok also interviewed him, but when Mark Twain read the result, his refusal to let it be published was adamant. His letter to Bok reads in part:

> For several . . . reasons, an "interview" must, as a rule, be an absurdity . . . It is an attempt to use a boat on land or a wagon on water . . . Spoken speech is one thing, written speech is quite another. Print is the proper vehicle for the latter, but it isn't for the former. The moment "talk" is put into print, you recognize that it is not what it was when you heard it; . . . an immense something has disappeared from it. That is its soul. You have nothing but a dead carcass left on your hands . . . everything that gave that body warmth, grace, friendliness, and charm . . . is gone and nothing is left but a pallid, stiff, and repulsive cadaver. Such is "talk" almost invariably, as you see it lying in state in an "interview." The interviewer seldom tries to tell *how* a thing was said; he merely puts in the naked remark . . . When one writes for print his methods are very different. He follows forms which have but little resemblance to conversation, but they make the reader understand what the writer is trying to convey. And when the writer is making a story and finds it necessary to report some of the talk of his characters, observe how cautiously . . . he goes at that risky and difficult thing. "If he had dared to say that thing in my presence," said Alfred, taking a mock heroic attitude and casting an arch glance upon the company, "blood would have flowed."
>
> "If he had dared to say that thing in my presence," said Hawkwood, with that in his eye which caused more than one heart in that guilty assemblage to quake, "blood would have flowed."

> "If he had dared to say that thing in my presence," said the paltry blusterer, with valor on his tongue and pallor on his lips, "blood would have flowed."
>
> So painfully aware is the novelist that naked talk in print conveys no meaning that he loads, and often overloads, almost every utterance of his characters with explanations and interpretations . . .
>
> Now, in your interview, you have certainly . . . set down the sentences I uttered as I said them. But . . . what my manner was at certain points is not indicated. Therefore, no reader can possibly know where I was in earnest and where I was joking; or whether I was joking altogether or was in earnest altogether. Such a report . . . can convey many meanings to the reader, but never the right one. To add interpretations which would convey the right meaning is a something which would require — what? An art so high and fine and difficult that no possessor of it would ever be allowed to waste it on interviews.

Such delicate distinctions and fine-drawn shadings between spoken art and written art should help to refute the general impression of Mark Twain as the careless writer who simply wrote as he talked.

In 1908 he wrote to a friend, "There are times — thousands of times — when I can expose the half of my mind and conceal the other half," and such mental legerdemain increases the complexity of the Mark Twain problem. Mr. Wagenknecht takes account of this quality in him in words which recall Jane Clemens's early joke about striking his average and accepting what was left as perfect truth without a flaw. Mr. Wagenknecht warns that at the outset we must keep in mind that we are dealing with a humorist and that "the problem is to decide just what percentage to take. It is always extremely difficult to tell when Mark Twain is reporting and when he is elaborating, when he is actually conveying information to his auditor and when he is 'stringing him along.'" Yet Mr. Wagenknecht himself apparently gives serious consideration to Mark Twain's letter to a little girl, Elsie Leslie Lyde, in which he tells her that he began a slipper he has embroidered for her "with the first red bar . . . without ulterior design, or plan of any sort — just as I would begin a Prince and Pauper or any other tale"; he compares the making of a story and the putting together of the slipper, until finally "there's your book all finished up and never cost you an idea." Elsewhere Mr. Wagenknecht implies that to Mark Twain the business life was "worth two" of the literary life, since in business he could feel power in his hands: "When he finds in himself even a little aptitude along this line, he swells up like a pouter pigeon; no purely literary achievement could for a moment be compared with it."

A good deal of the evidence tends to refute this statement. In 1909, in "The Turning Point of My Life," as he looked backward over a long life spaced with various business ventures and acquisitions of wealth, he said, "To me, the most important feature of my life is its literary feature." And in 1902 he wrote congratulating his old friend Joe Goodman, who had devoted years to a study of the Mayan civilization and inscriptions: "You think you get 'poor pay' for your twenty years? No, oh no. You have lived in a paradise of the intellect whose lightest joys were beyond the reach of the longest purse in Christendom." That he himself had experienced those joys he revealed to his daughter Clara. In *My Father, Mark Twain*, she tells how he once complimented her for being so absorbed in her musical studies that she cared for no other pleasures; then he continued: "It is as I used to be with the pen long ago, and it is life, life, LIFE — there is no life comparable to it for a moment. Genius lives in a world of its own . . . Everybody lives, but only Genius lives richly, sumptuously, imperially." He was speaking with the voice of authority and experience. His own power of absorption in his writing will be attested in the pages to follow.

But in praising Howells for the particular excellences in fiction that he felt he himself lacked, he once declared, "I can't write a novel, for I lack the faculty." Mr. Brooks considers this statement in connection with another of Mark Twain's: "I like history, biography, travels, curious facts and strange happenings, and science. And I detest novels, poetry, and theology." In spite of the declaration that he couldn't write a novel, he repeatedly referred elsewhere to his own books as novels. And the kind of novels he detested included the namby-pamby products of sentimental "lady authoresses" and books blighted by what he called "niggling analysis" and "jejune romanticism." Mr. Brooks, however, was led to write: "Do we ask, then, why Mark Twain 'detested' novels? It was because he had been able to produce only one himself and that a failure."[10]

But it is time to turn from the critics to Mark Twain — this man who "detested" novels, who was "indifferent" to literary effects and "insolent" toward his own literary work. In 1894, in an essay called "What Paul Bourget Thinks of Us," he wrote a reasoned discussion on the importance of the novel which gives it an authority only recently yielded to it by men of our own time. He placed the novelist above the mere compiler of data (the statistician) or the "naturalist" with his collection of bugs which he studies and labels (the equivalent of our modern sociologist with his case studies):

> The Observer of Peoples . . ., when he is at home, observing his own folks, . . . is often able to prove competency. But . . . when he is abroad observing unfamiliar peoples the chances are heavily against

> him. He is then a naturalist observing a bug . . . He could explain . . . the bug to himself. But to explain the bug to the bug — that is quite a different matter.
>
> A foreigner can photograph the exteriors of a nation, but . . . no foreigner can report its interior — its soul, its life, its speech, its thought. I think that a knowledge of these things is acquirable in only one way . . . *absorption*; years and years . . . of intercourse with the life concerned; of living it, indeed. . . . Observation? . . . One learns peoples through the heart, not the eyes or the intellect.
>
> There is only one expert who is qualified to examine the souls and the life of a people and make a valuable report — the native novelist . . . How much of his competency is derived from conscious "observation"? The amount is so slight that it counts for next to nothing . . . Almost the whole capital of the novelist is the slow accumulation of *un*conscious observation — absorption . . .

To return to novel-building. Does the native novelist try to generalize the nation? No, he lays plainly before you the ways and speech and life of a few people grouped in a certain place — his own place — and that is one book. In time he and his brethren will report to you the life and the people of the whole nation . . . And when a thousand novels have been written, there you have the soul of the people, the life of the people, the speech of the people; and not anywhere else can these be had. And the shadings of character, manners, feelings, ambitions, will be infinite.

Mark Twain brought to the writing of such books as *Huckleberry Finn* and *Pudd'nhead Wilson* the sort of "unconscious observation — absorption" that he specifies here as the equipment of the novelist. But that he also gave a deal of time to thinking about the writing craft must begin to be evident.

Nevertheless, it must be freely admitted that much of his work shows artistic weaknesses. In his first book about Mark Twain, Mr. DeVoto comments on his intrusion of burlesque into superb literary material and, more recently, on his "painful disharmonies." The most damaging charge made by Mr. Brooks is that the true satirist must substitute a new and personal ideal for the satirized "racial ideal" (as he terms it) and that Mark Twain has no ideal to set up as the measure of society; in other words, he lacks a "norm." Mr. Wagenknecht says that he lacked the ability to project himself very far and that there is an intermediate stage in the creative process that he seemed never quite able to master. His abundant creative energy was "never more than imperfectly under his own command. The natural result is that hardly any of his books achieve unity of tone or succeed in maintaining anything like a standard of uniform excellence." Painful disharmonies, lack of a norm, failure to achieve unity of tone — there is a basic similarity in these critical strictures against the work of Mark Twain. Granting that much of the time he worked consciously towards a foreseen and desired end — and this is what the evidence shows — how are we to explain such weaknesses in his work?

The shadowy outlines of the Mark Twain problem begin to appear. Obvious questions concern the effects of this disharmony, this lack of unity, upon the artistic quality of his literary work. But, beyond that, an analysis of what Mr. DeVoto calls "the bases of Mark Twain's mind" seems called for. And then, what conflict or conflicts existing at the "bases of his mind" made it impossible for him to achieve the norm demanded by Mr. Brooks, the harmony found lacking by Mr. DeVoto, or the unity of tone desired by Mr. Wagenknecht?

NOTES

1. Calvin H. Higbie, recorded by Albert Bigelow Paine in *Mark Twain: A Biography*, I, 195 (hereafter referred to as *Biography*).

2. Edward Wagenknecht, *Mark Twain: The Man and His Work*, 143.

3. Paine, *Biography*, III, 1394-95.

4. *Ibid.*, I, 386.

5. Wagenknecht, *Mark Twain: The Man and His Work*, 102.

6. Mort Weisinger, in "Listen! Mark Twain Speaking", *Saturday Evening Post*, Vol. 221, No. 1 (July 3, 1948), disclosed that the Voice Library at Yale University, collected by G. Robert Vincent, contains a record of Mark Twain's voice.

7. See, for example, Bernard DeVoto, *Mark Twain's America*, 154.

8. *Ibid.*, 92, 240; see also pp. 127, 154, 158, 243, 245, and 252.

9. Mr. Brooks speaks of Mark Twain as "a shorn Samson" led about by a "simple Delilah" who held complete sway over him and steadily weakened his literary strength. Both Livy and Howells toned him down somewhat, and their criticism was often sound; neither effected any real change in him. Early in their married life he gave up smoking to please Livy — "just as I would . . . quit wearing socks if she thought them immoral." The reform was short-lived, and he was soon back to chain-smoking. It should be noted that Livy, reared in strict orthodoxy, followed Mark Twain into religious unorthodoxy (Paine, *Biography*, II, 650-51). The turn of this vital issue I regard as conclusive evidence of which of the two wielded the stronger influence over the other.

10. Quoted in Wagenknecht, *Mark Twain: The Man and His Work*, 48. In justice to Mr. Brooks, it should be noted that Mr. Wagenknecht used the 1920 edition of The Ordeal of Mark Twain, not the revised edition of 1933.

2

Realism, Romanticism and Politics in Mark Twain

—William F. Byrne

MARK TWAIN AND IRVING BABBITT

Imagination Shapes Society and Politics

According to Irving Babbitt, the imagination plays an "all-important role in both literature and life." For Babbitt, society and politics are shaped by the imagination, because it is within the context of the imagination that one's reason and will inevitably must function. He explains that

> man is cut off from immediate contact with anything abiding and therefore worthy to be called real, and condemned to live in an element of fiction or illusion, but he may . . . lay hold with the aid of the imagination on the element of oneness that is inextricably blended with the manifoldness and change and to just that extent may build up a sound model for imitation. One tends to be an individualist with true standards . . . only in so far as one understands the relation between appearance

> and reality—what the philosophers call the epistemological problem.[1]

Imaginative Truth and Error

For Babbitt, the development of a sound ethical center involves a degree of imitation and adherence to standards. What Babbitt has in mind is not slavish imitation of artificial external models but the careful building up of sound models for imitation. To accomplish this, one must be solidly anchored in reality and able to glimpse what Babbitt calls "the one in the many." Claes Ryn has said that Babbitt's solution to the epistemological problem is "to move closer to the truth above all by training the imagination, which is intimately related to the will. This is done negatively by unmasking perversions, . . . positively by discovering and absorbing the visions of the imaginative master-minds."[2] For Babbitt and Ryn, the work of artists and writers helps to shape one's imagination and, hence, one's will, which in turn further shapes the imagination. The shaping of the imagination may help one move closer to, or further from, truth. Works which move one toward truth are those which are anchored in reality. This does not mean that they flatly and indiscriminately portray a shallow empirical 'reality,' but that they possess a deep sense of the "oneness that is always changing." Such works help men to "find . . . concrete modes of ordering their lives, individually and in social cooperation, which are directly experienced as conducive to happiness and a heightened sense of reality."[3]

If it is true that artists and writers have played, and continue to play, significant roles in shaping the American imagination, one of the most important influences must surely be that of Mark Twain. In addition to achieving enduring popularity and becoming a part of the American literary canon, Twain, and, in particular, his Adventures of Huckleberry Finn have been the subjects of extensive discourse in many fields of study, including political philosophy. The purpose of this article is to offer a unique interpretation of Twain, one that approaches his work from a perspective informed by the thought of Irving Babbitt. Twain and Babbitt have something in common: they both viewed the romantic imagination, at least in some of its forms, as failing to move man toward truth. In Rousseau and Romanticism Babbitt offers an excellent account of the nature of the romantic imagination and its influence on modern thought and politics. Various literary scholars have observed that "Twain's literary opinions have been ti ed to realism because they seem to be based on an ingrained hostility toward romantic literature . . ."[4] Twain is typically classified as a member of the loosely defined 'school' of American Literary Realism associated with his friend William Dean Howells, although in recent years certain scholars have questioned the appropriateness of this classification. This question will be left for others to pursue. What is important here is that Twain would have wholeheartedly agreed with Babbitt's contention that the romantic imagination is one of the "perversions" which must be "unmasked."

Liberal Democracy Threatened

While Twain does not philosophically examine the subject of romanticism, Babbitt has written extensively in this area. Babbitt's objections to many common forms of romanticism derive from his view of man, a "classical" view which he regards as generally Aristotelian. He conceives of man's inner life as essentially a struggle between a lower and higher will; the higher will serves as an "inner check" on certain undesirable impulses of the lower will. While this higher will has a 'universal' quality, it must also be individually developed if it is to be successful in its task; the individual must find an ethical center with the aid of the imagination and sound models. Romantic literature, according to Babbitt, rejects "decorum" and, in doing so, fails to offer the reader sound models and standards, while "decorum is for the classicist the grand master-piece to observe because it is only thus he can show that he has a genuine centre set above his own ego."[5] Romanticism, in fact, not only fails to recognize t he need to check the impulses of the lower will but, instead, exalts those expansive impulses. This unanchored romantic imagination is a danger to liberal democracy because "no amount of devotion to society and its supposed interests can take the place of this inner obeisance of the spirit to standards."[6] If liberal democracy is to survive, the moral imagination, which Babbitt associates with Burke and with classical (but not most neo-classical) art and literature, must prevail over the expansive Rousseauesque imagination which Babbitt associates with romanticism. According to Babbitt:

> One may . . . regard the battle that has been in progress in the field of political thought since the end of the eighteenth century as being in its most significant phase a battle between the spirit of Burke and that of Rousseau. And this opposition between Burke and Rousseau will itself be found to turn, in the last analysis, on the opposition between two different types of imagination.[7]

Unreal Realism

A study of Twain provides an excellent opportunity to develop an understanding of the nature and effects of the Rousseauesque romantic imagination identified by Babbitt. This article will both explore Twain's critical portrayal of romanticism and uncover the romantic, Rousseauesque origins of his own realism. While Twain offers valuable insight into romantic influences on human behavior, it will be shown that he nevertheless fails to possess the kind of classical or moral imagination which characterizes the "spirit of Burke" and that an uncritical reading of Twain's literature can lead the reader to a moral and philosophical dead end. In addition to offering insight into the role romanticism can play in politics, the study of

Twain is important because of the likelihood that he has influenced, and continues to influence, American politics and society through the role that literature plays in shaping the imagination.

Before turning to Twain's literature it is important to make an observation about the man himself. In 1920 biographer Van Wyck Brooks remarked that "to those who are interested in American life and letters there has been no question of greater significance, during the last few years, than the pessimism of Mark Twain . . . his oft-expressed belief that man is the meanest of the animals and life a tragic mistake."[8] The "pessimistic cynicism" which Twain increasingly exhibited during his life has always been a problem for his biographers. Some have attributed it to personal misfortunes regarding family and finances, but, as Brooks points out, Twain experienced no more than his fair share of such troubles, and in general could be said to have led an enviable life. Moreover, despite his cynicism, Twain's personality is typically viewed as upbeat, and he described himself as a basically happy person; he certainly did not appear to suffer from anything like clinical depression. Brooks's explanation for the emergence of Twain's pessimism and misanthropy is that Twain was a frustrated artist who yearned to produce timeless, serious works of literature but ended up as a mere humorist, storyteller, businessman, and celebrity. Brooks also attempts a psychological evaluation of Twain and argues that he suffered from a kind of "arrested development." Brooks's approach to Twain is controversial, and ultimately it is not much more satisfying or convincing than more conventional views. Beyond this basic observation, this study will not attempt to analyze Twain's life or determine the relative accuracy of the various explanations offered by biographers for his cynicism and pessimism. This article will, however, argue that, regardless of whether Twain's pessimism can be viewed as psychological or circumstantial, it is also unquestionably philosophical in nature. By utilizing a 'Babbittian' approach it will be demonstrated that Twain's pessimistic misanthropy is intimately related to his particular brand of realism and to his relative success or failure in producing the kind of literature that helps develop the moral imagination and move one toward truth.

TOM AND HUCK

The Dynamics of the Romantic Imagination

The contrast between the characters of Tom Sawyer and Huck Finn is used by Twain to illustrate the romantic imagination. Tom has led a quintessential middle-class American existence. He attends school and church, is comfortable materially, and has an unexciting but stable, and certainly bearable, home life with his Aunt Polly. In contrast, Huck's life, though sometimes viewed as happy-go-lucky, has been by objective standards a nightmare. He has been raised in complete poverty by a worthless and shiftless father who is rarely present and often drunk, who sometimes treats Huck cruelly and has failed to have him educated, and who demonstrates a wide range of bad personality traits. When Huckleberry Finn opens Huck's situation has recently changed; he has been adopted by the Widow Douglas and has been going to school, and is adapting to his new situation. Still, Huck's personality and outlook remain basically the same as they were in The Adventures of Tom Sawyer. One notable characteristic of Huck is that he seems to remain outside society, looking in Another characteristic is his curious lack of a boyish imagination. It is as if the harsh realities of his life have forced Huck to grow up fast, and to focus exclusively on the practical concerns of the world immediately around him. Forced by necessity to live by his wits, Huck is constantly striving to work with the actual circumstances at hand. Huck's imagination actually functions remarkably well in helping him solve real-world problems; for example, he elaborately and convincingly fakes his own murder in order to escape from his father, and he is able to make up complex stories instantaneously when needed to deceive a stranger. However, Huck cannot suspend disbelief even for boyish play; he does not fantasize. In contrast, Tom is spectacularly imaginative in the boyish, romantic sense. He has learned some history, geography, and religion, and, we are reminded again and again, he has filled his head with romantic adventure novels. This material has shaped Tom's worldview and feeds his fantasies, which he is constantly trying to act out.

Numerous examples exist in both Tom Sawyer and Huckleberry Finn of Tom's vivid imagination and Huck's corresponding flatness. Perhaps the best example is the "band of robbers" that Tom establishes at the beginning of Huckleberry Finn. Tom's vision for the gang is very specific, and shamelessly romantic: "We ain't burglars. That ain't no sort of style. We are highwaymen. We stop stages and carriages on the road, with masks on, and kill the people and take their watches and money." Some victims will not be killed but ransomed. Tom isn't sure what 'ransomed' means, but "I've seen it in books, and so of course that's what we've got to do." Women, of course, will not be killed but taken back to their cave, "and by-and-by they fall in love with you and never want to go home any more." An objection is made that "soon we'll have the cave so cluttered up with women, and fellows waiting to be ransomed, that there won't be no place for the robbers," but this objection, like all others, is dismissed by Tom. Such mundane practical considerations are irrelevant in Tom's imaginary universe, and in any case cannot override the authority of the romantic literature he has read. As Tom says, "Do you want to go to doing different from what's in the books, and get things all muddled up?" While Tom's imagination may be vivid, we discover that it is also slavishly imitative (26-28).[9]

Huck tells us that,

> we played robber now and then about a month, and then I resigned. All the boys did. We hadn't robbed nobody, we hadn't killed any people, but only just pretended. We used to hop out of the woods and go charging down on hod-drovers and women in carts taking garden stuff to market, but we never hived any of them. Tom Sawyer called the hogs "ingots," and he called the turnips and stuff "julery" and we would go to the cave and pow-wow over what we had done and how many people we had killed and marked. But I couldn't see no profit in it (30-31).

Huck Finn's interest is in "profit," not pretending; he decides "that all that stuff was only just one of Tom Sawyer's lies" (33). While this lack of imagination in Huck is similar to that which he often displayed in Tom Sawyer, an interesting shift has occurred. In the earlier book Huck was the odd man out on issues of the imagination; the other boys welcomed the opportunity to share Tom's dreams. In this case, however, we are told that all the boys resigned; it is Tom who is the odd man out. The other boys are perhaps getting too old for this kind of imaginative play, but not Tom. He alone remains determined to re-enact the kinds of dramatic events he has read about in fiction. The change between the two books is significant; it signals that Mark Twain is now at war with the romantic imagination. As Babbitt and countless others have pointed out, children are romantics. Therefore, as a children's book, Tom Sawyer would have been a singularly inappropriate place for a vigorous attack on romanticism; Twain doe s address the issue there, but in limited and subtle ways. Huckleberry Finn, on the other hand, was written for adults, and here Twain would not hesitate to drive home his points.

The "Half-Educated Man"

The character of Tom can be likened to the "half-educated man" employed by Babbitt to illustrate "the particular craving that is met by Rousseauistic idealism," while Huck is his foil, the "uncultivated man." According to Babbitt,

> the half-educated man may be defined as the man who has acquired a degree of critical self-consciousness sufficient to detach him from the standards of his time and place, but not sufficient to acquire the new standards that come with a more thorough cultivation. It was pointed out long ago that the characteristic of the half-educated man is that he is incurably restless; that he is filled with every manner of desire. In contrast with him the uncultivated man, the peasant, let us say, and the man of high cultivation have few and simple desires . . . But what is most noteworthy about the half-educated man is . . . that these desires are so often incompatible. He craves various good things, but is not willing to pay the price—not willing to make the necessary renunciations.[10]

Huck's desires are indeed remarkably few and simple. Tom, on the other hand, seems to want a great deal out of life. He wants adventure and romantic drama; he wants to be a hero, to be dashing, to be important, to have "style." Life in St. Petersburg, Missouri, does not seem to offer any of this; real adventure lies far away, among "A-rabs and elephants." But at the same time Tom remains committed to middle-American life. In fact, he requires Huck to conform to this lifestyle. Huck tells us that he originally was not going to remain with the Widow Douglas, but Tom told him he could only join the band of robbers "if I would go back to the widow and be respectable" (18). In Babbitt's words, the half-educated man wants "to have his cake and eat it too." If Tom were an adult, he could be called a hypocrite, and Twain had a marked distaste for hypocrisy. When considering whether to write a book about Tom Sawyer's growing up, Twain concluded that "if I went on now and took him into manhood, he would just lie, like all the one-horse men in literature, and the reader would conceive a hearty contempt for him."[11] Of course, one could argue that here Tom is only a boy, and therefore could not be expected to actually have adventures such as he imagines. Nevertheless, at the end of the book it is Huck who heads out for the Western territories, where many real-life adventures no doubt lie in store for him. While it was Tom who first talked about going out West, we end the book suspecting that he will actually head back to Aunt Polly, to "respectability," and to the adventures of his imagination.

Dreamers can Hurt Those around Them

Twain paints an unflattering portrait of Tom and his imagination. We are all familiar with such childhood fantasies, however, and are prepared to dismiss them as harmless, even healthy. This creates a problem for Twain, for he wants to convince us that the romantic imagination is not just silly, but downright dangerous. In the latter part of the book, after Huck and the runaway slave Jim float down the Mississippi on their raft, Huck, through an unlikely coincidence, is reunited with Tom. Jim has been recaptured, and it so happens that he is being held on the farm where the boys are staying. Huck wants to free Jim, and Tom agrees to help. Of course, Tom immediately takes over. While freeing Jim could be accomplished quite easily, Tom is not about to pass up a golden opportunity to live out one of his fantasies. He has learned from his adventure books that the crude but efficient methods preferred by Huck and Jim are not suitable for a romantic hero. Tom therefore concocts a "stylish" but outlandishly elaborate scheme, prolonging Jim's captivity. In addition to making the escape much more difficult, complicated, and dangerous than it needs to be, Tom also wants to bring Jim rats to train as pets in his "prison cell" and wants Jim to grow a flower and water it with his tears. Tom also designs for Jim a coat of arms, displaying impressive knowledge of heraldic terms and devices. Ultimately, Tom goes so far as actually to send Jim's captors anonymous warnings of the upcoming escape attempt, greatly increasing the likelihood that they will be caught.

Tom's antics mask the fact that this is deadly serious business. Jim originally ran away because he was to be sold and separated from his wife and children. His only hope to be reunited is to escape to freedom and then buy them. Although Tom professes to be helping Jim, his actual callousness is striking. For Tom, Jim's plight pales beside the imperative of attaining the romantic vision. Increasingly, it becomes evident that Tom has difficulty distinguishing between fantasy and reality. When the escape finally occurs, Tom gets shot, suffering a potentially serious wound. Even then, as Huck goes for a doctor, Tom tells him to "blindfold the doctor tight and fast, and make him swear to be silent as the grave, and put a purse full of gold in his hand . . ." (345). In the end, we discover that before leaving St. Petersburg Tom had learned that the Widow Douglas had set Jim free in her will; all of this was unnecessary. Tom has prolonged Jim's captivity and risked all their lives, purely for the sake of a romantic vision.

Behind the facade of boyish fun, Twain has accomplished a devastating portrayal of the dangers lurking in the romantic imagination. Tom feels compelled to be a romantic hero; of course, since Jim has technically already been set free, the best Tom can do is to be a fake hero, but even this illusion of heroism is so important to Tom that he practically becomes a villain in order to create it, forsaking the real interests of his own friends. The need to attain the romantic vision is allowed to overrule the demands of reality, resulting not only in foolishness, but in something bordering on cruelty. This latter part of Huckleberry Finn, full of Tom Sawyer's antics, is a jarring shift from the middle of the book, which had been dominated by Huck and Jim's trip down the river. The ending section is tiresome, and is often considered a failure. However, one commentator, Catherine Zuckert, argues that Twain had a definite purpose in mind: "he tries to separate the reader's viewpoint even further from the narrator's at the end—by making the reader sick and tired of all the boyish tricks. Failing to perceive the critical thrust of the disgust that Twain purposely engendered, however, most commentators have simply concluded that his art ran out at the end."[12] It is true that by the end of the book we begin to wish that Tom would just grow up. It can be argued, however, that it is not simply "boyish tricks" we grow sick of, but Tom's romantic imagination which is fueling them. We recognize that the antics serve no purpose, and wish Tom would get done with them. Sandwiched between the book's Tom Sawyer-dominated beginning and ending sections, Huck and Jim's trip down the river, free of Tom and his romantic role-playing, is like a breath of fresh air.

Visions Need Anchor in Reality

Twain sees Tom Sawyer's imagination as the shaper and driver of his will. On the one hand, Tom is hindered by his imagination, since it blurs the line between reality and fantasy and impairs both the effectiveness and morality of his actions in the real world, leading him into trouble. On the other hand, Tom's imagination provides him with an unusual energy, spurring him to action. Adventure novels, supplemented by a romantic reading of history, have become Tom's idealized models for life. He has become dissatisfied with his mundane life in St. Petersburg and instead wants to lead the life of an adventure novel; indeed, Tom wants to become the hero of an adventure novel. A problem exists here; the real world, at least the vast majority of the time, is not much like an adventure novel. Tom nevertheless wants to be important, special, a man with "style"; to accomplish this, he needs to re-create in the real world the romantic images that he has encountered. To re-create these images, he needs to secure the cooperation of others. Thus, Tom's romantic imagination is manifest, in part, as a drive to dominate those around him. Tom develops a strong will. It is manifest not only in his drive to dominate but in his high level of activity and creativity, which gives him a certain charisma and makes him attractive to others. Tom is a natural leader, who achieves a certain 'success'; but his plans end in disaster. Disaster results because the original vision was not solidly grounded in reality; the real world ultimately cannot conform to it. In fact, in putting the plans into action important real-world considerations are downplayed or ignored, because they conflict with the vision. Further, attempts to resolve the incompatibility between the romantic vision and the real world prompt Tom to take actions which are at best inconsiderate and at worst immoral.

Romantic Tyranny

What is particularly troubling is the response of Huck to Tom's antics. For one, he does not seem to mind that Tom has deceived them. More important, Huck goes along with the elaborate, prolonged scheme to free Jim. Of course, Huck is unaware at that point of Tom's deception. Nevertheless, numerous opportunities exist for Jim to escape easily, but Huck encourages Jim to stick to Tom's romantic plans instead. Why does Huck do this? After all, although he is uneducated, he is clearly not stupid, and at times he demonstrates exceptional resourcefulness and good sense for a boy. Nevertheless, Huck allows Tom to dominate him; he acquiesces in Tom's romantic vision. Perhaps Huck has learned too well the art of meeting the world on its own terms. His adaptability serves him well under most circumstances, but makes him too accommodating in the face of a dominating will armed with a romantic vision. Unlike Tom, Huck himself has no delusions of grandeur, so he has little trouble deferring to others; in fact, one could say that he demonstrates an excessive level of humility. Even though Huck does not fully share in Tom's romantic vision, he is impressed by the elaborateness and drama of Tom's plan and automatically takes it to be superior to his own effective but humdrum suggestions. Obviously, one can see strong political implications in Tom's dominance, Huck's acquiescence, and the resulting disaster. It should be noted that Mark Twain was undoubtedly well aware of his friend William Dean Howells's "ideas about the connection between literary 'romanticism' and political tyranny."[13] Here Twain has made use of Tom Sawyer to demonstrate this connection.

Why are Huck and Tom fast friends, when they are so different? What do they see in each other? From Tom's perspective, Huck's ready submission makes it easy for Tom to live out his fantasies. Huck has no competing fantasies of his own, and serves both as supporting actor and audience for Tom. Moreover, Huck helps Tom to feel superior; not only does Huck let Tom lead, Huck plainly recognizes Tom as his social better. Also, as a romantic, Tom may be attracted to Huck's uniqueness. Unlike the other boys in town, Huck is an outsider to mainstream society and has lived a life very different from Tom's, an 'exciting' life that could be viewed romantically. Like "A-rabs and elephants," Huck is slightly exotic, and therefore worth associating with. It is a little harder to pin down what Huck sees in Tom. For one, it is certainly clear that Tom offers Huck friendship and that this is important. Huck has no family, with the exception of his terrible father, and is quite alone in the world; Tom offers a respite from Huck's aloneness. Also, Tom is entertaining. Although Huck does not really share Tom's romantic fantasies, he enjoys participating in the escapades. Anchored solely in his immediate physical world, Huck tends to get bored easily; this is seen when he is hiding on Jackson's Island. Although Huck does possess boyish curiosity and indulges it frequently, we have seen that he lacks a boyish imagination and is incapable of fantasy or reverie; this may make him more dependent on Tom for fun. Huck wants Tom's leadership. In any case, it is not Tom's romantic visions themselves, but Huck's desire to spend time with Tom, that prompts Huck to agree to assist Tom in indulging his imagination.

Babbitt has stated that "the poet who reduces poetry to the imaginative quest of strange emotional adventure, and the plain citizen who does not aspire beyond a reality that is too literal and prosaic, both suffer."[14] The friendship between Huck and Tom may ultimately reflect an intuitive awareness by Twain of a close relationship between these two approaches, and an understanding that neither boy is really approaching life in the right way. The uniting of Tom and Huck perhaps reflects a desire to bridge the gap between romantic and myopically utilitarian, empirical approaches to life, in the vain hope that the result will somehow be a complete person.

Aristocracy, Tyranny and Complicity

Twain further demonstrates the political implications of an excessively humble and acquiescing attitude in Huck's response to the 'duke' and the 'dauphin.' When these men join Huck and Jim on their raft, Huck lets them take over; he becomes their servant and addresses them with the various exalted titles they prefer. Of course, Huck really has little choice in this matter; he and Jim are but a boy and a runaway slave. The real significance lies in Huck's remarks to the reader:

> It didn't take me long to make up my mind that these liars warn't no kings nor dukes, but just low-down humbugs and frauds. But I never said

> nothing, never let on; kept it to myself; it's the best way; then you don't have no quarrels, and don't get into no trouble. If they wanted us to call them kings and dukes, I hadn't no objections, 'long as it would keep peace in the family . . . . If I never learnt nothing else out of pap, I learnt that the best way to get along with his kind of people is to let them have their own way (166).

Huck's way is to 'go along to get along,' and he has no qualms about deferring to others if this is what is necessary to keep the peace. Resistance is not his way. He has learned this behavior through his need to deal with the capricious violence of his father; it has made Huck into a sheep. The broader implication here is that if a person with a strong will asserts himself and attempts to place himself over his fellows, the tendency is for others to simply let him have his way, even if they know better. People will not stand up for themselves, or for any democratic or egalitarian convictions; they instead take the path of least resistance and go along with whatever fiction is being perpetrated. As Twain once put it,

> the universal conspiracy of the silent-assertion lie is hard at work always and everywhere, and always in the interest of a stupidity or a sham, never in the interest of a thing fine or respectable . . . For ages and ages it has mutely labored in the interest of despotisms and aristocracies and chattel slaveries, and military slaveries, and religious slaveries, and has kept them alive . . . the silent assertion that nothing is going on which fair and intelligent men are aware of and are engaged by their duty to try to stop.[15]

Noble Aspiration Equated with Falsehood

Twain takes care explicitly to connect the duke and dauphin with real royalty and hereditary aristocracy. Huck tells Jim that "all kings is mostly rapscallions, as fur as I can make out," and later comments, "what was the use to tell Jim these warn't real kings and dukes. It wouldn't 'a' done no good; and, besides, it was just as I said: you couldn't tell them from the real kind" (199-201). Twain was a champion of democracy, and he saw a very strong connection between the romantic imagination and a kind of impulse which results in monarchy and in aristocratic rule. This 'aristocratic impulse' is not a desire for true self-improvement, but a desire for sham self-improvement achieved though setting oneself over others; it is an image of superiority. While Twain associates this tendency with the hereditary nobility of Europe, it is not actually confined to kings and dukes; Huck tells us plainly that his Pap is of the same type. We know, in fact, that, in addition to dominating Huck physically, Huck's Pap forbids Huck to learn to read, lest Huck become his better. He is furious to see a black who is a college professor. He also tells Huck that he was going to vote, "if I warn't too drunk to get there; but when they told me there was a State in this country where they'd let that nigger vote, I drawed out. I says I'll never vote again" (50). Pap is unwilling to participate in the democratic process on an equal basis with others; he must maintain his superiority, a ridiculous requirement given his extreme poverty and complete lack of virtue. This connection of the aristocratic impulse to racial issues is another recurring theme in Twain's writings. It is primarily this impulse that prompts whites to keep blacks down; by such means they can demonstrate their superiority. In addition, it was this desire for aristocracy which engendered slavery in the first place. Moreover, the twisted desire for status prompts individuals to 'buy into' a complete social system; even if a man is not near the top, he has an incentive to preserve the power structure as long as he is superior to someone. Some people, like Huck and Jim, have no reason to support society's existing structures and conventions; they are at the bottom, view themselves as outsiders, or simply have no interest in social status. However, through oppression they have been taught meekness, and they remain passive, going along with the system "to keep peace in the family."

Twain saw a relationship between the aristocratic impulse and the latter nineteenth century's burgeoning romantic interest in the Middle Ages. A Connecticut Yankee in King Arthur's Court serves in part as Twain's vehicle to destroy romantic images of the past and make the Arthurian legends appear ridiculous. In the process, the medieval class structure is attacked, along with tradition and the Catholic Church. However, Twain is again careful not to let us think that it is only overseas nobility and old institutions that we need fear. Hank Morgan, the book's American protagonist, is no hero. He has nothing but contempt for the romantic world he has entered, so he sets himself up as "Sir Boss," takes over, and tries to remake the medieval world in a modern image. In some ways, he is Tom Sawyer grown up. This may seem unlikely, since Tom's vision was highly romantic, while Morgan's appears at first glance to be an aggressively 'modern,' anti-romantic view. His motivations, however, are closely aligned with Tom' s, and not just because the boy and man both desire to dominate their surroundings. While for Tom "style" is all-important, for Morgan everything is done for "effect." It becomes evident that one of his primary motivators is a twisted sense of aesthetics; at the core, Morgan is just as much a romantic visionary as Tom. Morgan's drive to achieve his vision becomes increasingly violent, and this dark and depressing book culminates in an orgy of death and destruction made possible by the modern weapons that Morgan has built. Twain seems to be issuing a warning that the dangers of the romantic imagination are not receding with time, but growing, as man comes to have greater technological powers at his disposal. This parallels Babbitt's view of the dangers inherent in the modern experiment. Babbitt argues that scientific progress has given man new confidence while breaking his ties to standards of good and evil, and that "to work outwardly and in the utilitarian sense, without the inner working that can alone save from ethical anarchy is to stimulate rather than repress the most urgent of all the lusts—the lust of power."[16]

THE FEUD

Romanticism, Will and Character

In the Grangerford-Shepherdson feud episode in Huckleberry Finn, Twain explores the relation of the romantic imagination to the will in ways that move beyond the romanticism/tyranny formula. The Grangerfords, with whom Huck comes to stay for a few days, are a particularly 'aristocratic' southern family. The clan is large, owns several farms, and is headed by Colonel Grangerford, who

> was very tall and very slim, and had a darkish-paly complexion, not a sign of red in it anywheres; he was clean-shaved every morning . . . and every day of his life he put on a clean shirt and a full suit from head to foot made out of linen so white it hurt your eyes to look at it . . . He carried a mahogany cane with a silver head to it. There warn't no frivolishness about him, not a bit, and he warn't ever loud. He was as kind as he could be—you could feel that, you know, and so you had confidence (143-44).

The Grangerfords are embroiled with the Shepherdsons in a feud, which had begun thirty years ago over an obscure legal issue. This is a feud fought by "splendid young men" on "fine horses."

The Grangerfords have considerable respect for the Shepherdsons, and a Grangerford boy tells Huck that "there ain't a coward" among either family. The nobility of the Grangerfords isn't completely phony; in some respects one could argue that they truly are embodiments of such virtues as honor, courage, duty, kindness, and generosity. Their home is decorated with a mix of pictures of the American Revolution and dark, morbidly romantic charcoal drawings made by a member of the family. The effect is almost surreal when, amid the pleasant surroundings, Huck asks his new friend "Has anybody been killed this year, Buck?" and the casual reply is "Yes, we got one and they got one. 'Bout three months ago, my cousin Bud, fourteen year old . . ." (147). When Buck tells his father about shooting at a Shepherdson, the Colonel's eyes first blaze with pride, but he then gently admonishes his son for shooting from behind a bush. Eventually, we learn that a young man and woman from the two families are engaged in a secret love affair, and it happens that while Huck is visiting they run off and get married. Rather than take advantage of the opportunity to unite the families, open war breaks out, ending in the death of many family members including Colonel Grangerford and, most tragically, Huck's young friend.

Twain's treatment of the romantic imagination here is in some ways more sympathetic than in his other examples. The Grangerfords and Shepherdsons are not really trying to establish sham superiority or to dominate or 'lord it over' anyone else. Nor do they, like Tom Sawyer, spend their time in a world of fantasy. They have taken their romantic vision to heart and allowed it to shape their lives completely. Armed with their romantic ideals and with romanticized models such as the heroes of the American Revolution, the Grangerfords have developed high standards of behavior, and have in fact done quite a good job of living up to them. They certainly stand in marked contrast to the seedy and shiftless characters who tend to populate Huckleberry Finn. The Grangerfords, unlike Tom Sawyer, have in a sense actually become romantic heroes. They want to be noble, and understand that this requires not just surface appearances but a certain nobility of character; they have not tried to live out their romantic dreams 'on the cheap' as Tom has, with his mere illusions of heroism. The problem with the Grangerfords, of course, is the feud itself. They are knowingly and deliberately perpetuating a situation that places their lives, including the lives of young boys, at great risk, for no good reason. Why would otherwise good and reasonable people do something as shockingly foolish and immoral as this?

Imagery over Reality

Something, it appears, has become more important to the Grangerfords than the lives of their family members. One possibility is that it is their hatred for the Shepherdsons, but there is no indication of this. Another possibility is that it is an exaggerated and twisted sense of honor, which stops them from coming to terms with their enemies. This may be closer to the mark, but Twain never actually brings out this point. More than anything, Twain creates the impression that the two families have made, in today's parlance, a 'lifestyle choice.' In this alternative lifestyle, neighbors shoot each other. They have chosen this life because it fits so well into their romantic vision. The feud provides a perfect opportunity for them to demonstrate virtues like courage, duty, and honor; it may even have helped them to build these virtues. Although their virtues have a certain degree of reality, something is rotten at the core. There is no compelling reason for the feud, and one cannot be truly virtuous while valuing human life so cheaply. Ultimately, the Grangerfords are living a lie; imagery has won out over reality. They are not fighting a just cause; the only 'cause' served by the feud is the re-creation of the romantic ideal. As in Twain's other examples, immorality results from the attempt to bridge the gap between impossible romantic imagery and the real world. Because the model that inspires the families is not firmly anchored in reality, it has skewed their priorities and warped their perception of reality, devaluing their lives and the lives of their children. They lack a sound ethical center, because, as Babbitt says, "there is no such thing as romantic morality"; the models upon which they have built their lives are not sound. Romanticism's potential for darkness and violence, signaled by the macabre drawings, emerges once again. By decorating their home with these drawings, the Grangerfords reveal that they have embraced death and darkness as an unavoidable component of their romantic dreams; they are willing players in the tragedy. However much the families may have benefited from the inspiration of the romantic imagination, they are ultimately its victims.

Twain has again demonstrated his belief that the romantic imagination is a powerful shaper and driver of the will. Man is inspired by romantic ideals, and the desire to realize these ideals spurs one to action in the world. In some cases, such as that of Tom Sawyer, this spurring to action is manifest in part as a drive to dominate others; this has strong negative connotations but is also an inspiration for leadership. In the case of the Grangerfords, the spurring to action is in part directed at the self, appearing as a desire to act nobly and to build sound character. Twain has shown us, however, that Tom Sawyer and even the Grangerfords are not sound models. If, then, Twain rejects those who are possessed by romantic dreams, what does he think of those who are not so possessed?

In general, Twain tends to depict the 'common folk' with contempt. Not long after the Grangerford-Shepherdson episode, Huck finds himself in a poorly kept "lazy town," where it appears that most of the men prefer to sit around idly, occasionally entertaining themselves by setting fire to a stray dog. One Colonel Sherburn, "a proud-looking man about fifty-five—and he was a heap the best dressed man in that town, too," kills an annoying but apparently harmless drunk who was threatening him (185). Eventually a mob forms outside Sherburn's house, and he addresses the crowd scornfully:

> The idea of you lynching anybody . . . Why, a man's safe in the hands of ten thousand of your kind—as long as it's day-time and you're not behind him . . . The average man's a coward. In the North he lets anybody walk over him that wants to, and goes home and prays for a humble spirit to bear it. In the South one man, all by himself, has stopped a stage full of men, in the day-time, and robbed the lot . . . You didn't want to come. The average man don't like trouble and danger . . . But if only half a man—like Buck Harkness, there—shouts 'Lynch him, lynch him!' you're afraid to back down—afraid you'll be found out to be what you are-cowards—and so you raise a yell, and hang yourselves onto that half-a-man's coat tail . . . The pitifulest thing out is a mob; that's what an army is . . . but a mob without any man at the head of it, is beneath pitifulness . . . If any real lynching's going to be done, it will be done in the dark, Southern fashion . . . (190-91).

Contempt for "Average Man"

The crowd, of course, goes home. One cannot help but wish that a Grangerford or Shepherdson were there. They are men and would not hesitate to see justice served. They are not Twain's "average man." Tom Sawyer is not an "average man" either. Tom is of course a boy, so it is hard to place him in this situation, but he certainly likes trouble and danger, after a fashion. The townsfolk are not just cowards; they are lazy and cruel. They lack the drive to stand up to the Colonel, to make something of themselves, to cultivate virtue; they are base, passive, lifeless, and lacking in self-respect. Setting fire to a dog is not beneath them. As Sherburn indicates in his speech, the average man is not a 'real man.'

The "will to be a man," encompassing such traits as being a "man of action" and possessing a sense of moral responsibility as well as traditional masculine virtues, was central to the Howellsian realism with which Twain was familiar.[17] Is Twain putting an ironic twist on Howells and telling us that one must be a slave to the romantic imagination if one is to be anything like a 'real man'? Twain seems to feel that without the romantic imagination spurring one on, one's "will to be a man" is too weak to accomplish much. Are our only options then to be contemptible "average men" or to be Grangerfords and end in disaster? For Twain, it appears that one can either seek inspiration in romantic, unrealistic ideals which are unattainable, or have no ideals or inspiration at all and sink to an almost sub-human level. In neither case are we truly soundly anchored morally. But, are all models and ideals in which we can seek inspiration out of touch with reality, by definition? Is there no third way, no way in which one can learn to live one's life in an ennobling manner, to build sound character, to make something of oneself, while remaining solidly grounded and meeting the world on its own terms, avoiding the pitfalls of romantic idealism? Is it impossible for one to perceive "the one in the many" and to move towards truth? These questions are met by Twain with a deafening silence.

TWAIN'S ROUSSEAUESQUE MORALITY

Huck, Jim and Morality

Twain seems to distinguish quite sharply between being a 'real man' and being truly moral. Those inspired by romanticism may be real men, but they are nevertheless led into moral error. In contrast, Jim and Huck do not display the same kind of bravery or bravado, but, on occasion, they both behave not just particularly morally but, one could say, almost heroically. Jim abandons his escape attempt to stay with Tom when he is shot. Huck protects Jim, refuses to turn him in, and helps him to escape, even though he believes that he may go to hell for doing so, since Jim is after all the Widow Douglas's legal property. In examining Huck's and Jim's actions, it is important to observe that they are unique characters in the novel; they, far more than any others, are portrayed essentially as standing outside of society looking in. There is a Rousseauesque suggestion here that man is inherently good, and that his moral instincts become corrupted in society. Another important Rousseauesque suggestion is that man's initial impulses are good, and that it is by second-guessing and controlling those impulses that one falls into error. Huck makes a better study than Jim in this respect, because we can see inside Huck's head. We see that Huck's moral actions are not the result of any effort on his part; they just come naturally. This contrasts sharply with Babbitt's "Aristotelian" view that one must work at morality. In fact, Huck's conscious efforts are actually working against moral action. Huck accepts all of society's conventions as gospel. When his own views on a particular matter conflict with those of society, Huck assumes his views are the bad ones, although he sometimes follows them anyway. Whenever Huck wrestles over the issue of helping Jim, his compassion urges him to stick by him, even though it is "wicked" to help a runaway slave and he may even go to hell. Nevertheless, he keeps trying to convince himself that he really should do the right thing, which is to turn Jim in. Huck, like everyone else, is participating in Twain's "universal conspiracy of the silent-assertion lie." However, Huck, living on the fringes of society, has not fully internalized the lie; as a result his better instincts sometimes win out.

What is Twain saying here about the source of moral action? Does a study of Huck's actions help equip us for life? Twain is certainly telling us that we should not blindly accept society's conventions as ultimate truth; this is helpful. What else? Perhaps that we should trust our 'gut' or follow our compassion. But Twain often casts a wary eye toward compassion, and he generally portrays common men as base, and not particularly moral. It appears that for Twain only the 'gut' of someone in something like a state of nature, one who has not been corrupted by society, is likely to be right. It is not even clear whether Twain believes that all men in a state of nature necessarily possess Huck's goodness. This question appears to be moot for Twain, since we have all presumably been corrupted by society and are not like Huck Finn. Since Huck's morality just flows naturally and does not have to be worked at, he is of limited value to us as a model. In fact, Huck is not even particularly desirable as a model for life in the real world, since, like others lacking in romantic inspiration, he suffers from meekness, passivity, and excessive humility. As a result, Huck's moral instincts do not always translate into moral action.

Does Twain suggest that one can learn, that one can improve? Huck does manage to learn some things; actually, he appears to be the only character in the book who learns anything. Everything Huck learns seems to center on Jim. Huck moves beyond his, and society's, stereotypical images of blacks and learns to respect and care for Jim. He discovers that Jim cares deeply for his family and comes to appreciate him as a real human being. Huck plays tricks on Jim, but then regrets it and decides not to do so again. We do see positive learning here, but it is extremely limited. Huck does not really seem to move toward any broader truths or to change as a character. He goes back to playing tricks with Tom Sawyer, and he never questions the legitimacy of slavery or of any of society's other conventions. When, in the latter part of the book, Tom tells Huck he will help him rescue Jim, Huck comments to the reader, ". . . I'm bound to say Tom Sawyer fell, considerable, in my estimation. Only I couldn't believe it. Tom Sawy er a nigger stealer!" (285). Huck never really demonstrates significant moral growth.

It is noteworthy that the only places where even hints of growth and of particularly moral behavior are demonstrated are in areas surrounding the relationship between Huck and Jim. This material is not typical of the book. While Twain is generally something like a 'realist' in style, it is widely recognized that he did not hesitate to switch to sentimentalism in special cases. This is one such case. Twain was opposed to the way blacks were treated in American society, and he wanted to drive home certain points in this regard and move the reader toward his own position. This sort of social preaching, more than a desire to get at deeper philosophical truths, was probably at the top of Twain's mind when he was writing this particular material.[18] Therefore, it may be appropriate to discount attempts to draw broader lessons here, and to consider the lack of positive examples in the rest of the book to be more representative of Twain.

Twain's doubts about man's improvability are evident in the fact that, although he does sometimes engage in sentimentalism and in humanitarian causes, he goes out of his way to ridicule those sentimental humanitarians who believe that people are easily reformed. Early in the book, Huck's "Pap" is arrested, and the new judge, who does not really know him, decides to reform him:

> So he took him to his own house, and dressed him clean and nice, and had him to breakfast and dinner and supper with the family, and was just old pie to him, so to speak. And after supper he talked to him about temperance and such things till the old man cried, and said he'd been a fool, and fooled away his life; but now he was agoing to turn over a new leaf and be a man nobody wouldn't be ashamed of, and he hoped the judge would help him and not look down on him. The judge said he could hug him for them words so he cried, and his wife she cried again; pap said he'd been a man

> that had always been misunderstood before, and the judge said he believed it (42).

Friendly Persusasion, then the Gun

The scene goes on, with more earnest pledges and melodrama. Then, that very night Pap gets drunk, trashes the judge's guest room, crawls out the window, breaks his arm, and is found the next morning lying almost frozen. Huck tells us that "the judge he felt kind of sore. He said he reckoned a body could reform the ole man with a shot-gun, be he didn't know no other way" (44). One commentator writes that what Twain is showing is that "Americans generally tend to vacillate between an overly sentimentalized view of nature and the use of unadulterated force."[19] Reformers of humanity may begin with friendly persuasion, but end by getting the gun. It is important to expand on this analysis and understand why people "vacillate" this way—because they are suffering from another hopeless romantic vision. The reformist ideal for which they are working cannot be realized. The underlying implication here is that in Twain's view people generally cannot be changed, and, perhaps, cannot really even change themselves for the better.

TWAIN'S 'REALISTIC' IMAGINATION

No Sound Models to Inspire Reader

As was observed in the first section of this chapter, the "training" of the imagination involves both a "negative" and "positive" dimension. Mark Twain has done an excellent job on the "negative" side, at least in the area of unmasking the romantic imagination and helping us understand its dangers. To the extent that Americans may have avoided some of the worst nightmares that can result from the influence of romantic visionaries, perhaps some thanks can go to Twain and to the members of the literary realism movement. Unfortunately, it is difficult to find much to applaud in Twain on the "positive" side. He offers us little in terms of role models or help in "finding concrete modes of ordering" our lives. One could say, in fact, that he doesn't even offer us hope. It appears that for Twain all men in society are essentially corrupt and only two options exist. The first option is to embrace the romantic imagination; this can help one develop a strong will, spur one to become a man of action, perhaps even inspire one to cultivate virtue and develop a kind of a noble character. It will not, however, provide one with a sound ethical center, but will end in immorality and disaster: the result of desperate attempts to make real an impossible dream. The second option is to reject the vision and become meek, passive, base. Under this model one may perhaps avoid the worst disasters, but one is not really a good person; in fact, one may be quite detestable. There appear to be no other options. Twain is very skeptical of the belief that one can really learn or change for the better. It is pointless for us to aspire to move toward truth or to rightly order our lives. If we insist on trying, perhaps Twain's characters offer us examples of what not to do, of how not to be. However, we are on our own from there. We have not been equipped for life.

Babbitt maintains that realism and romanticism are two sides of the same coin. What happens is that

> the Rousseauist begins by walking through the world as though it were an enchanted garden, and then with the inevitable clash between his ideal and the real he becomes morose and embittered. Since men have turned out not to be indiscriminately good he inclines to look upon them as indiscriminately bad and to portray them as such. At the bottom of much so-called realism therefore is a special type of satire, a satire that is the product of violent emotional disillusion . . . [W]hat lurks most often behind this pretense to a cold scientific impassiveness in observing human

> nature is a soured and cynical emotionalism and a distinctly romantic type of imagination. The imagination is still idealistic, still straining, that is, away from the real, only its idealism has undergone a strange inversion; instead of exaggerating the loveliness it exaggerates the ugliness of human nature . . .[20]

A Disillusioned Romantic

It is not difficult to recognize Twain here, or to see the philosophical origins of the cynicism and pessimism which became increasingly pronounced over the course of his life. While Mark Twain does not go quite so far as to view men as indiscriminately bad, or human nature as exclusively ugly, he comes close to such views; certainly, he expresses an attitude toward society that is quite similar to that of Rousseau. Brooks notes that Twain's "closest friends were accustomed to little notes like this: 'I have been reading the morning paper. I do it every morning, well knowing that I shall find in it the usual depravities and baseness and hypocrisies and cruelties that make up civilization and cause me to put in the rest of the day pleading for the damnation of the human race.'"[21] His misanthropy is that of the disillusioned romantic, and his 'realism' is actually a product of the romantic imagination.

Realism, Romanticism both Repudiate Decorum

According to Babbitt, "what binds together realism and romanticism is their common repudiation of decorum as something external and artificial."[22] Here we see the source of Twain's frustration. He is able to understand decorum only as the hackneyed romantic ideals which circulate in literature and life, or as the corrupt social conventions that derive from those ideals. Again one hears echoes of Rousseau, who complained,

> What would I gain from changing course? If I were to adopt the teaching of my persecutors, should I also adopt

their morality—the rootless and sterile morality which they expound so grandiloquently in their books or with bravado in their plays, but which never makes its way to the heart or the reason, or else the cruel secret morality, for which the other is only a mask . . .[23]

While Babbitt argues that one must distinguish between true decorum and artificial decorum, for Twain and Rousseau all decorum is artificial; it does not exist as something which can actually provide useful models and standards and thereby help one through life. Unlike Rousseau, however. Twain is skeptical about the universality of man's 'good' natural instincts, or at least he doubts that there is any way in which those instincts can emerge in men in society. As a result, Twain is at a dead end; self-improvement is impossible.

Inner Control not Attained

As Brooks observes, Twain denied free will. He compared man to a "coffee mill" and stated that man simply responds to external stimuli and "is merely a machine and entitled to no personal merit for what he does."[24] Brooks believes that Twain liked his mechanistic philosophy because it absolved him of responsibility for failing to develop and exploit his true artistic talents. Artistic talents aside, Babbitt would no doubt emphatically agree that a lack of personal responsibility is a big part of Twain's problem. Twain does not recognize the need to develop, or the possibility of developing, a morally anchored higher will which checks one's undesirable expansive impulses. Brooks comes close to hitting this on the head when he describes Twain as "a great genius, in short, that has never attained the inner control which makes genius great, a mind that has not found itself, a mind that does not know itself, a mind that cloaks to the end in the fantasy of its temporal power the reality of some spiritual miscarriage."[25] Brooks identifies a tendency toward megalomania in Twain, due to "that lack of inner control which makes one's sole criterion the magnitude of one's grasp over the outer world."[26] This is the great modern danger identified by Babbitt as arising from a Rousseauesque lack of "inner obeisance of the spirit to standards."

Road to Despair

Babbitt observes that "the democratic idealist is prone to make light of the whole question of standards and leadership because of his unbounded faith in the plain people."[27] Twain was a political commentator from the start, and it has been said that the "first importance" of Twain is "the democratizing effect of his work."[28] Yet his portrayal of the common man became increasingly contemptuous throughout his career. Twain is a "democratic idealist" who has lost his "unbounded faith in the plain people." Originally blaming societal evils on would-be aristocrats and tyrants, Twain becomes increasingly aware that the common folk actually help perpetuate those evils and are in fact no better; they have failed him. Twain realizes that his faith in democracy is itself a romantic dream. Democracy aside, Twain has lost his faith in man. Able to conceive of the good only in terms of romantic ideals, Twain becomes disillusioned when they are not realized, and becomes deeply disappointed with what he habitually called "the damned human race." Building upon Babbitt's philosophy. Claes Ryn has stated that man must "cultivate, through proper willing, the kind of imaginative openness that embraces the real terms of life."[29] In failing to achieve this, Twain has failed to "build up a sound model for imitation" for himself or for those whose imaginations have been shaped by his work. A question exists as to whether the influence Twain has exerted on the American imagination and, thereby, on American political life has been a net benefit or detriment. On the one hand, Twain warned his readers of the dangers of romantic dreams; on the other, he provided them with little help in developing the "moral imagination" or in becoming equipped for life in the real world. He offered cynicism as the only alternative to romanticism, suggesting that attempts at moral self-improvement are futile. For Twain himself, it appears that his disappointment in humanity and society could lead nowhere philosophically but to despair.

NOTES

1. Irving Babbitt, *Rousseau and Romanticism* (New Brunswick, NJ: Transaction Publishers, 1991), lxxv-lxxvi.
2. Claes G. Ryn, *Will, Imagination and Reason* (New Brunswick, NJ: Transaction Publishers, 1997), 180.
3. Ryn, 178.
4. Michael Davitt Bell, *The Problem of American Realism* (Chicago: University of Chicago Press, 1993), 42.
5. Babbitt, *Rousseau and Romanticism*, 265.
6. Irving Babbitt, *Democracy and Leadership* (Indianapolis: Liberty Fund, Inc., 1979), 283.
7. Babbitt, *Democracy and Leadership*, 91.
8. Van Wyck Brooks, *The Ordeal of Mark Twain* (New York: E. Dutton & Company, Inc., 1920, Rev. 1933), 11.
9. All parenthetical notes refer to Mark Twain, *Adventures of Huckleberry Finn* (New York: Random House, Modem Library Edition, 1985).
10. Babbitt, *Rousseau and Romanticism*, 194-95.
11. Quoted in Brooks, 25.
12. Catherine H. Zuckert, *Natural Right and the American Imagination* (Savage, MD: Rowman & Littlefield Publishers, Inc., 1990), 149.
13. Bell, 69.
14. Babbitt, *Rousseau and Romanticism*, 88.
15. Mark Twain, "My First Lie, and How I Got Out of It," orig. pub. in *New York Sunday World*, Christmas 1899,

anthologized in *Mark Twain an the Damned Human Race*, ed. Janet Smith (Clinton, MA: The Colonial Press, 1962), 30.

16. Babbitt, *Rousseau and Romanticism*, 331.
17. Bell, 66.
18. Gregg Camfield, *Sentimental Twain* (Philadelphia: University of Pennsylvania Press, 1994), 11.
19. Zuckert, 138.
20. Babbitt, *Rousseau and Romanticism*, 105.
21. Brooks, 17.
22. Babbitt, *Rousseau and Romanticism*, 105.
23. Jean-Jacques Rousseau, *Reveries of the Solitary Walker*, trans. Peter France (New York: Penguin Books, 1979), 60.
24. Brooks, 39.
25. Brooks, 38.
26. Brooks, 37.
27. Babbitt, *Democracy and Leadership*, 288.
28. Bernard De Voto, "Mark Twain and the and Valley," in *Mark Twain*, ed. Harold Bloom (New York: Chelsea House Publishers, Modern Critical Views series, 1986), 22.
29. Ryn, xv.

3

Beneath the Veil: Clothing, Race and Gender in Mark Twain's Pudd'nhead Wilson

—Linda A. Morris

> And thus in the land of the Color-line I saw, as it fell across my baby, the shadow of the Veil.
>
> —W.E.B. Du Bois, *The Souls of Black Folk*

> Now who would b'lieve clo'es could do de like o' dat?
>
> —Mark Twain, *Pudd'nhead Wilson*

The idyllic opening of Pudd'nhead Wilson, with its description of Dawson's Landing's modest dwellings with whitewashed exteriors and a cat asleep in a flower box, concludes with the description of the village bounded on the front by the Mississippi River and on the back by a row of high hills that, Mark Twain writes, were "clothed with forests from foot to summit."[1] Thus, unobtrusively and in the context of a tranquil landscape, he introduces what is to become one of the major subtexts of the novel: namely, clothes as markers of identity, race, and gender.

The text is rich with masquerading, with layering of clothing, with cross-dressing and misleading gender markers, with foppery, veiling and unveiling, and with clothing as cues (and mis-cues) to sexual and racial identity. Yet across the novel's critical history, Twain's preoccupation with clothing in the text has been all but invisible.[2]

For the first generation of critics and reviewers of Pudd'nhead Wilson, even the multiple acts of cross-dressing performed by both the slave heroine, Roxana, and her son escaped public notice. The reviewer for Cosmopolitan, for instance, called attention to a host of melodramatic elements in the novel, but made no mention of cross-dressing:

> exchanges of infants in the cradle, a hero with negro taint in his blood substituted for the legitimate white heir, midnight encounters in a haunted house between the false heir and his colored mother, murder by the villain of his supposed uncle and benefactor, accusation of an innocent foreigner, and final sensational acquittal and general unraveling of the tangled skein . . .[3]

This reviewer goes on in familiar nineteenth-century terms to extol the virtue of the text's black language: "How deliciously rich, racy, and copious is, for instance, his negro talk. The very gurgling laugh and cooing cadence seems, somehow, implied in the text."[4] The reviewer for the Spectator, responding to the wry humor of the novel, wondered if Twain had "found Missouri audiences or readers slow to appreciate his jokes,"[5] while the Bookman focused on the novelty of fingerprint records that ultimately reveal the true identity of the false heir who murders his purported uncle.[6] These reviewers, as others across the work's critical history, responded to Pudd'nhead Wilson's deeply disturbing critique of racial categories, but none of them perceived how metaphors of clothing and cross-dressed performances complicate and complement the racial issues at the core of the novel. More recently, Pudd'nhead Wilson criticism has taken two distinct directions. Scholars such as Hershel Parker have taken pains to understand how Twain composed Pudd'nhead Wilson, not being content to accept the author's flippant description of how he simply removed the Siamese twins from his original manuscript by Cesarean surgery once the slave Roxana and her son "took over" the text.[7] By delicate surgical procedures of their own, these scholars have reconstructed Twain's composing and revising processes that led to the ultimate creation of two texts, Pudd'nhead Wilson and Those Extraordinary Twins. They note, for example, that in the original manuscript, now known as the Morgan Manuscript, there were no changelings; Tom Driscoll was white, not black; and the Italian twins were Siamese twins who were ultimately hanged by the good citizens of Dawson's Landing. (More accurately, only one of the twins was hanged; but as the citizenry deduced about Wilson's dog at the beginning of the story, killing one halt of the animal would for all practical purposes also kill the other.)

A second strand of modern scholarship, as represented in Susan Gilman and Forrest Robinson's collection of essays, Mark Twain's Pudd'nhead Wilson: Race, Conflict, and Culture, reads the text historically and interprets late nineteenth-century culture through the text.[8] Critics such as Eric Sundquist and Shelley Fisher Fishkin recontextualize the novel in ways that emphasize the relationship between Pudd'nhead Wilson and the racial politics of the day, while Carolyn Porter and Myra Jehlen read the racial and gendered subtexts of the novel.[9] Susan Gilman explores the relationship between twins, duality, and identity in the novel, and positions the novel in relationship to Twain's late dream narratives.[10] Most of these critics, especially those exploring the intersections of race and gender, note that cross-dressing occurs at key crisis points in the novel and that it contributes to and highlights crises of race and identity, but none pursues this subject in depth. Nor has anyone yet noticed how relentlessly the text enacts more conventionally defined issues of dress and clothing.

This essay will focus in particular upon dress and clothing as markers of identity, race, and gender as played out in relation to two of the primary characters in the novel, Roxana and her son Chambers, also known as Tom. Representations of their clothing simultaneously confound the already problematic categories of race and make problematic the categories of gender.[11] Such confounding, we will see, further destabilizes the precarious social order of Dawson's Landing and the post-Reconstruction South of Twain's own time.

In our first introduction to Roxana, the slave woman who propels the major plot into motion, we do not see her, only hear her, as she exchanges witticisms with a slave named Jasper. We do not need to see her, however, to know by her dialect that she is "black": "Oh, yes, you got me, hain't you. 'Clah to goodness if dat conceit o'yo'n strikes in, Jasper, it gwyne to kill you, sho'. If you b'longed to me I'd sell you down de river 'fo' you git too fur gone". The narrator immediately both confirms and contradicts our assumptions: "From Roxy's manner of speech, a stranger would have expected her to be black, but she was not: Only one-sixteenth of her was black, and that sixteenth did not show". In Mark Twain's South—whether the antebellum era in which the story is set or the post-Reconstruction era in which it was written—"by a fiction of law and custom," Roxana is "black." In the text her otherwise ambiguous racial identity is marked, finally, by the fact that her "heavy suit of fine, soft [brown] hair" is concealed "by a checkered handkerchief". Set against her "white" appearance, Twain chooses here one of the most powerful and persistent of racial markers with which to identify Roxana, her head rag.[12] From this moment on,

Roxana is "black"—her race does "show." The head rag as a marker of racial identity is reinforced later in the text when Roxana becomes a fugitive slave, hotly pursued by her "master"; following the practice of the day, the master has a "wanted" poster made for Roxana: "The handbill had the usual rude wood-cut of a turbaned negro woman running, with the customary bundle on a stick over her shoulder, and the heading, in bold type, '$100 Reward'" (89). In other words, the handbill evokes the stereotyped image of the escaped slave woman, and it pins that stereotype on Roxana. For her part,

> Roxana continually undercuts all racial stereotypes throughout the novel, and the patriarchal order as well.[13]

Two infant boys born on the same day are entrusted wholly to Roxana's care: Thomas a Beckett Driscoll, son of one of the "first" white families in Dawson's Landing, and Roxana's own son, Valet de Chambres, who like his mother looks white but by Missouri law is black and a slave. The infants can be distinguished from one another only by their clothing. Tom's clothes are described briefly, but in detail, calling attention to their fabric and their ruffles, while Chambers is dressed in the unmistakable clothing of a slave child: a "tow-linen shirt which barely reached to its [sic] knees". The transformative event of the novel—Roxana's exchanging the babies' clothing and thereby altering their public identities and personal fortunes—begins quite simply when Roxana privately declares her intention to drown herself and her baby. She plans to do so not to save the two of them from slavery, but to save her son from the possibility of being sold down the river, a fate she sees as literally worse than death. However, her action is arrested as she catches "sight of her new Sunday gown," a chance event that sets the plot in motion in a different direction. She looks down at her own slave's clothing, her linsey-woolsey dress, and vows not to be "fished out" looking so "misable."

In the passage that follows, Twain displays his clear fascination with the details of female clothing, for nothing in the plot requires him to give so much attention to Roxana making her "death-toilet." Central to the process of preparing her death attire, Roxana sheds the marker of race, her head rag, and lets her "white" hair hang loose.

> She put down the child and made the change [into the dress]. She looked in the glass and was astonished at her beauty. She resolved to make her death-toilet perfect. She took off her handkerchief-turban and dressed her glossy wealth of hair "like white folks;"she added some odds and ends of rather lurid ribbon and a spray of atrocious artificial flowers; finally, she threw over her shoulders a fluffy thing called a "cloud" in that day, which was of a blazing red complexion. Then she was ready for the tomb.

What Roxana sees when she looks in the mirror is her own beauty—that is, her constructed white self—in contrast to the equally constructed black image reflected back to her by Southern society. The faintly mocking tone of the narrator goes unheard by Roxana, who is clearly pleased by the image of herself that she creates. This image empowers her, just as later dressing as a man will empower her. Roxana may be "ready for the tomb," but her son is not. Having completed her toilette, she turns her gaze on her son, and is appalled by "his miserably short little gray tow-linen shirt and noted the contrast," not, as we expect at this moment, between her son's clothing and Master Tom's, but between his dress and her own. When she "noted the contrast between its pauper shabbiness and her own volcanic irruption [sic] of infernal splendors, her mother-heart was touched, and she was ashamed". She was ashamed, that is, not of her own dress, but of her son's racially marked clothing, which she characterizes as "too indelicate" for the heaven to which they are bound. Ever resourceful (and spontaneous), Roxana dresses Chambers in the only fine clothing available, which is Tom's, and echoing her surprise at her own image in the mirror, she is now astonished at how "lovely" Chambers appears dressed in "white" clothing. Only then does she conceive the plan to exchange her "black" son with her "white" charge.

Roxana's exchange of the babies in the novel, as Carolyn Porter has so cogently argued, is a powerfully subversive act, one that challenges and disrupts the patriarchal order of Dawson's Landing. For Chambers to assume his new identity as Tom, however, he has to be stripped naked; only then can he don his "dainty flummery of ruffles". Tom, too, is "stripped of everything" and dressed in tow-linen, which marks him in everyone's eyes as a slave. By this act, Tom is stripped of his name, his identity, his inheritance, his paternity (although both children have been fathered by two of the town's most distinguished citizens), and his freedom. Roxana stands back to view her handiwork and exclaims, "Now who would b'lieve clo'es could do de like o' dat?".

In the early pages of Pudd'nhead Wilson, then, Twain establishes that clothing and dress will carry the weight of race as it is performed (and deconstructed) in the novel. The expected, indeed purportedly "indelible" stamps of race, both black and white—facial features, hair, skin color—are unreliable from the beginning. Moreover, clothing codes, which we would expect to be the more mutable markers of race, are unfailingly enforced by social dictate. The supposedly "natural" boundaries between the races were disappearing through racial mixing at the time of the novel's writing, leading to demands that they be reinforced by new boundaries and powerful markers. Yet Roxana's action demonstrates that these, too, are unreliable, even deceptive. Dawson's Landing, unbeknownst to its principal citizens, is in the midst of a cultural crisis; its socially constructed codes are unraveling before its very eyes.

As a young boy, the changeling Tom, who knows nothing of his identity as a changeling, is the master of Chambers, and he is spoiled by both Roxana and the white families with whom he resides. Pampered, undisciplined, indulged, he tyrannizes over Chambers and treats Roxana with contempt. Chambers, in contrast, is quickly taught his place as a slave. The relationship between the two boys is expressed in part through metaphors of clothing. Tom, who is cowardly and a bully, makes Chambers do all his fighting for him; consequently, Chambers earns a reputation as an accomplished fighter, until "by and by . . . Tom could have changed clothes with him, and `ridden in peace,' like Sir Kay in Launcelot's armor". There is no hint of irony in this passage, no sense that Twain is making a conscious joke about the exchange of identities that has already taken place, although the passage evokes in its readers that ever-present knowledge. The literal "armor" that Chambers wears is Tom's cast-off, worn-out clothes that are described ironically by Twain as "holy": "`holy' red mittens, and `holy' shoes, and pants `holy' at the knees and seat".

Twain's exploration of the childhood relationship between Tom and Chambers comes to an end when Chambers saves Tom from drowning, which earns him only insults for his trouble. Their playmates tease Tom that Chambers is his "Nigger-pappy—to signify that he had had a second birth into this life, and that Chambers was the author of his new being." Infuriated by the taunting, Tom orders Chambers to attack the boys; when he fails to do so, Tom "drove his pocket knife into him two or three times before the boys could snatch him away and give the wounded lad a chance to escape". And escape he does. After this scene, Twain has no more interest in

Chambers until the end of the story; he slips out of sight while Tom takes center stage as the (wrongful) heir to the Driscoll name and fortune.

When he is nineteen, Tom is sent off to Yale, where he learns to "tipple," gamble, and affect "eastern fashion." Upon returning to Dawson's Landing, he particularly offends the young people of his social set by wearing gloves. He also "brought home with him a suit of clothes of such exquisite style and cut and fashion—eastern fashion, city fashion—that it filled everybody with anguish and was regarded as a peculiarly wanton affront". In a scene rich with foreshadowing, the young people of Dawson's Landing set about to cure Tom of his affectations by mocking his style of dress. They tailor a suit that burlesques Tom's and fit it to the town's "old deformed negro bellringer." He follows Tom through the streets, "tricked out in a flamboyant curtain-calico exaggeration of his finery, and imitating his fancy eastern graces as well as he could". The mockery works: "Tom surrendered, and after that clothed himself in the local fashion".

In commenting on this scene, Myra Jehlen rather enigmatically asserts that "it is unclear just what is being satirized: is it simply foppish pretensions, or rather some absurdity of black foppery? Because the characters are unaware that their parody of Tom possesses this additional dimension, it becomes a joke shared by the narrator and the reader, a joke with a new target."[14] Eric Lott reads the incident as "a sort of minstrel gag in reverse; the black man burlesques Tom's acquired graces, and does so at the behest of an audience of village white boys . . . it also suggests that Tom's whiteness is itself an act, a suggestion that is truer than either the bell ringer or Tom can know since Tom's identity is precisely a black man's whiteface performance."[15] Both Jehlen and Lott raise important points, but both critics quickly slip past the specific image of the "flamboyant curtain-calico exaggeration of his finery." Jehlen's focus is on who is the target of the joke, while Lott's is on the performance of race. More fundamentally, we might wonder why this scene has such a haunting quality about it. We are left with the image of the black bellringer shadowing Tom through the streets of Dawson's Landing, mirroring Tom in a distorted mirror that reflects both his costume and his manners. Tom has been perceived by his contemporaries as feminized, as suggested by reference to his "fancy eastern graces." Later, as we shall see, when Tom cross-dresses as a young girl and like Huck Finn practices being a girl, this same language is echoed in the text. By then he will know that by society's definitions, he is really a black man, and he will assume a series of masquerades only to deceive. The bellringer, by contrast, is a figure used to re-establish, at least temporarily, Dawson's Landing's social order, which its young male citizens believe has been disrupted by Tom's putting on airs. In Bakhtinian terms, the scene is carnivalesque, with the most lowly member of the community, the deformed Negro bellringer, dressed in clothing intended to mock a member of the town's most privileged class. While the black bellringer is not protected by the customs of a festival as he would be in Bakhtin's ceremonial world, he is protected by the cover of the white youths on whose behalf he performs.[16] Nothing in the text suggests that the black bellringer is himself foolish or absurd, and to assume the joke is somehow on Tom because he is "really" black but does not know it misses the point. Lott's notion that Tom's whiteness is itself a performance comes much closer to the mark; nonetheless, his analysis stops with this observation, thereby missing the opportunity to investigate the convergence of a racialized and gendered performance.

Cured of his worst pretensions, Tom nonetheless continues to commit offenses against the social order. He accrues a sizable gambling debt that will, if revealed, cause him to be disinherited, so he resorts to theft and deceit to pay off his creditors. In order to steal from the villagers of Dawson's Landing, he assumes a series of disguises to mask his identity. Most powerfully and most successfully, he cross-dresses as both a young girl and an old woman. The first time we see him cross-dressed as a girl, we watch him through Pudd'nhead Wilson's eyes, although neither the reader nor Wilson knows at that moment that the "girl" we are watching is Tom. The scene is in fact represented twice in the text, first from David Wilson's perspective and then from Tom's.

In the first instance, Wilson chances to look out of his window across a vacant lot into Tom's bedroom window in Judge Driscoll's house. There he sees a girl in a pink and white striped dress "practicing steps, gaits and attitudes, apparently; she was doing the thing gracefully, and was very much absorbed in her work". Wilson wonders what a girl is doing in Tom's bedroom, and for some time tries unsuccessfully to discover her identity. Three chapters later, Twain repeats the same scene, but this time from Tom's point of view. This second time the scene is dramatized much more fully and more elaborately, and we do not know at first we are witnessing what we have seen before. Until close to the end there is no mention at all of David Wilson.

> He [Tom] arrived at the haunted house in disguise on the Wednesday before the advent of the Twins,—after writing his Aunt Pratt that he would not arrive until two days later—and lay in hiding there with his mother until toward daylight Friday morning, when he went to his uncle's house and entered by the back way with his own key and slipped up to his room, where he could have the use of mirror and toilet articles. He had a suit of girl's clothes with him in a bundle as a disguise for his raid, and was wearing a suit of his mother's clothing, with black gloves and veil. By dawn he was tricked out for his raid.

While Wilson had seen only a girl in a striped summer dress in Tom's room, we now see Tom cross-dressed not once but twice, first in his mother's clothing, then as the young gift Wilson sees. The added detail of the second female identity assumed by Tom is further intensified by the new information that he had slipped into his own room at his uncle's house so that "he could have the use of [a] mirror." While David Wilson is watching Tom, not knowing who he is, Tom is gazing at one of his female selves in the mirror. He is in the act of performing a gender as surely as his life has become an act of performing a race. Further, the scene and imagery recall his mother's act of looking at herself in the mirror just before she chances upon the scheme to exchange the babies, turning the "black" Chambers into the "white" Tom. That is to say, Tom's identity as a "white" man began with his mother's glance in the mirror, just as one of his identities as a woman is likewise reflected in a mirror.[17]

The scene is filled with images of performing, posturing, mirroring. Just after this passage, Tom notices that Wilson is watching him from his house. The two men, in Twain's words, "caught a glimpse" of each other peering through their respective windows. Far from being upset by his discovery that Wilson is watching him, Tom "entertained Wilson with some airs and graces and attitudes for a while". Tom deliberately performs for Wilson as a girl, and as a girl he is apparently wholly convincing. Only after Wilson is confronted with other, overwhelming evidence that Tom is an impostor does he "see" beyond the female masquerade: "Idiot that I was! Nothing but a girl would do me—a man in girl's clothes never occurred to me.". This is the admission of one of the two founders of the Society of Free Thinkers in the town; in spite of his reputation as being a Pudd'nhead, David Wilson is a shrewd and discerning man. If he is unable to see beyond Tom's cross-gendered disguise, who can?[18]

After his performance, however, Tom is not entirely confident that he has thrown Wilson off track and so changes back into his mother's clothes before leaving the house. Just as Twain had repeated the performance scene twice, he now repeats twice in three sentences the same information about Tom's changing into his mother's clothing, under scoring the intensity of his preoccupation with cross-dressing in this text:

> Then [Tom] stepped out of sight and resumed the other disguise, and by and by went down and out the back way and started downtown to reconnoitre the scene of his intended labors.
>
> But he was ill at ease. He had changed back to Roxy's dress, with the stoop of age added to the disguise, so that Wilson would not bother himself about a humble old woman leaving a neighbor's house by the back way in the early morning, in case he was still spying.

Tom's cross-dressing in order to commit burglaries sets the scene for even more complex gendered and racial crossing that follows. It is both a symptom and a cause of the category crisis that is at the heart of the novel. As the story progresses, Tom's debts mount; he is disinherited by his uncle, written back into the will, then threatened with being disinherited again. In as ugly an action as the story holds, Tom knowingly sells his own mother into slavery, and down the river, to pay his creditors. Some months pass before Roxana shows up again in the story, now as a fugitive. To escape detection in St. Louis, where she has fled from the deep South, Roxana has cross-dressed as a man, putting on men's clothing and "an old slouch hat," and blackening her face. That is to say, she has altered all the visible markers of her former identity: the planter from whom she escaped is looking for a "white" black woman, so she turns herself, ironically, into a "black" man. Her disguise is so effective that it fools even Tom, whom she tracks down in St. Louis. When Tom first sees her, he notices only "the back of a man"; when the man turns around, he sees only "a wreck of shabby old clothes sodden with rain and all a-drip . . . ."Then the man says, "in a low voice—`Keep still—I's yo' mother!'" (84-85).

It is an arresting moment. While Tom "gasped" out a few feeble "incoherently babbling self-accusations" about why he has done such a terrible thing, Roxana takes off her hat, and her hair "tumbled down about her shoulders." Now she stands before Tom, and before us, as a "white" woman in blackface, dressed in men's clothes. At this critical moment in the text, Roxana embodies us all, black and white, man and woman. She is "every man" and "every woman." For this woman who has already been a forceful actor in her own life, this moment represents the most powerful embodiment of her strength. Roxana then proceeds to tell her story of enslavement, one that invokes and re-enacts the genre of slave narratives—stories of brutal physical treatment, of ultimately striking back at the overseer (Roxana "snatch[ed] de stick outen his han' en laid him flat" [86]), and of escape. Roxana's story, seemingly a long and moving digression from the main plot of the novel, propels the novel inexorably toward the tragedy that it becomes.

With Roxana back on the scene (and in near total command of her son), Tom becomes more desperate in his efforts to steal money both to pay off his debts, and thus ensure his inheritance, and to buy his mother's freedom, as she demands. Desperate, he ultimately plots to steal from his uncle. Taking his cue from his mother (and evoking the tradition of minstrel theatre with its complex socially constructed images and enactment of blackness),[19] Tom also blacks up to commit the robbery. Surprised by his uncle in the act of stealing from his safe, Tom thrusts a knife into him, killing him instantly, then flees upstairs to his own room. There, still in blackface, Tom disguises himself as a girl to escape from the house. The scene is represented in only one sentence, but it is crucial:

> Tom put on his coat, buttoned his hat under it, threw on his suit of girl's clothes, dropped the veil, blew out his light, locked the room-door by which he has just entered, taking the key, passed through his other door into the back hall, locked that door and kept the key, then worked his way along in the dark and descended the back stairs. (95)

That is to say, Tom commits the murder in his own clothes (minus his coat), and in blackface. Then he puts on his "girl" clothes over his male clothes, drops a veil over his blackened face, and flees from the house. What is the meaning of the layering here? Is it, perhaps, a mistake, a glitch in the manuscript such as those remnants of the Siamese twins carelessly left in the Pudd'nhead Wilson story? All evidence suggests that it is not. Twain had hinted at just such layering before the murder. In preparing to commit the robbery, Tom "laid off his coat and hat . . . unlocked his trunk and got his suit of girl's clothes out from under the male attire in it, and laid it by. Then he blacked his face" (93). The male clothes in the trunk have concealed the female clothes, while after the murder, Tom's female clothes hide his male clothes (and identity). In a move that mirrors his mother's triumphant moment of embracing white and black, male and female, Tom puts on layers of identities over the layers he already "wears." The whiteness of his skin hides his blackness; passing for white hides his true relationship to Roxana; blacking up hides his whiteness; female clothing covers up his maleness; a veil covers his blackface. Tom, aka Chambers, murderer of his benefactor and purported uncle, collapses all categories of socially constructed identities. Marjorie Garber, in discussing briefly the transvestite theme in Pudd'nhead Wilson, draws a connection between Twain's use of the "veil" and Du Bois' image of the veil in which to be "within the veil" meant to be "under the burden of blackness." According to Garber,

> when Tom dresses as a woman, he disguises his gender because he is ashamed of his race. To "drop the veil" is to pull it over his face, to voluntarily veil himself. Inadvertently, then, read backwards through Du Bois' compelling image, Tom's disguise, the woman's veil, becomes a signifier of that very blackness he is so anxious to conceal. The irony of Tom's desperate ploy—to pass as a woman because he has been passing as white, and then to obliterate the damning evidence, burning both male and female clothes—is that it marks him unmistakably, if only for a moment, as a black transvestite, the tree son of the mother he despises and sells down the river.[20]

This is a provocative observation, but one that is ultimately based on a misreading of the text. Garber fails to notice that Tom "drops the veil" over his blackface—the blackness he is so anxious to conceal is twice represented here—while the literal veil he wears is a socially encoded, unambiguous marker of gender. In order to escape detection, and literally to escape from the house, Tom thus goes forth, as his mother did in St. Louis, as both man and woman, as both black person and white. Like his mother's blackface cross-dressing, this represents a very powerful moment in Tom's life—he has acted, and he has acted decisively—but with two crucial differences. Although Roxana wears layered gender and racial identities, she pulls off her slouch hat and reveals her long, flowing hair; she strips off one layer to reveal herself. Tom, by contrast, piles on his layers only to deceive, to cover up the shame of his deed. And so his act, unlike his mother's, is an act of cowardice that puts him beyond the pale of human redemption.[21]

It has been clear to generations of readers that for all its vexing statements about the role of race in determining Tom's character (and by extension Chambers'), Pudd'nhead Wilson exposes the absurdity and arbitrariness of the very racial categories upon which the slave society depended. As both Eric Sundquist and Shelley Fisher Fishkin have demonstrated, the novel critiques as well the racial divisions of the 1890s, the era of the enactment of Jim Crow laws and the bolstering of racial boundaries where they were clearly threatened.[22] This essay has argued that the text is even more radical than these critics have suggested, for it also calls into question the socially constructed definitions and meanings of gender markers. In other words, in Pudd'nhead Wilson, the gender disguise is as hard to read as the racial disguise, and both reinforce the deconstructing of the other.

Pudd'nhead Wilson culminates with the trial of Luigi, one of the Italian twins, for the murder of Judge Driscoll. In the course of formally defending Luigi, David Wilson accidentally discovers the "true" identities of Tom and Chambers, and simultaneously reveals Tom to be the murderer of his uncle. The patriarchal social order has been thus only temporarily subverted by Roxana, for her worst fears are realized in the end as her son is deemed too valuable a piece of property to shut up in prison for life and he is sold down the river into slavery. From Roxana's perspective, the ending is like a Greek tragedy in which the very fate she had sought to escape is visited upon her son. Nonetheless, the social order has clearly been dealt a blow from which it is unlikely to recover fully. In a novel glutted with ironies, the ultimate irony may be that the one utterly reliable marker of identity that cannot be altered—finger prints—reveals nothing whatsoever about either the gender or the race of the individual. The community's carefully drawn and constructed racial and gender lines have been challenged and exploded. This is signified subtly, but forcefully, by the re-introduction into the text of the man called Chambers, the "white" man who had been condemned to a lifetime of slavery by the treachery of his "mammy" but who is ostensibly set free by Wilson's discovery of his "true" identity:

> The real heir suddenly found himself rich and free, but in a most embarrassing situation. He could neither read nor write, and his speech was the basest dialect of the negro quarter. His gait, his attitudes, his gestures, his beating, his laugh—all were vulgar and uncouth; his manners were the manners of a slave. Money and fine clothes could not mend these defects or cover them up, they only made them the more glaring and the more pathetic. (114)

The issue of gender, which seems not to play any role at all in Chambers' transformation back to being the white Tom, is hinted at after all in the language describing his "vulgarity": "His gait, his attitudes, his gestures." This is the language, we will recall, used to describe Tom when he performs his female gender for David Wilson. The fact that Chambers is at home only in the kitchen evokes not only race but also the female gender, or a feminized male identity.[23] A novel propelled into motion by the exchange of two babies, Pudd'nhead Wilson makes no effort, dramatically, to make the exchange reciprocal. Twain shows almost no interest in the white baby who is raised as a slave; most of his attention is focused on the black baby raised as white. In the terms of the novel, "really" being white does not mean much at all, or, as Lott puts it, "to be imitation black is to be black, to be imitation white is to be [a] mere mimic."[24] Nevertheless, Chambers, who has been absent from the novel for much of its duration, is left in the end on center stage. His clothes, taken from him at six months, are symbolically returned to him, but the power they had to undo him at the outset is not matched by a corresponding ability to restore him in the end. In this sense, the social order has not been restored in the end. Even the whitest of black men can be sold into slavery, but a white man, once "crossed by the shadow of the Veil," cannot ever be fully white again. While the old categories seem to be reinstated, they are now confounded to such a degree that the old order is shaken to its core.

NOTES

1. Mark Twain, *Pudd'nhead Wilson and Those Extraordinary Twins* (New York: Norton, 1980), 3. Hereafter cited parenthetically.

2. Two notable recent exceptions include Marjorie Garber's brief consideration of the text in *Vested Interests: Cross-Dressing and Cultural Anxiety* (New York: Routledge, 1992), which notes that "questions" of clothing and "the exchange of clothing" are part of the story from the beginning (289), and Eric Lott's "Mr. Clemens and Jim Crow: Twain, Race, and Blackface," which explores the relation of blackface and identity in the novel. Although issues of dress and disguise inform Lott's argument, his primary and provocative thesis focuses on racial performance. In *The Cambridge Companion to Mark Twain*, ed. Forrest G. Robinson (Cambridge: Cambridge Univ. Press, 1996), 129-52.

3. Hjalmar Hjorth Boyesen, quoted in Susan Gilman, *Dark Twins: Imposture and Identity in Mark Twain's America* (Chicago: Univ. of Chicago Press, 1989), 53.

4. *Cosmopolitan*, 18 (January 1895), 379.

5. *The Spectator*, 74 (March 17, 1895), 367-68.

6. *The Bookman* 7 (January 1895), 122.

7. Hershel Parker, *Flawed Texts and Verbal Icons: Literary Authority and American Fiction* (Evanston: Northwestern Univ. Press, 1984), 115-46; Daniel McKeithan, *The Morgan Manuscript of Mark Twain's Pudd'nhead Wilson* (Cambridge: Harvard Univ. Press, 1961).

8. Susan Gilman and Forrest G. Robinson, *Mark Twain's Pudd'nhead Wilson: Race, Conflict, and Culture* (Durham: Duke Univ. Press, 1990).

9. Eric Sundquist, "Mark Twain and Homer Plessy," in *Pudd'nhead Wilson: A Collection of Critical Essays*, ed. Eric Sundquist (Englewood Cliffs: Prentice-Hall, 1994), 169-83; Shelley Fisher Fishkin, "Race and Culture at the Century's End: A Social Context for Pudd'nhead Wilson," *Essays in Arts and Sciences* 19 (1990): 1-27; Carolyn Porter, "Roxana's Plot," in Sundquist, ed., *A Collection of Critical Essays*, 154-68; Myra Jehlen, "The Ties that Bind: Race and Sex in Pudd'nhead Wilson," in *Mark Twain's Pudd'nhead Wilson: Race, Conflict, and Culture*, 105-20.

10. Gilman, *Dark Twins*.

11. Susan Gilman argues that in the novels following Pudd'nhead Wilson Twain questions traditional categories of gender identification: "If `male' and `female' are as readily interchanged as `black' and `white,' then gender difference may prove to be as culturally constituted as much `a fiction of law and custom' as racial difference." Gilman, *Dark Twins*, 79. A recent article by Laura Skandera-Trombley focuses on cross-gendered shorter works Twain wrote in the late 1890s and 1900s: "Why Can't a Woman Act More Like a Man? Mark Twain's Masculine Women and Feminine Men," *OVERhere* 15 (1995): 49-57. In the same issue of *OVERhere*, John Cooley writes about Twain's "heroic but also tragic maidens and inadequate males" (3447). None of these scholars, however, addresses the relationship between gender and race in the major works.

12. See Patricia Turner, *Ceramic Uncles and Celluloid Mammies: Black Images and Their Influence on Culture* (Berkeley: Univ. of California Press, 1994). Of particular interest is the chapter "Back to the Kitchen," 41-61.

13. See Porter, "Roxana's Plot."

14. Jehlen, 110.

15. Lott, 145.

16. Mikhail Bakhtin, *Rabelais and His World*, trans. Helene Iswolsky (Bloomington: Indiana Univ. Press, 1984).

17. On female identity and being seen see, for instance, Laura Mulvey, "Visual Pleasure and Narrative Cinema," *Screen* 16 (Autumn 1975): 6-18.

18. Carolyn Porter is less patient with Wilson, saying that he "is remarkably dull witted when it comes to reading his evidence. Most noteworthy is his persistent and blundering confusion over the identity of the `young woman' in Tom's room, `where properly no young woman belonged'" (164).

19. In addition to Eric Lott's "Mr. Clemens and Jim Crow," see also his *Love and Theft: Blackface Minstrelsy and the American Working Class* (New York: Oxford Univ. Press, 1993).

20. Garber, 290-91.

21. Eric Lott characterizes Tom's going forth in female dress as "an element of blackface revenge for the master's rape of slave women, one of whose issue is Tom himself." "Mr. Clemens and Jim Crow," 149.

22. Eric J. Sundquist, "Mark Twain and Homer Plessy"; Shelly Fisher Fishkin, "Race and Culture at the Century's End."

23. See Myra Jehlen, who argues that "the subversion in Tom's usurpation of white identity turns Chambers into a woman, for femininization is the lasting result of that unfortunate man's slave upbringing." But Jehlen never makes clear precisely how Chambers is feminized, except to suggest that the black man, in white men's stereotypes, is either an over-sexualized, threatening being or "contemptibly effeminate" (112). Chambers clearly is not the former.

24. Lott, "Mr. Clemens and Jim Crow," 147.

4

Carnival in Mark Twain's "Stirring Times in Austria" and "The Man That Corrupted Hadleyburg"

—Peter Messent

The publication of the 29 volume *The Oxford Mark Twain* in 1996 provided, both for the writers and critics involved in the project, and for its readers, an unusual opportunity for an overview and reassessment of the work Twain published during his lifetime. Essays like that written by Toni Morrison on Adventures of Huckleberry Finn, where she speaks eloquently of her responses to different "encounters" with the novel, focusing in particular on what she has come to see as "the silences that pervade it ... entrances, crevices, gaps, seductive invitations flashing the possibility of meaning. Unarticulated eddies that encourage diving into the novel's undertow" (Morrison xxxi, xxxiii, xxxvi), promise to become the critical lens through which a new generation of readers approach the text.

Another result of the project, however, has been to remind us of the original context in which some of Twain's best-known short fictions appeared. So Cynthia Ozick, in her introduction to the 1900 collection, The Man that Corrupted Hadleyburg and Other Stories and Essays, draws revealing comparisons between the title story and the little-known essay, "Stirring Times in Austria," which appears later in the same volume. I use Ozick's essay, and also Bruce Michelson's analysis of "The Man That Corrupted Hadleyburg" in his fine recent book, Mark Twain on the Loose,[1] as twin points of departure for my own critical work here.

It is not, though, merely the connections between the lead story and the later essay about Austrian politics that emerge when re-reading Twain's Hadleyburg book. However casual Twain and his publishers might have been in pulling together the stories and essays written between 1893 and 1900 that make up the collection (Jeffrey Rubin-Dorsky dismisses all but three of them as "periodical literature, written for the moment and for money" [1]) a set of recurring concerns do bring it some unity, however loose that may be. Most noticeable are the references to the Dreyfus Case scattered through the book. Twain makes direct reference to this case on four different occasions (144-46, 170, 270, and 388-89). Moreover, he wrote "The Man That Corrupted Hadleyburg" in 1898 in Vienna, the same year Zola published J'accuse, and Ozick astutely draws connections between Twain's story and this wider historical context when she writes that:

> the notion of a society—even one in microcosm, like Hadleyburg—sliding deeper and deeper (and individual by individual) into ethical perversion and contamination was not far from a portrait of Europe undergoing the contagion of its great communal lie. The commanding theme of "The Man That Corrupted Hadleyburg" is contagion; and also the smugness that arises out of self-righteousness, however rooted in lie it may be. (xxxv)

Ozick's reference to the "communal lie" directly echoes the idea of the "colossal National Lie" (180) that Twain analyzes in "My First Lie, And How I Got Out Of It," another essay in the Hadleyburg book. Communal hypocrisy, ethical perversion, the Dreyfus Case, failures of systems of justice, and anti-Semitism, provide a cluster of related themes that draws together much of the material in the collection.[2] There are, too, other repeated themes that both further unify the book and connect it to the other work Twain was producing in the period. The subjects of mistaken and twinned identities, and of personal dislocation and alienation, obsessed Twain throughout his career, and especially in its final stages. In Hadleyburg, the comic potential inherent in the former pairing is exploited, to varying degree, in two pieces: "My Debut as a Literary Person" and "My Boyhood Dreams." In the first, Twain has a contribution on the shipwreck of the Hornet (a story fully reprised in this essay) accepted by an important New York magazine, but his dreams of literary glory are dashed by the publication of his nom de plume not as "MARK TWAIN" but as "'Mike Swain' or 'MacSwain,' I do not remember which" (85). In "My Boyhood Dreams," the gap between dreamed and actual career becomes comic source, as Twain plays off the figures of friends like Howells, Hay, and Cable, reporting on their supposed "dream-failure[s]" (389). Thus he claims that Cable, for instance, once dreamt of being a "ring-master in the circus" but has ended up instead "Nothing but a theologian and novelist" (393).

Sketches like "My Boyhood Dreams" may be slight, but Twain's improvisations on themes of career reversal, the relationship between identity and career, and between dream and reality, will take more thematic weight, and more somber resonance, in his other later writing. And though the Mark Twain/MacSwain confusion is a passing reference, the additional comment that the name Mark Twain "had some currency on the Pacific coast" keys into another repeated theme in the book: that of exchange, currency, and the existence—or lack of it—of some kind of firm gold standard (here, the authorial identity). This takes us from the "gold coin" (4) that turns out to be "virgin lead" (67) in "The Man That Corrupted Hadleyburg" to the metaphoric analogy between fraudulent gold and false language running throughout the story, with early description of the "golden remark ... worth forty thousand dollars, cash" (20) followed by later reference to the "magic document [the stranger's letter], each of whose words stood for an ingot of gold" (41).[3] The question of relative values (and currencies) later features as the central theme of "The Esquimau Maiden's Romance," a comic story in which ethnocentric assumptions are undermined in the representation of cultural difference and alterity that occurs (Kruse). The defamiliarizing disjunctions represented in this story, and undermining of any firm value base, relates in turn to the epistemological uncertainty that always shadows Twain's writing. Mary's remark in "The Man That Corrupted Hadleyburg" that "the foundations of things seem to be crumbling from under us" (28) could act as a motto for much of the work he produced, and especially in his later years.

The theme of dislocation and alienation, too, is increasingly prominent in this period, and is often linked to that of self-division.[4] In "Is He Living or Is He Dead?," Twain narrates how a (fictional) Francois Millet fakes his own death, with the help of artist friends, and takes on a new identity; and how his works then rise phenomenally in price. This might be read biographically both in terms of some buried desire on the author's part to shuck off the burdens of his invented public persona, or as a fictional exploration at a time of some financial anxiety of the question of the "value" of that persona as measured both in personal and professional terms. The view given of Theophile Magnan (the renamed Millet), who now appears "alone in the world, . . . always looks sad and dreamy, and doesn't talk with anybody" (182), and who, despite his financial rewards, goes (it seems) ungreeted even by his previously "doting" and "inseparable" friend (184), speaks of anxieties about identity and estrangement that are repeated, in different ways, over and over in Twain's late fiction.

I am arguing, then, that the writings put together in the Hadleyburg collection are not quite the rag-bag of disparate materials we might expect, especially given the speed with which Twain was churning out books at this time (15 between 1889 and 1900; 12 from 1902 to 1909 [Rubin-Dorsky 1, 2]). The correlative of this is to suggest that we might gain critically by looking more closely at Twain's short stories and essays in the full context of the book in which they first appeared. Rather than extending my analysis of the other stories and essays in Hadleyburg, however, I narrow focus to set the one short story "The Man That Corrupted Hadleyburg" against the political essay "Stirring Times in Austria" (on a series of dramatic events in the Austrian parliament in late 1897). In doing this, I extend Cynthia Ozick's initial exploration of the complementary nature of these texts, where she writes of the Austrian parliament, as Twain represents it, as "a non-homogeneous Hadleyburg corrupted well past greed into the contagion of chaos and contumely." The trace of the word "Hapsburg" in "Hadleyburg" helps to reinforce the analogy made here.

If the Hadleyburg townspeople, unlike the Hapsburg parliament with its 19 national groupings, are apparently from the same ethnic background, Ozick notes that "their interests [too] conflict as if they held nothing in common" (xxxix).[5] For her, the crux of both pieces lies in the issue of language. In "Stirring Times in Austria," Twain explains how ratification of the Ausgleich, the treaty that formally links the Austro-Hungarian Empire, has been jeopardized by the deal Count Bedani, leader of the government, has made with the Czechs, "making the Czech tongue the official language in Bohemia in place of the German." The German-speaking minority, "incensed" (292) by this move, obstructs government business—in particular that of the Ausgleich—until the status of their own language should once more be restored. Ozick compares the 19 states in the Austrian parliament to the 19 worthies in Hadleyburg, and sees the way both the parliamentarians and leading citizens "furiously compete" as analogous: "we can recognize in Hadleyburg the dissolving Austria-Hungary of the 1890's" (xl).

Ozick's critical work here is extremely valuable, but it is noticeable that she does not quite pin down her point about the comparative use of the language theme in the two texts. Also, she remains curiously blind to what I see as their main point of comparison—the way in which description of the sessions of the Austrian parliament structurally mirrors the representation of the Hadleyburg town meeting. Prompted by the use of Bakhtinian terms in Bruce Michelson's analysis of "The Man That Corrupted Hadleyburg" (though he nowhere uses the Soviet theorist's name), I use Bakhtin as a lens through which the public meetings at the center of both texts can be analyzed. The conclusions I reach concerning social and political hierarchies and the way they work, and the view of human nature presented, will come as no surprise to those familiar with Twain's late work. They serve, though, to further illustrate the close relationship between these two "Austrian" texts.[6]

Bakhtin's notion of carnivalization provides an ideal model to apply to "The Man That Corrupted Hadleyburg." It can also be applied to "Stirring Times in Austria," even if its relevance here is less immediately obvious. Bakhtin's consistent interest is in the way language serves as a site of conflict, registering the power relations in any particular culture, as one "social speech type" (that is, the voice of a particular professional, regional, ethnic, age-related, or other social or political group) is set against another in a multi-layered whole.[7] He sees centripetal impulses within any given socio-political world as in dynamic tension with centrifugal ones. The centripetal is the unhealthy urge toward the closed system—the establishing of a single officially-recognized language—and toward "cultural centralization" (Bakhtin, Dialogic 271), while the centrifugal "endlessly develop[s] new forms which parody, criticize and generally undermine the pretensions of the ambitions toward a unitary language" (Murray 119). In his favoring of the centrifugal, Bakhtin asserts his commitment to social diversity and change rather than to the hierarchical. For a culture is not, for him, something fixed, rigid and ordered. He emphasizes rather its multi-languaged aspects, assigning qualities of health and vitality to those ongoing forces of disunification and decentralization that the authorities and ruling classes of any society would try to deny.

"Carnivalization" is a key term for Bakhtin and one directly related to the centripetal-centrifugal axis. For it is the model of carnival festivity "transposed into the language of literature," life turned upside down as conventional hierarchical barriers are removed (Bakhtin, Problems 122). Bakhtin's preference for "low" languages over "high" is evident in the emphasis in carnival on the comic overturning of official systems of life and thought by an unofficial folk culture, and the energies with which the latter is associated. Carnival is a time of masquerade, as masks and false identifies are assumed that blur the boundaries between high and low and decenter authoritative systems and structures. And carnival is associated with public space (and especially the public square) where normal hierarchies are suspended as the festival runs its course and where all types of people can meet and mingle freely and easily together. Carnivalization primarily means laughter, a laughter "directed toward something higher—toward a shift of authorities and truths." What results is the relativizing of "all structure and order, of all authority and all (hierarchical) position" (Bakhtin, Problems 127, 124). In communal performance, the very essence of carnival, the language and structure of officialdom (law, prohibition and restriction) are overturned on behalf of the vital and indecorous folk-energies there allowed release.

The version of carnival that takes place in "Stirring Times in Austria" is a distorted one, with the idea of folk energy[8] and the laughter that accompanies it present only in corrupt form. The language and structure of officialdom are subject to contest and potential overthrow, with energies loosed that are normally harnessed, but such action takes place primarily in a limited arena, and any sense of a life-affirming folk culture ("the folk as an untamable, rebellious, and regenerative force that will destroy the status quo") is absent.[9] Such an absence, and the way the essay portrays the relationship between authority and social diversity, points (despite the difference in setting between the Vienna represented here and the small American town of Hadleyburg) both to the intertextual connections traversing Twain's work, whatever its generic form, and to the bleak view of human behavior, and the way social hierarchies function, that underlies it.

The parliamentary meetings described in "Stirring Times in Austria" differ from the town meeting in "The Man That Corrupted Hadleyburg," but the centrality of these public assemblies in both texts is highly significant. The parliament in "Stirring Times" is not the carnival area (the public square) where all types of people can mingle freely together, but it is, to an extent, a microcosmic version of the pluralistic Austro-Hungarian whole, with a membership representing "peoples who speak eleven languages" (292), and coming "from all the walks of life and from all the grades of society" (316). Moreover the sense of the multi-layered communal whole indicated here—something we might expect in a representative body—is reinforced in the way Twain carefully structures his essay to draw links between what occurs within and outside the parliament. Thus the essay starts with a striking metaphor of diffuse electrical energy in which this connection is immediately made: "The atmosphere is brimful of political electricity. All conversation is political; every man is a battery, with brushes overworn, and gives out blue sparks . . ." (284). Despite public confusion about the real nature of the political situation,[10] energies within the parliament have their counterpart on the streets outside. "Stirring Times" both starts and finishes with larger public restlessness, the final references to "a popular outbreak or two in Vienna" and rioting elsewhere (340) a direct result of the parliamentary turbulence described at the essay's core.

Parliamentary events, then, are linked to the release of energies in the larger community in the essay. And within the parliament, elements of the carnivalesque are clearly apparent. As governmental authority is challenged, so events in parliament take on (sporadically) a masquerade quality with formal debate drowned in the "general exuberance" (320) bursting forth. Dr. Lecher does finally get a hearing for his 12-hour speech, holding up the attempt quickly to push through the Augsleich, but he commences in "pantomime," his voice drowned out by the "wild and frantic and deafening clamor" (299-300) from the house floor. At another point in the proceedings Lecher and Wolf (another key member of the opposition) "spoke at the same time, and mingled their speeches with the other noises, and nobody heard either of them" (308). All types of wild energies are loosed as language (reasoned or otherwise) is drowned out, first by "explosions of yells" (299), later by the "slam-banging" of desk-boards (305), and then by a form of music, as Wolf "struck the idea of beating out a tune with his board" (308). This festive overturning of officialdom, as normal parliamentary business is disrupted, is paralleled in the next sitting of the house when "ceaseless din and uproar, . . . shouting, stamping and desk-banging" (320) are followed by the bursting forth of personal insults, first singly, and then in the form of communal song:

> in their rapture [the Christian Socialists] flung biting epithets with wasteful liberality at specially detested members of the Opposition; among others this one at Schonerer: "Bordell in der Krugerstrasse!" Then they added these words, which they whooped, howled, and also even sang, in a deep-voiced chorus: "Schmul Leeb Kohn! Schmul Leeb Kohn! Schmul Leeb Kohn!" and made it splendidly audible above the banging of desk-boards and the rest of the roaring cyclone of fiendish noises. (325)

The unruly nature of these parliamentary events have a carnival element about them, but, as I have indicated, the urge toward heterogeneity and the celebration of communality that Bakhtin associates with that term are denied here. Laughter is present (see 325) but far outweighed by forms of irony and abuse. Any antithesis between authority systems and a festive and pluralistic community is interrogated by the fact that the government is associated both with an extra-legal exercise of power (the President "persistently ignoring the Rules of the House in the interest of the government side" [320]) but also with the centrifugal impulse, since the very fact of "disunion" has kept this [Austro-Hungarian] empire together (285). And not just the opposition but the government benches too share in the carnival nature of the events taking place, in the latter's own use of "pure noise" (308) to short-circuit the legislative process. Most crucially, given Bakhtin's celebrations of linguistic diversity and social difference, it is the government that, as a means of retaining its authority, works toward linguistic pluralism (allowing Czech as the official language in Bohemia) while the opposition fights for linguistic purity: "that the country's public business should be conducted in one common tongue, and that tongue a world language—which German is" (293). The fact that the boundaries are so blurred in this (microcosmic) parliamentary context between the imposition of authority and a carnivalistic sense of release, and between the acceptance of heterogeneity and the demand for a unitary official language system, completely undermines any note of celebration concerning the positive expression of diversity, the regenerative nature of the communal performance, and the fulfilling release of folk energies, we might otherwise (from a Bahktinian perspective) hope to expect. Indeed it is the more sinister and pessimistic notes that sound in this essay that remain most strongly with the reader. For if the dark carnival Twain describes, with energy loosed to no positive end, may be no more than accurate reportage of events, the ambition for German as a potential "world language" and the racial intolerance loosed within the parliament, are, from a later historical perspective, chilling. As Ozick says:

> the parliamentary upheaval [Twain describes] is an indelible precursor that not merely portends the profoundly unforgettable Viennese mob-events of 1938, but thrusts them into our teeth with all their bitter twentieth-century flavor. Here is no deja-vu, but its prophesying opposite. Or, to say it otherwise: a twenty-year-old rioter enjoying Mark Twain's Vienna easily becomes a sixty-year-old Nazi enjoying Anschluss Vienna. (Ozick, "Introduction" xlii-xliii)[11]

Carnival is swiftly ended in the parliament with the sudden introduction (on the government's command) of "an invasion of brute force ... a uniformed and helmeted battalion of bronzed and stalwart men marching in double file down the floor of the House" (339), and this is soon followed both by the collapse of the government and by public riot. The mix of racist and anti-Semitic abuse within parliament ("'You Jew, you! . . .' 'East-German offal tub!'" [321,325]) is thus transformed into open violence on the streets. This is no open expression of a Bakhtinian "folk energy," though, but its corrupt, narrowly nationalistic, and anti-humanistic underside (the uses to which Hitler would put the celebration of "the folk" come quickly to mind). For Twain reports that, in the outbreaks that take place (in Vienna, Prague and elsewhere), "in some cases the Germans [were] the rioters, in others the Czechs—and in all cases the Jew had to roast, no matter which side he was on" (340). Twain's figure of speech provides another example of that prophesying opposite of deja vu to which Ozick refers, as images of the festivity, entertainment and laughter associated with carnival are entirely obliterated in the anti-Semitism, racial hatred, and destructive mob violence then released. The events that Twain describes in "Stirring Times in Austria" are non-fictional and occur in a turbulent European political setting. Nonetheless, the central sequence in his essay (completed on 9 December 1897 [Dolmetsch 72]) significantly foreshadows the portrayal of the town meeting in his short story, "The Man That Corrupted Hadleyburg," written in Vienna late in the following year.[12] The essay also bears certain comparison with the short story in their different depictions of the way in which a particular community functions, and in what we can construct of the notion of folk energy from each such representation.

Carl Dolmetsch briefly alludes to the similarity between the two texts when he compares the technique used in the climactic sequence of "Hadleyburg" to that in the main section of "Stirring Times":

> Depicting the same atmosphere of "delightful pandemonium," the scene is theatrically staged, with the chair attempting to keep order while

> raucous taunts and insults are exchanged and speaker after speaker is jeered or shouted down by a "storm," a "cyclone," or a "tornado" of voices, the same imagery he had used in "Stirring Times." (Dolmetsch 234)

There is more to it than this, though. Both texts have public meetings at their center. In "Stirring Times" this takes a representative form, with a certain separation between parliamentary members, crowded viewing galleries inside the House, and general public outside. Whereas in the small town of Hadleyburg (called, like St. Petersburg in The Adventures of Tom Sawyer, "town" and "village" variously) the whole community pack into the Town Hall, its numbers boosted by a variety of "strangers," including "a strong force of special correspondents who had come from everywhere" (38) and even a representative from Barnum's (66). However, the form and progression of both meetings are similar, as, in "Hadleyburg" too, ordered process gives way to pandemonium and reasoned discussion to "all manner of cries . . . scattered through the din" (53-54). Again, individual speech is replaced first by "Many Voices" (58) acting as communal chorus, and then by outbreaks of musical festivity. Such festivity, as the local worthies are mocked, takes the shape both of parodic hymn, "a massed and measured and musical deep volume of sound (with a daringly close resemblance to a well known church chant)" (59), and travesty of light opera:

> "Hooray! hooray! it's a symbolical day!"
>
> Somebody wailed in, and began to sing this rhyme (leaving out "it's") to the lovely "Mikado" tune of "When a man's afraid of a beautiful maid"; the audience joined in, with joy [adding further lines to that first] . . . Then the happy house started in at the beginning and sang the four lines through twice, with immense swing and dash . . . (55-56)

If the transition from speech to uproar to song is the similar in both texts,[13] the version of carnival represented in "Hadleyburg" is a fuller and more positive one, as Bruce Michelson suggests in describing how, here:

> a too-settled social order gives way to folklife, to a springtime of human society in which collective talk and humor flow free, overcoming repression, inhibition and decorum. It is a springtime with power and identity residing nowhere and everywhere. (Michelson 182)

In the town meeting, the established social order is turned upside down. The discredited and "best-hated" (9) man in the community, Rev. Mr. Burgess, is given authority as chairman, and the chief citizens of the community are made fun of, as their greed and hypocrisy is exposed. During the meeting "the monolithically serious" life of this firmly hierarchical community is undermined by the typical form of carnival laughter, where "ridicule [is] fused with rejoicing" (Bakhtin, Problems 125, 127). "The pandemonium of delight" that follows banker Pinkerton's humiliation was, we are told, "of a sort to make the judicious weep. Those whose withers were unwrung laughed till the tears ran down" (53). Laughter becomes king here (as it never fully is in "Stirring Times") and the jester who shares its crown is Jack Halliday, the town's "loafing, good-natured, no-account, irreverent" (22) who helps instigate the festival that the meeting becomes.[14] As the town-hall becomes the meeting place for the variety of social types that make up the community, as the exchange of gifts (associated with carnival abundance [Bakhtin, Problems 125])—first the gold sack, then the large checks—occurs, and as the "nineteen principal citizens and their wives" (21) are reduced from beaming self-congratulation to public humiliation while indecorous folk energies find expressive release, all the conditions of carnival literature appear successfully complete. If my use of Bakhtin is more explicit, the analysis I propose here has much in common with Michelson's. But my main interest is not (as his is) in the nature of the gap between the dissolve of individual identity, with its celebration of a foundational version of folk life where all subjects merge in a healthy communal whole, and a countering awareness of the way selfhood is defined both by the nature of external events and by social and psychological circumstance. I am more concerned with the representation of social diversity that Twain gives us here. For if in my reading of "Stirring Times in Austria" I noted how any opposition (in the way parliament functioned) between centralizing and decentralizing impulses were blurred, so—and to an extent analogously—the portrayal of social hierarchy in "Hadleyburg" is less clear cut than it at first seems. Both this fact, and the narrative closure that occurs, undercut the impact of that celebration of communal energy in the town hall meeting. The conclusions I reach here do not significantly differ from those of prior critics, but my focus on the issues of class and authority that are engaged, and the ironic attitude toward folk culture I identify, help both to twin this text thematically with Twain's Vienna essay, and to place it in the context of other texts by Twain—and particularly Huckleberry Finn—that can be read from a similar thematic perspective.[15]

Carnival depends on the upsetting of established hierarchies, and, at first view, this is exactly what happens in "The Man That Corrupted Hadleyburg," with 18 of its 19 principle citizens exposed as "liars and thieves" (64) by a stranger who had once received "deep offence" (63) while passing through the town. The only name we have for this stranger is "Howard L. Stephenson," signed to a letter (supposedly from a quite other "stranger") written to put the plan of revenge in action. At the public meeting, as exposure occurs, these 18 "Symbols of Incorruptibility" (54) become the object of complete public ridicule, as the remainder of the community loose their voices in exuberant mockery of them. Thus, to quote Bakhtin, "the joyful relativity of all structure and order, of all authority and all (hierarchical) position" occurs as the "high" town authorities (the first three men exposed are the Deacon, Lawyer and Banker) are brought low, and "mass actions . . . and . . . the outspoken carnivalistic word" are given their day (Bakhtin, Problems 124, 123).

The social reversal that takes place here is compromised, however, by the position of the main protagonists in the narrative, Mary and Edward Richards. Edward is, we have to assume, one of the 19 principal citizens of Hadleyburg. He gets one of Stephenson's letters, and it is he who is left unexposed, his (nineteenth) letter claiming the gold unread by Burgess, due to an old debt he owes to Edwards. For the latter once warned Burgess, on the occasion of his unspecified disgrace, of the town's plans to "ride him on a rail" (11). The fact that the "town" as a whole is early identified with a violent act against an innocent man warns us not to take the opposition between "the authorities" and "the folk" too seriously here. And if the town is socially heterogeneous (the tanner, we are told, cannot get recognition as one of the 19), any clear gap between high and low is interrogated by the Richardses role.

For Edward Richards is the cashier at the bank. An old man who is neither rich nor successful, his working life consists of being "always at the grind, grind, grind, on a salary—another man's slave" (6). What he is doing here among the "aristocracy" (65) is never explained. The town meeting expresses its respect, honor, and love for Richards: ironically as he tries to interrupt it to confess his own greed and guilt. Jack Halliday validates that judgment, in a resonant metaphor, as the "hall-marked truth" (57). And if, to recall Michelson, power and identity come in the story to reside nowhere and everywhere as folk-life erupts at the meeting, then we might take the Richardses very name as signaling their membership of the general mass rather than the aristocracy. I am thinking here of his similarity of name to Henry Edwards in The Great Dark, and Michelson's description of the Edwardses as a couple who do "not exist, not as real folk nor even in some respect as characters, for they are . . . presented as middle-class American everybodies and nobodies ... nonpeople" (Michelson 218). If this description itself calls the definition of "real folk" into question, that does not seem inappropriate once we return to "Hadleyburg." Here it might be argued that in the use of the Richardses, "the town's representative consciousness" (Briden 131), Twain deconstructs the opposition he appears to construct between classes, and between town authorities and folk-life, to suggest a lack of essential difference in kind between them.[16] In "Concerning the Jews," he famously wrote: "I think I have no color prejudices nor caste prejudices nor creed prejudices. All that I care to know is that a man is a human being—that is enough for me; he can't be any worse" (254). This statement might be applied, I would suggest, (with the possible exceptions of Sam Halliday and the dead Barclay Goodson) to the community of Hadleyburg. Class difference and social status matter very little if to be a man is to be a human being, and to be a human being is to be a self-interested hypocrite. Any positive conception of folk-life collapses with this equation.

Even Sam Halliday, unbound by the social constraints of others in the town, is by no means an entirely positive folk figure. The mocking laughter associated most strongly with him, then shared by others, brings, as I shall argue, no sense of communal renewal. Moreover, despite his position on the fringes of the community, he does not see entirely clearly. This text is one in which human behavior remains largely impenetrable and the "free familiar contact" of carnival is never entirely achieved (Bakhtin, Problems 123). The story has a striking early image of Halliday carrying "a cigar-box round [like] a camera and [saying],

"Ready!—now look pleasant, please," but the Howellsian idea of realist transparency does not work here. Halliday is puzzled by the changing expressions of the 19 couples' faces at various stages following the receipt of Stephenson's letters, "and didn't know what to make of it" (37). "Stephenson" himself, the manipulator of events, is taken in by the apparent innocence of Richards. Burgess does not know Richards, the warmth of his feelings based on partial ignorance; for Richards in fact has proof that Burgess is innocent of his supposed crime, and "could have saved him" (10) from his disgrace had he chosen to do so. And Richards does not know Burgess, seeing the latter's concealment of his letter as an act of vengeance and not of gratitude. Finally, at the end of the narrative, the townsfolk know Burgess little better than at the beginning, his "impassioned" denial of the motives attributed to him by Richards in the latter's death-bed confession falling "on deaf ears" (83). In a community where the thoughts and motives of others are rarely transparent, the full expression and free familiarity of carnival is never properly achieved, neither in the town meeting nor in the subsequent behavior of the town's inhabitants.

Indeed any celebration of the folk spirit seems well and truly quashed by the narrative's end. If Bakhtin, in his celebration of Carnival, tends to underestimate the fact that such festivity only temporarily upsets established hierarchies, Twain does not. As the town meeting concludes, "Dr." Harkness buys the sack of bogus coins and uses them to ensure his election to the Legislature. In doing so, he "reviv[es] the recent vast laugh" (77), but directs it away from himself to the single person of his political opponent, Pinkerton. The festivity that has occurred is finally ended, then, with the public energies that have been released channeled to selfish and power-oriented ends: for we are told that what is at stake here in the election are the "two or three fortunes" to be made in the routing of a new railway (70). That the election itself is contested by two of the discredited 18 suggests that nothing fundamentally has changed in the town, despite the humiliation that has occurred, and that social hierarchies have been immediately restored.

The claim that a change in moral sensibility results from the carnival that has occurred (Scharnhorst, among many others, sees the story as "Twain's parable of the Fortunate Fall" [64]) also seems highly dubious. For the final line of the story—"[Hadleyburg] is an honest town once more, and the man will have to rise early that catches it napping again" (83)—might rather be seen as, in James D. Wilson's words, "fraught with irony." As he explains:

> The first clause is patently absurd, for Hadleyburg was never an honest town; furthermore, the syntax suggests a restoration, not a transformation—a return to pride in a deceptive, misconceived self-concept. The second clause . . . implies not that Hadleyburg has changed morally but that it is simply cleverer, less naive—no one will catch "it napping again." (Wilson 212)[17]

The final focus on the town as a collective whole, moreover, undermines the sense of conflict between "the folk" and the "aristocracy" that gives the scene of the town meeting its energy and power. Such a stress on community may seem logical if we read the story as illustrating how folk values have helped to reform the whole town. But if we take the more ironic option sketched above, the very notion of a life-giving folk energy is placed under erasure, as all toxin members are represented as a collective, and unimproved, social and moral unit. The structural movement of "Stirring Times in Austria" is from populace to parliamentary meeting, and thence back to public riot and racial hatred, with the events that take place in the centrally-placed representative forum containing strong elements of the carnivalesque. In

"Hadleyburg," the carnival structure is even more pronounced and the idea of communal renewal appears to carry much more positive resonance. But the folk laughter released in "Hadleyburg" turns out, under close analysis, to lack transformative power. Indeed the very difference between folk-values and those of the authorities they would upset is subject to question. The essay and the story in the Hadleyburg volume can then (despite obvious difference in genre, location and subject matter) be read as twinned texts, both of which hinge on public meetings and their loosing of (types of) carnival. If the one text ends with everything back in its ordered social place, and the other with the possibility of political revolution, neither conclusion has much of a positive ring. The attitude toward democratic values and folk energies is ambivalent even in Twain's earliest works, but by this stage in his writing career it has darkened very considerably. "About Play-Acting," another essay in the Hadleyburg collection, glosses a play Twain had recently seen and admired in Vienna (The Master of Palmyra). He writes here of the figure of Death appearing on stage, and how "always its coming made the fussy human pack seem infinitely pitiful and shabby and hardly worth the attention of either saving or damning" (239). Such a judgment, I would suggest, could be applied with equal justice in both "Stirring Times in Austria" and "The Man That Corrupted Hadleyburg."

NOTES

1. See especially 175-88.

2. Ozick's critical analysis of Twain's "Concerning the Jews," another piece in the Hadleyburg volume, is sharply relevant here in its discussion of the problematic nature of Twain's attitudes toward Jewishness. See "A Tale" 10-14.

3. See Ozick, "Introduction" xxxviii-xxxix.

4. For discussion of the brief narrative of "treacherous self-divisions" in *Following the Equator* (1897), concerning the "young American boy raised . . . in the Sandwich Islands, whose cross-cultural background erupts in delirium," and a fascinating analysis of it in terms of the function of Hawaii in Twain's career as "a kind of imperial unconscious of national identity," see Kaplan 237-48. The quotations used here are on 238.

5. As Ozick's words here suggest, her distinction between a "homogenous" Hadleyburg and a "non-homogenous" Austria-Hungary does not entirely hold.

6. Twain lived in Vienna from September 1897 to May 1899 and wrote both his essay and short story during this time. Carl Dolmetsch's "Our Famous Guest": Mark Twain in Vienna is an invaluable resource on this period of Twain's life.

7. I am here radically condensing Bakhtin's complex arguments, and, in particular, the importance he gives to novel form, for him (because of the "multiplicity of social voices" it represents) the one literary form in "living contact with unfinished, still evolving contemporary reality (the open-ended present)." See Dialogic Imagination, 264 and 7. The quotation in the main text is from 262. For a fuller analysis of Bahktin's theories, and their application to Adventures of Huckleberry Finn, see Messent, *New Readings* 204-42. I borrow from that text in my explication here.

8. A term that relates closely to Bakhtin's "folk-carnival life." What Bakhtin says about the decline of carnival life (and the cutting off of carnival forms from their "folk base") is relevant to the argument that follows. See Problems 130-31. For a short but pertinent discussion of carnival in a contemporary literary context, see McHale 171-75.

9. See Katerina Clark and Michael Holquist (310). They are commenting here on the way Bakhtin "consistently idealizes the folk" in his work. The status quo (the Badeni

regime) is, as I will describe, finally upset in "Stirring Times" but to no positive end.

10. Due to repressive mechanisms employed by the political authorities, and especially the censorship of the public press (287-92). See also Ozick, Introduction li.

11. Jeffrey Rubin-Dorsky's incisive account of the shift in tone of the essay from "Marx Brothers movie" to "Lenny Bruce nightmare" (10) is also relevant to my discussion.

12. Dolmetsch writes that it was completed in October (232). James D. Wilson says December (199).

13. Bruce Michelson also notes the relationship between writing and oral discourse in "The Man That Corrupted Hadleyburg." While "written words prove part of Hadleyburg's crisis," Michelson sees the "oral discourse of talk and song" linked to a "dream of primordial freedom—from social conformity, from culture-founded ideas, and from selfhood as a modern construct." See Michelson 183.

14. Though see Michelson (182) on Halliday and the "tide of namelessness" that comes to take over the text.

15. I cannot develop this argument here, but would direct the reader to my *New Readings of the American Novel and Mark Twain* (86-109), where the status of carnival and folk energies in Huckleberry Finn are discussed.

16. Susan K. Harris sees the Richardses as "aliens to the town," sharing the harshly realistic views Barclay Goodson (a "psychological outsider") has of the town. This view does not hold water, since it is clear at the town meeting that other members of the community, too, see through the chief citizens' facades. See Harris 483, 474.

17. Wilson sees the final focus on the Richardses as illustrating the larger message that "humans do not make moral choices at all but behave as they must according to nature, conditioning, and circumstance" (211). Earl F. Briden places the story in the context of Twain's other

writings of the time to argue strongly that "'Hadleyburg' thematizes the inoperability of the fortunate-fall doctrine in a world far gone in depravity." He presents the Richardses as initially motivated (after the town meeting) by public opinion, and shows how, at the narrative's end, "the pair obviously can learn no abiding lesson from their sin because they lose their reason." See Briden 128, 131.

REFERENCES

Bakhtin, M.M. *The Dialogic Imagination: Four Essays*. Trans. Caryl Emerson and Michael Holquist. Austin: U of Texas P, 1981.

—. *Problems of Dostoevsky's Poetics*. Trans. Caryl Emerson. Manchester: Manchester UP, 1984.

Briden, Earl F. "Twainian Pedagogy and the No-Account Lessons of 'Hadleyburg.'" *Studies in Short Fiction* 28 (1991): 125-34.

Clark, Katerina, and Michael Holquist. Mikhail Bakhtin. Cambridge, Massachusetts: Harvard UP, 1984.

Dolmetsch, Carl. *"Our Famous Guest": Mark Twain in Vienna*. Athens: U of Georgia P, 1992.

Harris, Susan K. "'Hadleyburg': Mark Twain's Dual Attack on Banal Theology and Banal Literature." *American Literary Realism* 16 (1983): 240-52. Rpt. Sloane 469-88.

Kaplan, Amy. "Imperial Triangles: Mark Twain's Foreign Affairs." *Modern Fiction Studies* 43 (1997): 237-48.

Kruse, Horst H. "Mark Twain and the Other: A Contextual Reading of 'The Esquimau Maiden's Romance.'" Elmira Conference on The State of Mark Twain Studies. Elmira College. Elmira, New York. August 1997.

McHale, Brian. *Postmodernist Fiction*. New York: Methuen, 1987.

Messent, Peter. Mark Twain. *Basingstoke*: Macmillan, 1997.

—. *New Readings of the American Novel: Narrative Theory and Its Application*. Basingstoke: Macmillan, 1990.

Michelson, Bruce. *Mark Twain on the Loose: A Comic Writer and the American Self*. Amherst: U of Massachusetts P, 1995.

Morrison, Toni. *Introduction. Adventures of Huckleberry Finn*. [1885]. By Mark Twain. *The Oxford Mark Twain*. Series ed. Shelley Fisher Fishkin. New York: Oxford UP, 1996. xxxi-xli.

Murray, David. "Dialogics: Joseph Conrad, Heart of Darkness." *Literary Theory at Work: Three Texts*. Ed. Douglas Tallack. London: Batsford, 1987.

Ozick, Cynthia. Introduction. Twain xxxi-xlix.

—. "A Tale of Two Scholars." *Commentary*. August 1995: 10-14.

Rubin-Dorsky, Jeffrey. *Afterword*. Twain 1-11.

Scharnhorst, Gary. "Paradise Revisited: Twain's `The Man That Corrupted Hadleyburg." *Studies in Short Fiction* 18 (1981): 59-64.

Sloane, David E.E., ed. *Mark Twain's Humor: Critical Essays*. New York: Garland, 1993.

Twain, Mark. "The Man That Corrupted Hadleyburg" and *Other Stories and Essays. The Oxford Mark Twain*. Series ed. Shelley Fisher Fishkin. New York: Oxford UP, 1996.

Wilson, James D. *A Reader's Guide to the Short Stories of Mark Twain*. Boston: Hall, 1987.

5

Through a Glass Eye, Darkly: The Skeptic Design of 'Life on the Mississippi'

—Earl F. Briden

Mark Twain's Life on the Mississippi is generally regarded as an uneven, disjointed work, one part cub-pilot memoir, three parts pedestrian reportage. As critics point out, the book was conceived as a journalistic project: Twain would revisit the river, "make notes" (p. 178),[1] and use them to expand "Old Times on the Mississippi," his 1875 Atlantic articles, into a subscription-length work. It has not been noted, however, that Twain's 1882 return to the river and to "Old Times" activated a skepticism about the nature and grounds of knowledge that complicated his journalistic agenda. As a consequence, the 1882-83 section of Life on the Mississippi is reportage with a Twainian stamp, journalism that wryly subverts its own claims to factual authority. The book as a whole presents a series of variations on the theme of epistemic (and thus representational) limitation—the boatman's, the writer's, humanity's; and skepticism defines the domain of its humor, a site where epistemological failure and the self-satisfying "truths" that shape experience intersect.

To many readers the "Old Times" section of Life on the Mississippi is vintage Twain, while the 1882-83 chapters (1-3, 21-60) amount to little more than hack-work. For Edgar J. Burde, "Old Times" is imaginatively controlled narration, but the balance of the book shows Twain slaving under "the tyranny of literalism and direct observation."[2] A similar falling-off is noted by Ronald Lycette: "Old Times" is a coherent initiation story, while the later section "breaks down into a looser, more rambling description of river life."[3] John R. Brazil suggests that in "Old Times" Twain effectively opposes romantic and pragmatic consciousness; however, the cost of his alliance with pragmatism is that the rest of the book consists of anecdotal "reportage."[4]

Such criticism overlooks the emergence, in conscious, discursive form, of Twain's skeptic epistemology and its significance in unifying the 1882-83 chapters and linking them securely to the "Old Times" section. Outlined in his river notebooks and in an essay written in February 1883, Twain's skeptic scheme establishes the thematic rhythm of Life on the Mississippi as a whole. These later chapters explore a theory of knowledge new to Twain in its breadth and reach but old in its rudiments, an epistemology that universalizes the meaning of "Old Times" by positing the boatman's engagement with the river as the paradigmatic story of the mind's engagement with its world. The later chapters serve as a gloss upon "Old Times," explicating the cub's repeated demonstrations of inability to master the river's mysteries and the pilot's achievement in fabricating a "river . . . in [his] head" (p. 72). These chapters register Twain's awareness that most people see (as he said of James Fenimore Cooper) "through a glass-eye, darkly"[5] and that "reality" is a product of Twainian man's constituting activity. The comedy of Life on the Mississippi resides in this conjunction of blindness and fabrication, which, to Twain, represents a primary condition of human happiness.

When Twain revisited the Mississippi in the spring of 1882, he evidently intended to write a "standard work," a book of recognized factual authority on the culture and history of the river.[6] Among his notes, however, he roughed out a theory of knowledge that would destabilize his plan and transform Life on the Mississippi into a richly ironic production. He set down his doubts about the mind's capacity for originating ideas, asking himself, "Who can think wise or stupid things at all that were not thought of in the past?" He recorded his sense of a world characterized by perpetual change and thus eluding recognition: "I found that the river was as brand new to me as if it had been built yesterday & built while I was absent. I recognized no single feature of it." He also noted that he was a stranger to his boyhood home: "Alas! everything was changed in Hannibal except the mud." He transcribed an anecdote the import of which is that humanity occupies a universe of encoded fictions, and experience is thus a matter of reading linguistic and natural texts. On board the Gold Dust he met an Irish literature-vendor who extolled the benefits of reading "fiction": "When you rade the Greek and Latin languages you're rading fiction. Go to-night and rade the firmament; the stars {are} ivery {o} wan of 'em tells of fiction." And he recorded ideas about cowardice and selfishness, traits that affect humanity's way with its truths: "Is anybody brave when he has no audience? Is anybody or any action ever unselfish? (Good theme for Club essay)."[7]

The essay was "What Is Happiness?," which Twain dashed off one month after completing Life on the Mississippi and presented to the Hartford Monday Evening Club. As Twain later recalled, "What Is Happiness?" represented "one chapter of [his] gospel,"[8] the gloomy philosophical scheme that would find its fullest expression in What Is Man? (1906). The essay coupled ideas recorded in his 1882 notebooks with a mechanistic view of man and mind, arguing that man is "merely a machine automatically functioning without any of his help or any occasion or necessity for his help." Lacking free-will, man-the-machine is driven by the one imperative behind all action, the satisfaction of self. Yet the mind is stocked entirely with derivative ideas, since "the human machine gets all its inspirations from the outside and is not capable of originating an idea of any kind in its own head."[9]

Twain's experiences on his trip west confirmed the general truth-value of a number of ideas developed, in concrete, particular terms, in his "Old Times" articles. Thus the cub illustrates both the derivative nature of the ideas in which one is (as Twain would say) "trained"[10] and the difficulty of decoding the text of a river that, to the writer in 1882, figured the entire Heraclitean world-in-flux. At the outset, the cub is a Tom Sawyer figure, his mind a storehouse of the second-hand romantic notions shared by all village boys and steamboat passengers - that piloting is pure glamor, that the river is pure poetry. Like Tom, he takes vast satisfaction in his romantic banalities, as his lurid description of sunset on the river indicates (pp. 83-84). But unlike Tom, who never has to abandon his bookish romanticism, the cub is put through a retraining program that displaces dulce with utile. He must learn the pilot's science of reading "the language of the river" (p. 83) under all perceptual conditions and despite never-ending changes in channel, depth, and shape. Twain closes the "Old Times" sequence by remarking that "In due course I got my license" (p. 177); yet he never dramatizes the cub's epistemelogical success. "Old Times" is patterned by the cub's complacency-deflating moments of defeat by the enigmatic river; the sequence is structured, in other words, by Twain's comic strategy of building up and then shattering the cub's confidence that he is mastering his subject. To the cub, apparently, the Mississippi is always as "brand new" as it seemed, in 1882, to Twain, whose return entailed a rediscovery of cub-consciousness—his own and all mankind's.

Twain seems to have fleshed out his epistemology by generalizing from the pilot's story as well, which further defines the nature, sources, and uses of knowledge. The pilot's authority stems from knowing "the shape of the river," which enables him always to "steer by the river that's in [his] head, and never mind the one that's before [his] eyes" (p. 72). Yet for Twain (as for Kant, whose Critique of Pure Reason Twain mentions in an 1882 notebook entry),[11] the pilot's scientific knowledge is not knowledge of an objective reality—of the material river-in-itself. Rather, the pilot's river is a synthetic approximation of the real, built up from pieces of information. Out of his interpretation of the details comprising his world of sensation, the pilot constructs his river, an abstraction of the specialized mind generated by the need for technical control.

The pilot's scientific truth is as much a construct, then, as the cub's romantic truth (or any truth viewed from the position of Twain's skepticism). Each is a product of training—of the pilot's technical education, of the cub's environmental conditioning. Nor does the river in the pilot's head amount to his original idea. "Old Times" indicates that pilots are trained to read their river-text by stringent protocols that serve to standardize their readings and eliminate the idiosyncratic. In addition, owing to the river's dizzying changes, the individual pilot must depend for much of his data upon the pooled observations of a community of fellow pilots—first, an informal society, later, an elite Pilots' Association (pp. 132-134). Since the river can be modeled only as it evolves, the pilot's constituting activity must go on perpetually and so is expanded to the proportions of a life-form. Other craftsmen can interest themselves in nontechnical matters: "Not so with a pilot; he must devote himself wholly to his profession and talk of nothing else . . . He has no time or words to waste if he would keep 'posted'" (pp. 134-135). In Emersonian terms, the epistemological demands of his work turn man piloting into the Pilot, the whole person into the specialized fraction; and though piloting develops the mind into "a very colossus of capability," this development occurs "only in the matters it is daily drilled in" (p. 111).

The pilot's prowess is also a function of his automation; a figure of Bergsonian comedy, he is arguably a source of Twain's theoretic conception of man—and mind—as machine. The old-time pilot's memory does its work "unconsciously," effortlessly laying up "its vast stores, hour by hour, day by day." Though attending to other things, he notes the leadsman's call of "quarter twain" in the midst of a seemingly endless series of "half twain" calls. "The cry of 'quarter twain' did not really take his mind from his talk, but his trained faculties instantly photographed . . . the important details for future reference without requiring any assistance from him in the matter." His mind is "patiently and laboriously trained to do that sort of thing mechanically" and operates independently of —even in spite of—his will; his "faculties could not help noticing landmarks and soundings, and his memory could not help holding on to them with the grip of a vise" (pp. 110-111).

The description of the somnambulist steersman crowns Twain's portrayal of the pilot as machine. Fast asleep at the wheel on a dark, drizzly night, Mr. X manages a "marvel of steering" (pp. 98-99). Though exaggerated, the episode dramatizes the reliability of the river in the pilot's head and, at the same time, his machine-like performance. Oblivious to the phenomenal world and steering down his mind's river, Mr. X is the automatic pilot, functioning without any need for his waking self's help.

An ambiguous epistemological hero, the pilot of "Old Times" prefigures Twain's Connecticut Yankee in his hard-headed practicality, his tyrannous authority, and his self-aggrandizing showmanship. A man of technical know-how, he is the antithesis of poetry and sentiment. His expertise may make him "the only unfettered and entirely independent human being that lived in the earth" (p. 119); but he is the technocrat, the "Boss" whose power is likely to become despotic, as Twain's remarks on the "snarling, fault-finding, mote-magnifying tyrant" Mr. Brown suggest (p. 159). Like Hank Morgan, the pilot has a "circus side" and stages spectacular feats of showmanship, as Chapter 7 reveals.[12] Brave before his pilot-house audience, Mr. Bixby demonstrates the relationship between self-gratification and knowledge in Twain's "gospel," which proposes that man satisfies the absolute need for his own self-approval by asserting his truth—in the case of the pilot, the truth of his river-model.[13]

In the 1882-1883 chapters of Life on the Mississippi Twain explores the epistemology adumbrated in "Old Times," validated by his experiences on the river in 1882, and central to his emergent "gospel." This section restages his return to the Mississippi, a drama that amounts, finally, to an etiology of epistemological weaknesses. Twain multiplies examples of the derivative, authoritative truths - of law and politics, science and religion, romance and history - in which the mind is grounded and by which its reach for knowledge is circumscribed. Figured by the river, reality is marked in these chapters by the deceptive appearances and relentless changes that vexed the cub and now bedevil the author of a projected "standard work." These chapters reflect his ironic discovery that the would-be transcriber of the real willy-nilly authors a "fiction of words" (p. 120), since the real is escaping him even as he sets it down. Life on the Mississippi dramatizes Twain's recognition that signs constitute rather than represent, that we occupy worlds fashioned from words, images, dreams, and memories—the static, opaque signs that define experience. In this book Twain's comedic strategy is essentially a matter of inverting conventional hierarchic orders, valorizing our self- and world-constituting fictions and the epistemological darkness in which they flourish.

Twain's original intention of writing a "standard work" is inscribed as a source of ironic humor in *Life on the Mississippi*. The book opens with the ostensible purpose of educating the reader in the history and culture of the river: Twain promises that the Mississippi is "well worth reading about" (p. 15), supports his claim with impressive statistical details, and outlines the structure of his book by historical "epoch" (p. 18). In the opening chapters, however, the voice of serious reportage modulates into a skeptical counter-voice that quietly questions the status of his "facts"; and by the book's end he has educated himself in the ramifications of the epistemology of his "gospel" and abandoned all pretense of factual authority.

In these opening chapters there is the familiar juxtaposition of nature-in-process with Twainian man's self-interested invocations of his signs. Here, however, Twain shows how legal and political ideas lose touch with the reality of ongoing change, since the river refuses to conform to the abstractions people impose upon it. Disposed to straighten itself by cutting off necks of land and so to play "havoc with boundary lines and jurisdictions" (pp. 16-17), the Mississippi frustrates the mind's ordering efforts. Twain also stresses the self-aggrandizing motive behind the ideological structuring of the natural and human orders, an act which reveals the opacity of our signs. The European appropriation of the Mississippi valley was essentially a matter of training the native inhabitants in religious and political signs to which, as the explorers piously believed, the geography and culture of the new world simply had to be conformable. La Salle set up a cross bearing the arms of France and so dispossessed the natives of their land, while the priest explained "by signs" the faith which is to compensate the "savages" for their loss (p. 27).

The chapters on Southern romanticism place the second-hand, static, and fictive nature of people's world-constituting truths in bold relief. The South cleaves to "obsolete forms and a dead language" (p. 349), a change-denying romanticism authored by Sir Walter Scott and perpetuated by cub-consciousness. Scott is "probably responsible" for the Capitol building at Baton Rouge, an imitation castle that in itself should be harmless; "but as a symbol and breeder and sustainer of maudlin Middle-Age romanticism . . . it is necessarily a hurtful thing and a mistake" (p. 309). Scott's books may be at the bottom of the region's problems, in other words, but, like any ideology, romanticism has a way of multiplying its symbols and adherents. Having been trained in Scott's "dreams and phantoms" (p. 347), Southerners, like all people everywhere, find satisfaction in symbolic elaborations and validations of their truth. So the literary text gives rise to the architectural, which in turn has its progeny, as the mind adds to and objectifies its importations.

Twain piles up examples of texts that take on an authoritative significance owing to the various ways in which epistemological limitation and the imperative of self-satisfaction are conjoined. Some are designed to deceive their readers for selfish reasons. There is the letter, supposedly written by one "Jack Hunt" (p. 391), that dupes clergymen by appealing to their sentimental beliefs. There is the antedated marriage license contrived, in order to inherit his in-laws' money, by the steamboat clerk. Twain's comment on this vignette suggests his view that any fact has a fictive quality; though comprised of "actual facts," the story competes with fiction, for "not all novels have for a base so telling a situation" (p. 366). Then there are texts that deceive their authors as well as their auditors.

The book contains a pair of quixotic autobiographies, one told by the night watchman whose life is a romantic invention worked up out of "wildcat literature" (p. 52), the other by the Lynch-destroying carpenter whose "poor romantic head [has been] turned" by reading the "Jibbenainosay." Both talk themselves into identities constructed from their reading and win the credit of the young Twain. Thus identity, the story we tell to and about ourselves, is one more derivative, reified notion; the self is constituted from texts, making everyone a "plagiarist" (p. 411).

Twain's return to Hannibal is marked by the experience of alternative worlds- the reified past and the ever-changing present. His one enduring idea of the town is his memory of it as he had known it when he left it in 1853, an image that coexists with the novelty of a place that has been evolving all along. He sees the new houses, "but they did not affect the older pictures in my mind, for through their solid bricks and mortar I saw the vanished houses, which had formerly stood there, with perfect distinctness" (p. 393). A similar objectification of memory occurs in his encounters with young women who seem not to have changed but turn out to be daughters or granddaughters of the ladies he has in mind. "It takes some little time to accept and realize the fact that while you have been growing old, your friends have not been standing still, in that matter" (p. 407). Memories constitute an entire world that is standing still.

Personal identity involves a like division between the old, remembered self and an image of self shaped by the aging process. In Hannibal, Twain wakes each morning thinking that he is a boy and has "simply been dreaming an unusually long dream" (p. 394). In his dreams, "the faces were all young again." He also retires each night "a hundred years old," having seen the same faces "as they are now" (p. 407). He would not formulate his conception of a virtually autonomous dreamself for some fifteen years.[14] Yet here he probes the ways in which people displace an anarchic reality of aging bodies and shifting landscapes with the definiteness of dreams and memories.

The Hannibal sequence also reveals how conscience shapes perception. As Twain recalls, the children of his village interpreted natural events as signs of Divine judgment, and young Sam often spent nights in agonies of terror and repentance for behavior that went against the official religious culture. Thunder storms were manifestations of "celestial attention" to the boy "for sins which I knew I had committed, and for others which I was not certain about" (p. 400). Conscience is culturally derived, then, and determines the child's reading of the natural and human worlds.[15] Believing himself guilty of the death of a tramp he supplied with matches, Sam detected "suspicion in the most purposeless remarks" of those around him (p. 416).

Twain's etiology of epistemological problems embraces a number of subjective factors. Grief, for example, operates much like guilt. The undertaker he encounters in New Orleans humorously describes how grief invests the dead with a logic-defying value, enabling him to sell expensive embalming procedures. Partiality also governs perception. When Uncle Mumford calls attention to the "religious look" of Cape Girardeau, Twain remarks that "partialities often make people see more than really exists" (p. 200). Judgments of facts can be altered by reputations generated by the social environment. When the fast steamboat Eclipse passes an inattentive old man, he describes it as "loafin' along," and then, told its name, reverses opinion and judges that it "went by here a-sparklin'" (p. 239). Reputation likewise accounts for the homage paid by New Orleans to one of its dead, a pirate who, turning politician, fell out of favor. After his death, his sanguinary reputation is resurrected, and the public shows "respect for the pirate;

not the alderman" (p. 330). Society selectively rewrites its biographical texts, in other words; the object of public esteem is authored by the social mind.

Epistemological failure can be traced, of course, to a person's cublike inability to discriminate among phenomena. Owing to their customers' sensory limitations, "sagacious people" can doctor cotton-seed oil so that it passes for olive oil (p. 244) and manufacture oleomargarine that cannot be told from butter. There are people whose ability to simulate identities enables them to fool even the old-hands at deception and the educated, as in the case of the gambler who finds enormous satisfaction in passing as a figure of "countrified simplicity" (p. 285) and duping both a crew of fellow professional gamblers and a college professor. Some events are indeterminate owing to their unfamiliarity. When Twain samples cock-fighting, he comically notes that a stranger might have mistaken the pre-fight gathering for a prayer-meeting. Moreover, there are works of art that are utterly ambiguous without titles. Chapter 44 describes an oil-painting of Stonewall Jackson's last interview with General Lee, a picture that "means nothing without its label." The painting "tells one story," Twain remarks: that here are Jackson and Lee. But it was simply impossible for the artist to render details signifying a final interview, information which requires a verbal context (p. 332). John E. Bassett points out that the lesson embedded in this account is "the indeterminacy of meaning in texts."[16] However, this episode also emphasizes people's dependence upon outside sources - their "authorities," as Tom Sawyer would say—for the significance of their texts, for "meaning" that is, at bottom, arbitrary.

Perhaps the most suggestive testimony to the comic convergence of the textual and the real comes in Chapter 47, where the authors who meet in New Orleans describe their experience of giving fictional characters "next-to-impossible" names only to find, to their chagrin, that their choices designate actual "living bearers" of the names (pp. 351-352). In this account Twain inscribes one of the paradoxes at the heart of his epistemology and his river book: that a person's world-constituting fictions are always unoriginal, always plagiarisms, and yet inevitably present themselves as real.

Twain's skepticism also undermines the geographic polarity that Life on the Mississippi superficially seems to offer of a progressive, practical North as the antithesis of the romantic South. Yet, ironically, the very pace of progress along the upper river creates difficulties for Twain-the-writer. Citing population statistics for rapidly growing towns, he is compelled to confess the inadequacy of his numbers. The population figures set down for St. Paul and Minneapolis are several months old. "These towns are far larger now . . . This book will not reach the public for six or seven months yet; none of the figures will be worth much then" (p. 429). Approaching the end of his journey and his book, Twain sees that he has come the full epistemological circle. Like the cub, he is attempting to chart the contours of a world that is changing with vertiginous speed and thus outpacing his transcription of it. The fluidity of the real is acknowledged in his remarks on the railway station in St. Paul: "so large is it, that it seemed somewhat overdone, in the matter of size, at first; but at the end of a few months it was perceived that the mistake was distinctly the other way. The error," he concludes, "is to be corrected" (p. 446). Nor does he describe a building whose replacement will soon outdate his representation.

A reality under perpetual reconstruction defeats both the enumerating and the bounding function of the writer's signs. The concluding chapters of Life on the Mississippi bristle with statistics employed ironically, since numbers cannot stabilize their referents and serve only as obsolete indices of perpetual change. At one point, in fact, Twain gives up counting, admitting its futility, and simply notes that Minneapolis has mills "without number, so to speak" (p. 448). Lines of geographic and political demarcation have no more lasting significance here than they do on the lower river. Minneapolis and St. Paul "were ten miles apart a few months ago, but were growing so fast that they may possibly be joined now and getting along under a single mayor." In five years a stranger will not be able to tell "where one Siamese twin leaves off and the other begins" (pp. 447-448).

Nor do the methods of the historian serve to establish a comprehensible, stable order of past events. The historian's contextualizing strategy is put to the test when Twain observes that a date by itself is meaningless, but if "one groups a few neighboring historical dates and facts around it, he adds perspective and color" (p. 18). The whole enterprise of situating 1542 (the year white people first saw the Mississippi) in the context of other events is a waste of erudition, since it reveals that all points on the time-line are relative to one another. The effect of the exercise is to set the reader adrift in an encyclopedist's realm that lacks any absolute epistemological markers.

Similarly, the scientific approach to knowledge comes in for a drubbing. The geologist, extrapolating from figures on the shortening of the river, would conclude that one million years ago "the Lower Mississippi River was upward of one million three hundred thousand miles long, and stuck out over the Gulf of Mexico like a fishing-rod" (p. 151).[17] The scientist's personal limits are dramatized in the tale of Karl Ritter, whose quest for justice depends upon the "theory" that the one sure method of sorting out identity is the thumbprint (p. 253). Having detected his family's murderer, Ritter takes his vengeance, only to find that he has killed the wrong man. Clearly, scientific knowledge, even when precise, is likely to be employed by people who are otherwise blind. Nor does science provide one monolithic truth; rather, as Twain's remarks on the River Commission indicate, science offers competing truths, each with adherents, each tainted by politics (pp. 224-227).

Appropriately, Life on the Mississippi reaches its conclusion with a description of Twain's passage through Chicago, a city that he has no hope of definitively capturing in his text. For in "astonishing" Chicago "they are always rubbing the lamp, and fetching up the genii, and contriving and achieving new impossibilities." Thus "it is hopeless for the occasional visitor to try to keep up with Chicago—she outgrows his prophecies faster than he can make them." Chicago is forever a "novelty," he concludes, "for she is never the Chicago you passed through the last time" (pp. 451-452). Chicago will not stand still long enough to be authoritatively represented by the writer; and, as it turns out, the North in general is a magical Arabian Nights romance in its ever-renewed novelty; authored by its own strenuous, hard-headed Walter Scotts, it is, like the South, another realm of dream.

In sum, Life on the Mississippi is cognate with Twain's venture into philosophic system-building; indeed, as an exploration of the epistemological strand of his "gospel," it represents an integral part of that venture. Like Huckleberry Finn, much of which also grew out of Twain's 1882 return to the river, it is about the self- and world-defining ideas in which Twainian man is trained. It puts to the skeptic test society's various discourses - romantic, scientific, legal, historical—knowledge of which both constitutes authority and establishes a person's epistemological horizons. Like Huck's story, too, Life on the Mississippi humorously dramatizes the self-satisfaction inherent in fabrication—in both manipulating the signs that establish authority and embracing their truth-value.

NOTES

1. This and all subsequent page references to Life on the Mississippi are to the Author's National Edition (New York: Harper & Brothers, n.d.)

2. Edgar J. Burde, "Mark Twain: The Writer as Pilot," *PMLA*, 93 (October 1978), 882, 888.

3. Ronald Lycette, "Mark Twain Mapping His Territory," *ETC: A Review of General Semantics*, 29 (June 1972), 155, 162.

4. John R. Brazil, "Perception and Structure in Mark Twain's Art and Mind: Life on the Mississippi," *Mississippi Quarterly*, 34 (Spring 1981), 93-95, 97, 100.

5. "Fenimore Cooper's Literary Offenses," *Author's National Edition*, XXII, 85.

6. The phrase appears in Twain's letter of 27 November 1871 to his wife; see *The Love Letters of Mark Twain*, ed. Dixon Wecter (New York: Harper & Brothers, 1949), p. 166.

7. *Mark Twain's Notebooks & Journals*, ed. Frederick Anderson, Lin Salamo, and Bernard L. Stein (Berkeley: University of California Press, 1975), II, 512, 528, 479, 524, 497-498.

8. *Mark Twain in Eruption*, ed. Bernard DeVoto (New York: Harper & Brothers, 1922), p. 240.

9. *Mark Twain in Eruption*, pp. 239-240.

10. By "training." Twain meant the various forms of environmental conditioning brought to bear upon the individual. Probably his best-known statement on the subject is Hank Morgan's remark that 'training is everything; training is all there is to a person." See *A Connecticut Yankee in King Arthur's Court*, ed. Bernard L. Stein (Berkeley: University of California Press, 1979), p. 208.

11. *Notebooks & Journals*, II, 455. At about this time Twain also set down an entry which reads "Huxley's Hume"

(*Notebooks & Journals*, II, 463), suggesting his interest in still another major philosopher in the skeptic tradition.

12. For an analysis of the pilot and cub as a team staging vaudeville acts, see James M. Cox, *Mark Twain: The Fate of Humor* (Princeton: Princeton University Press, 1966), pp. 121-122.

13. *What Is Man? and Other Philosophical Writings*, ed. Paul Baender (Berkeley: University of California Press, 1973), pp. 184-185.

14. Twain first described the "dream self" in a notebook entry of 7 January 1898. See *Mark Twain's Notebook*, ed. Albert Bigelow Paine (New York: Harper & Brothers, 1935), pp. 348-349. Paine mistakenly dates this entry 1897.

15. Twain describes the cultural basis of conscience in an 1885 essay, "The Character of Man." See *What Is Man? and Other Philosophical Writings*, p. 61.

16. John E. Bassett, "Life on the Mississippi: Being Shifty in a New Country," *Western American Literature*, 21 (May 1986), 39.

17. Twain had satirized the epistemic methods of geologists and paleontologists in "Some Learned Fables, for Good Old Boys and Girls" (1874), Author's National Edition, XIX, 156-189. For a discussion of this fable, see Sherwood Cummings, *Mark Twain and Science: The Adventures of a Mind* (Baton Rouge: Louisiana State University Press, 1988), pp. 13-14.

6

'A Difficult Case': W.D. Howells's Impression of Mark Twain

—Lawrence I. Berkove

There is little doubt today about the nature and extent of the influence of William Dean Howells on Mark Twain, but what of the reverse situation? Is it possible that Howells restricted a long and close friendship with Twain to a personal level and that he never assimilated the relationship to the point of expressing it in his art? "A Difficult Case" (1900) is evidence that Twain did leave his mark on both Howells's thought and art, deepening him and inspiring him to write one of his richest, most skillful, and most powerful short stories.

The story, all Howells scholars agree, has been largely overlooked. Yet, paradoxically, most modern commentators on the story praise it as one of Howells's best. Although their interpretations of it vary, the main point of agreement among them is that a main character, Ransom Hilbrook, resembles Mark Twain. The first person to sense this resemblance was Mark Twain himself. Reading the story as it was published in July and August of 1900 in the Atlantic Monthly, Twain wrote Howells that "I read the Difficult Situation [sic] night before last, & got a world of evil joy out of it" (Smith et al. 719). What has led scholars to link Twain to Hilbrook is that character's objections to the doctrine of the immortality of the soul. In My Mark Twain (1910), Howells described the impact of Twain's belief on Livy Clemens: "After they had both ceased to be formal Christians, she was still grieved by his denial of immortality, so grieved that he resolved upon one of those heroic lies, which for love's sake he held above even the truth, and he went to her, saying that he had been thinking the whole matter over, and now he was convinced that the soul did live after death. It was too late" (32).

Although little has been written about the story, what there is covers a lot of ground. Henry James singled it out for brief praise in a letter to Howells, calling it "beautiful and admirable, ever so true and ever so done" (James 198).[1] Edwin Cady called it one of Howells's "most moving stories," finding it an affirmation of love (Cady 201-02). Edward Wagenknecht saw little in it beyond the story level of a minister who "wears out his health and strength in struggling with the doubts of an aged parishioner," and Howells's "most elaborate discussion of the immortality question in fiction" (Wagenknecht 242, 253). Kenneth Eble briefly describes the story as reflecting Howells's weak faith in a personal God and personal immortality, but recognizes in Hilbrook "a central character, suggestive of Mark Twain" (Eble 201-02). In a recent discussion of the story—and, apparently, the only extended one—John Crowley declares it to be "one of Howells's finest short works," and views it as representing both Howells's transition from realism to romance, and his virtual identification with the Rev. Ewbert's affirmation of "a willed belief in the ideal of love and a commitment to life itself, whatever its mysteries and imperfections" (Crowley 138, 144).

The salient features of "A Difficult Case" are easily summarized. The setting of the story is the town of Hilbrook, which changed its name from West Mallow when Josiah Hilbrook, one of its successful sons, endowed it with a university to be named after him. He also separately endowed a church building and a parsonage in the town, and a fund to support the preaching of the doctrines of the Rixonite church, a small sect to which he belonged, whose distinguishing characteristic was its belief in a "patient waiting upon the divine will, with a constant reference of this world's mysteries and problems to the world to come" (149).

Emily Ewbert, the wife of Rev. Clarence Ewbert, the town minister, admires her husband's verbal ability and resents that so few university people attend his sermons. When Rev. Ewbert discovers that Ransom Hilbrook, a cousin of Josiah, though raised a Rixonite, had lost his faith in an afterlife in the Civil War, he "set himself, with all his heart and soul, to dislodge Hilbrook from his deplorable conviction" (165). To Ewbert's surprise, he learns that Hilbrook, whom everyone assumed was only a bachelor farmer, had once had a wife and child—both of whom had died. He also discovers that although Hilbrook speaks in vernacular, he is actually deeply read in the literature of immortality, from Plato to Swedenborg to John Fiske, and that he is "a doubter whose doubt was hopeless through his knowledge" (165).

Ewbert attempts to win Hilbrook back to faith by engaging him in theological discourse. At first Ewbert seems successful, but after Hilbrook thinks over each of Ewbert's arguments he comes back with a rebuttal. What started out as a comfort mission becomes an intellectual contest that increasingly drains Ewbert and leads him to devise ingenious counter-arguments of whose truth he has doubts. Eventually, Hilbrook gives up on Ewbert and starves himself to death in the hope that death is the absolute end, and that there will be no afterlife. Ewbert preaches a funeral sermon for Hilbrook in which he teaches the lesson derived from the old man's death that his hearers should keep "themselves alive through some relation to the undying frame of things, which they could do only by cherishing earthly ties" (219). Many university people come to the sermon and are moved by it, and, in the story's last line, "Mrs. Ewbert augured the best things for her husband's future usefulness from their presence" (220).

It is impossible to do justice to the subtleties of a text by a plot summary, but even in this overview, readers familiar with Twain might be reminded of "The Man That Corrupted Hadleyburg" (1899) by the name change from West Mallow to Hilbrook. Another connection to Twain might be made to What Is Man?, which, though published in 1906, had its genesis in Twain's 1893 paper, "What Is Happiness?," which he had worked on in Vienna in 1898 (Wagner-Martin 783). In that work, an old man remorselessly assaults the idealism of a young man with a depressing but persuasive pessimism. Howells most probably read "The Man That Corrupted Hadleyburg" when it came out in the December 1899 issue of Harper's Monthly, and though Twain was overseas from January 1896 until October 1900, Howells had almost certainly learned from Twain the plan of the gestating What Is Man?[2]

Whatever external similarities there may be of "A Difficult Case" to one or another of Twain's works, the deepest and most convincing similarities lie within its text. The story is written with superb irony, both subtle and sharp. Attractive though he might seem, it is not at all the Rev. Ewbert who is the story's hero, but Ransom Hilbrook. Hilbrook is a character of austere integrity. He tests every doctrine and argument against the standard of truth, which he determines for himself by both his learning and his experience. There is no guile or pretense to him; he is "perfectly sincere" (177) and speaks his mind directly, plainly, and uncompromisingly. He objects with a simple "it ain't true" to the idea that people mourn all their lives over past sorrows. Calling on his own experience to support this judgment, he says of his grief at losing a sweetheart to Josiah, "It wore out." He recalls that he subsequently married and was pleased with his wife, but then "[s]he died when I was away at the war, and the little boy died after I got back. I was sorry to lose her, and I thought losin' him would kill me. It didn't. It appeared one while as if I couldn't live without him, and I was always contrivin' how I should meet up with him somewhere else. I couldn't figure it out . . . Well . . . that wore out too" (173-74).[3]

In contrast to Hilbrook, Rev. Ewbert is not very admirable. For one thing, he appears not to be doctrinally committed.[4] We are early told of him that "the version of his [Rixon's] gospel which his latest apostle gave taught a species of acquiescence which was foreign to the thoughts of the founder." Instead of encouraging his parishioners to take constant spiritual stock of themselves while interrogating "Providence as to its will concerning them," Ewbert preaches that "while they fulfilled all their plain, simple duties toward one another, God would inspire them to act according to his purposes in the more psychological crises and emergencies, if these should ever be part of their experience" (149-50). It is important to keep in mind that Howells is not, in this story, necessarily advocating or rejecting any real theological issue, but is primarily using a theological issue for the story's purposes. The real function in the story of what may seem a technical theological distinction is to provide a key to Ewbert's personality.

How it does this can be seen from several perspectives. First, it underlines the significance not of Ewbert's putting a slightly different emphasis upon Rixon's teachings, but of his teaching a doctrine "foreign" to Rixon's mind. In other words, though a Rixonite in name, he is not a Rixonite in belief or practice. There is quite a difference between Rixon's emphasis upon passively waiting for a sign from God, and Ewbert's position of embarking on a course of action and trusting—or expecting—that God will supply one with an inspiration whenever one needs it. Second, Ewbert is not shown to have any basis in Scripture or experience for his theological change. He is a young man, preaching of things beyond his ken, taking undue liberties with the doctrines of his church, and assuming authority that properly belongs to Rixon, supposedly his spiritual guide.[5] Third, his own theories do not work, or in the words of Hilbrook, "ain't true." Their most conspicuous failure is demonstrated with Hilbrook. Hilbrook has suffered several psychological and spiritual crises beyond anything Ewbert has ever endured: loss of a sweetheart, war, and the deaths of a wife and son, and God has not supplied him with any compensating inspiration. Hilbrook therefore bases his doubts on his own experience and is honest with himself, whereas Ewbert cannot claim any authority outside of his own mind for his theories, and is not honest with himself. The text, in fact, damningly describes his efforts to resuscitate Hilbrook's belief in an afterlife as having been undertaken "upon terms which, until he was himself much older, he could not question as to their beneficence, and in fact it never came to his being quite frank with himself concerning them" (216).

Finally, Hilbrook may be seen as a better disciple of Rixon than Ewbert. Hilbrook has spent his whole life passively waiting for a sign. One has not come, but then Rixon never promised that one would; his teachings were limited to recommending a spiritual discipline. It is Ewbert who commits God to delivering inspiration on demand, a promise that is patently undeliverable. As long as Hilbrook remains merely passive in his unbelief, he continues to live, but he precipitates his own death when he adopts the this-worldly "spin" on Rixonism that Ewbert advocates.

The situation and the language describing it are thoroughly ironic. Howells obviously realized that passivity could be inverted into a kind of action. Hilbrook takes his own life by active passivity; he decides to take no nourishment. The point is made with elegant irony in the scene in which Ewbert discovers Hilbrook in bed. To Ewbert's suggestion that he get up, Hilbrook responds, "I ha'n't got any call to get up" (211). The word "call" has a Rixonite connotation of a summons from God as well as its primary denotation of "reason." When Ewbert tries to entice Hilbrook into survival by asking him if he is hungry, "'Yes, I'm hungry,' the old man assented, 'but I don't want to eat anything'" (213). The sentence clearly puts a great deal of volitional weight on the verbal "don't want" and reinforces the emphasis by the locution "don't want to eat anything" instead of "don't want anything to eat." Hilbrook indifferently "submits" to the help offered by people called in, a farm-wife and a doctor, but says that "he would have no agency" in taking medicine. Instead, he displays "absolute apathy" as to what goes on about him. Hilbrook may be said to have turned Rixonism against itself, but it is Ewbert who starts him. The one thing that Ewbert truly teaches Hilbrook is the means of the logic he uses, which converts passivity into action.

The more Ewbert is frustrated by Hilbrook's refutations of his various arguments, the more his Christian compassion for the old man is shown to be a professional front—and the more he strains not so much to tell the truth as to win.

Some new thoughts had occurred to him [Ewbert] in corroboration of the notions they had agreed upon in their last meeting. But in response Ewbert found himself beset by a strange temptation—by the wish to take up these notions and expose their fallacy. They were indeed mere toys of their common fancy which they had constructed together in mutual supposition, but Ewbert felt a sacredness in them, while he longed so strangely to break them one by one and cast them in the old man's face. (196)

The most insidious of these notions is his disingenuous imputation to Hilbrook of a desire to have enough consciousness in an afterlife to enjoy his unconsciousness (179).[6] It tricks the old man at first, but he finally sees through it. "There ain't anything in that. I got to thinking it over, when you was gone, and the whole thing went to pieces. That idea don't prove anything at all, and all that we worked out of it had to go with it" (211). When Ewbert offers to put the notion together again, the old man says, dryly: "You can, if you want to . . . I got no interest in it any more; 'twa'n't nothing but a metaphysical toy, anyway" (212). The original magazine version of the story uses the much sharper "casuistical" instead of "metaphysical," thereby unmistakably denigrating Ewbert (Atlantic Monthly 215). It is the last straw for Hilbrook; after he figures out the fallacy of Ewbert's notion, he decides to die.

To give Ewbert his due, it was not his intention to push Hilbrook to this radical step. On the other hand, he entered into a debate on a tremendous subject with the old man without ever compassionately gauging how much the topic meant to him and without matching him in understanding or commitment, let alone honesty. Ewbert never appears to be quite as unChristian as his wife does when she rejects Hilbrook, "What did it matter whether such a man believed that there was another world or not?" (217), but his real motivation in carrying on the contest was not so much Christian as it was pride. He either does not realize or care to recognize his responsibility for the doctrine that he preaches: his last sermon reaffirms the this-worldly activism that contradicts the main tenet of the Rixonism to which he was supposedly dedicated. The final irony is that whatever success he has as a Rixonite minister with the university people who attend the funeral is owing to a non-Rixonite notion, and one whose fatal casuistry has been demonstrated.

It is now possible to link "A Difficult Case" more closely to Twain and his works. The biographical similarities that earlier critics have noticed can be specified. Hilbrook and Twain share a number of important qualities besides their denial of a belief in the soul's immortality and an afterlife: they are both self-taught vernacular philosophers, plain-spoken and direct, experiential rather than theoretical, and "realistic" rather than romantic. They have both known suffering and bereavement. They see life as hard, painful, and probably not worth the candle. And God does not appear to either of them as merciful and benevolent. They also both have a gritty integrity that consists of describing things exactly as they see them and of not being awed by authority or intimidated by sacrosanctity. They both penetrate to the essence of things and stick to their positions.

Of Twain's works, "The Man That Corrupted Hadleyburg" offers the richest number of connections to Howells's story. The convenient name change of Hadleyburg to something else is paralleled in "A Difficult Case" not only by the readiness with which West Mallow gives way to Hilbrook but also by the unexamined ease with which Ewbert slips from one religious and philosophical position to another, and by the revelation that his true character is quite different from the superficial pose he maintains. But, like the citizens of Hadleyburg, neither he, nor his wife, nor the townspeople are conscious of the ironic discrepancies between what they affirm and what they are.

It is not that Howells imitated "Hadleyburg" or any other Twain story, but rather that he appears to have assimilated Twain more deeply than has hitherto been realized. If Howells had attempted merely to parrot

"Hadleyburg," it would have been obvious long before this, and probably not much better than imitations usually are. But 30 years of friendship with someone as intense, forthright, and closely reasoned as Twain had to have left an impression on Howells, at least in terms of some of Twain's values, ideas, and ways of thinking.

"A Difficult Case" is unusual among Howells's stories in that it gives so much respect to a fatalist and pessimist. The tale is not, of course, simply a reflex of Twain's views; Howells loaded it with his own concerns, and his deft use of irony toward Rev. Ewbert's hypocrisy is in line with the realism Howells advocated and practiced. Still, in light of the impact that ideas and attitudes associated with Twain have in the story, a question may remain about how much of Howells, himself, is invested in it.

Eble reports that in "Eighty Years and After" (Harper's Weekly, December 1919) Howells related how he in his early life had had a "faith in an afterlife, which gave way to 'the prevailing agnosticism of the eighteen seventies and eighties'" (Eble 216). Howells was too serious and independent a thinker to have drifted into agnosticism on a prevailing fad; like Livy Clemens he must have come up against arguments he could not refute. The issue of immortality was not decided in this story for Howells but continued to vex him for years.[7] Undoubtedly, Howells encountered many agnostics and atheists, but his long-term and close friendship with Twain would have made him a prime influence in Howell's life. "A Difficult Case" may have involved Howells in some painful recollections and deliberations, but if the story is rare Howells it is nevertheless authentic Howells.

In addition to the superb artistry that makes it deserving of more recognition and consideration than it has received, "A Difficult Case" is a remarkable testimony to Howells's friendship with Twain. The position represented by the Twain-like Hilbrook was not one with which Howells wanted to identify. Troubled as he was with the tragic death of a daughter[8] and with his own spiritual doubts, Howells was himself in search of grounds for consolation and security. That he could embark upon such a personally painful topic and endow Hilbrook, under these circumstances, with such integrity is an eloquent compliment to Twain's spiritual depth and honesty and reveals a new aspect of the nature of the powerful bonds between these two friends.

NOTES

1. James's letter was written from Lamb House, Rye, on 10 August 1901, and was his response to his receipt of Howells's newly published *A Pair of Patient Lovers*, in which collection "A Difficult Case" was included.
2. Although no direct references to "The Man That Corrupted Hadleyburg" occur in the Twain-Howells correspondence, Howells and Twain regularly exchanged publications as soon as they came out, and Howells in his 14 January 1900 letter to Twain wrote that he hoped to review the volume of short works, in which "Hadleyburg" appeared, that was to come out later that year. As for What Is Man?, what Twain called "my Bible," specific allusions to it occur at least as early in their correspondence as Twain's letter of 2 April 1899, and the allusions are in a context that strongly implies Howells's familiarity with its content.
3. In a similar mood, Twain, some years after the 1896 death of his daughter Suzy, reflected: "It is one of the mysteries of our nature that a man, all unprepared can receive a thunder-stroke like that and live" (qtd. in Kaplan 335).
4. In response to a bereaved mother's pleas for assurance about seeing her child in a hereafter, "[h]e had not the heart to refuse her this consolation, and he had pushed himself, in giving it, beyond the bounds of imagination." When the mother confessed she did not understand his position, he responded by becoming more emphatic (168). On this occasion he experiences an inward collapse. The

increasing weariness he feels after his encounters with Hilbrook is related to this, in that in both situations he advocates positions that he does not believe in. Thus, he is attempting to overcome his own intimations of truth as well as honest questioners.

5. In this portrait of a young minister out of his depth and not true to the doctrines of his religion, Howells interestingly parallels Harold Frederic's *The Damnation of Theron Ware* (1896).

6. An eerie antecedent to this idea occurs in a letter from Twain's daughter Suzy, in a letter quoted by Clara Clemens. Supposedly written when she was 18 (1890), she confided some of her religious musings to her Aunt Sue: "While one can have a good sized piece of sky in one's sight, though, one must possess some consciousness of eternity—even if it be an unconscious consciousness" (Clara Clemens 64-65). At this point, one can only speculate how Suzy's phrase might have been brought to the attention of Howells.

7. In 1910 Howells wrote "A Counsel of Consolation" for the purpose of guiding those in bereavement. He made no attempt in this essay to speak with authority, preferring to "trust" rather than believe. Significantly, however, he described himself as one of those who "patiently wait for the fulfillment of the hopes which Christianity has worded from the Greek philosophers rather than from the Hebrew prophets" (5). He spoke of the apparition of "visions of the night, which I would have the sorrower at least passively accept, or not positively refuse" (6), and recommended the authority of a priest of any church or some strongly believing friend; "it is enough if either be sincere" (10). Howells's position more closely resembles Rixon's original doctrine than Ewbert's or post-Ewbert Hilbrook's, and his emphasis upon sincere belief again implies a rejection of Ewbert. I wish to thank Professor Don L. Cook of Indiana University for his assistance in locating this work.

8. Crowley suggests that through the story Howells dramatized "a dialogue between his best and worst

attitudes" toward the death of his daughter, Winifred, which occurred in 1889 (144).

REFERENCES

Cady, Edwin H. *The Realist at War: The Mature Years* (1885-1920) of William Dean Howells. Syracuse, NY: Syracuse UP, 1958.

Clemens, Clara. *My Father Mark Twain*. New York: Harper, 1931.

Crowley, John W. *The Mask of Fiction: Essays on W.D. Howells*. Amherst: U of Massachusetts P, 1989.

Eble, Kenneth E. *Old Clemens and W.D.H.: The Story of a Remarkable Friendship*. Baton Rouge: Louisiana State UP, 1985.

Howells, William Dean. "A Difficult Case." *A Pair of Patient Lovers*. New York: 1901.

——. "A Difficult Case," Part II. *Atlantic Monthly* 86 (August 1900): 205-17.

——. "A Counsel of Consolation." In *After Days / Thoughts on the Future Life*. New York: Harper, 1910. 3-16.

——. *My Mark Twain*. New York: Harper, 1910.

James, Henry. *Henry James Letters, 1895-1916*. Ed. Leon Edel. Cambridge: Harvard UP, 1984. Vol. 4. of Henry James Letters. 4 vols. 1974-84.

Kaplan, Justin. *Mr. Clemens and Mark Twain*. New York: Simon, 1966.

Smith, Henry Nash, William M. Gibson, and Frederick Anderson, eds. *Mark Twain-Howells Letters: The Correspondence of Samuel L. Clemens and William D. Howells*. Cambridge: Harvard UP, 1960. 2 vols.

Wagenknecht, Edward. *William Dean Howells: The Friendly Eye*. New York: Oxford UP, 1969.

Wagner-Martin, Linda. *"What Is Man?" Mark Twain Encyclopedia*. Ed. J. R. LeMaster and James D. Wilson. New York: Garland, 1993.

7

Literary Continuity in Sandra Cisneros's 'The House on Mango Street'

—Thomas Matchie

In 1963 in a collection of articles entitled Salinger, Edgar Branch has a piece in which he explores the "literary continuity" between Mark Twain's The Adventures of Huckleberry Finn and J. D. Salinger's Catcher in the Rye. Branch claims that, though these two books represent different times in American history, the characters, the narrative patterns and styles, and the language are strikingly similar, so that what Salinger picks up, according to Branch, is an archetypal continuity which is cultural as well as literary (239). I would like to suggest a third link in this chain that belongs to our own time, and that is Sandra Cisneros's The House on Mango Street. Published in 1989, this novella is about an adolescent, though this time a girl who uses, not the Mississippi or Manhattan Island, but a house in Chicago, to examine her society and the cultural shibboleths that weigh on her as a young Chicana woman.

Though not commonly accepted by critics as "canonical" (McCracken, 62), The House on Mango Street belongs to the entire tradition of the bildungsroman (novel of growth) or the kunstlerroman (novel inimical to growth), especially as these patterns apply to women. One can go back to 19th-century novels like Harriet Wilson's Our Nig (1859), where a black woman working in the house of a white family in Boston is treated as though she were a slave. Later, Charlotte Gilman's The Yellow Wallpaper (1889) depicts a woman who goes crazy when she is confined to a room in a country house by her husband, a doctor who knows little about feminine psychology. Finally, in Kate Chopin's The Awakening (1899), the protagonist literally moves out of the house to escape her Creole husband, but cannot find a male with whom to relate in this patriarchal culture.

In Mango Street, a hundred years later, Esperanza is actually part of a six-member family of her own race, but that does not prevent an enslavement parallel to Nig's. Though not limited to a single room as in Yellow Wallpaper, Esperanza's house is a symbol of sexual as well as cultural harassment, and she, like the narrator in Gilman's story, is a writer whose colorful images help her create a path to freedom. And as in The Awakening, Esperanza dreams of leaving her house, an action that like Edna's is related to all kinds of men who make up the power structure in her Chicana world.

So in a general way Cisneros's novel belongs to a female tradition in which culture and literary quality are important. But for her, far more significant as literary models are Huck Finn and Holden Caufield, primarily because they are adolescents growing up in culturally oppressive worlds. Cisneros's protagonist, like them, is innocent, sensitive, considerate of others, but extremely vulnerable. Like them, Esperanza speaks a child's language, though hers is peculiar to a girl and young budding poet.

And like her predecessors, she grows mentally as time goes on; she knows how she feels, and learns from the inside out what in Holden's terms is "phony," and what with Huck she is willing to "go to hell" for. There are, of course, other Chicano novels that are bildungsromans, such as Tomas Rivera's ...y no se lo Trago la Tierra, but none presents a better parallel to Huck and Holden than Cisneros's Esperanza.

It may seem that the two boy's books are really journeys, while Mango Street is limited to a house, and therefore set - the opposite of a geographical quest. But when one looks at the patterns of the novels, what the boys go out to see simply comes past Esperanza, so that the effect is the same. She is simply a girl, and does not have the cultural opportunity to leave as they do. What is more important is that Mango Street continues a paradigm of growth where a young person encounters an outside world, evaluates it in relationship to herself, and then forges an identity, something that includes her sexuality and the prominence of writing in her life. McCracken says that this character breaks new boundaries with her outward movement into "socio-political reality" (63-64).

Huckleberry Finn begins with young Huck leaving a father who has abused him, the Widow Douglas who has tried unsuccessfully to educate him, and nigger Jim's owner, Miss Watson, who perpetuates the system of slavery which Huck will undercut on his journey down the river. Catcher in the Rye, as we learn in the end, is really a story Holden Caufield tells. Recovering from a mental breakdown, he begins by saying he's leaving school, Pency Prep, where in his view the teachers, alumni, and students are all phony. Mr. Spencer, his history teacher, talks to him just before leaving, but is more interested in justifying his test, which Holden failed, than understanding what is actually happening to the boy. Holden then goes to New York City to visit, not his parents, but his little sister.

His father is a wealthy corporate lawyer and investor who is apparently too busy for Holden. Neither Huck nor Holden, however, is an arrogant individual, or sees himself as a rebel. They simply move out because, bored and lonesome, they object to the conditions they live under, and instinctively seek more comfortable worlds. The reader, however, cannot help but evaluate what is askew in the systems that fail these boys.

Esperanza actually loves her father, though as with Holden's he is virtually absent from the narrative. As Marcienne Rocard points out, Chicanas concentrate intensely on "human relationships between generations" (57)—something not stressed in Twain and Salinger. Esperanza thinks her father is brave; he cries after the death of a grandmother, and his daughter wants to "hold and hold and hold him" (57). But this same father perpetuates a structure that traps women. The girl's mother, for instance, has talent and brains, but lacks practical knowledge about society because, says Esperanza, Mexican men "don't like their women strong" (10). Her insight into an abusive father comes through her best friend Sally, whose father "just forgot he was her father between the buckle and the belt" (93). So Sally leaves home for an early unhappy marriage. Another friend, Alicia, goes to the university to break the pattern of her dead mother's "rolling pin and sleepiness" (31), but in studying all night and cooking, too, she begins to imagine that she sees mice, whereupon her father belittles her. Esperanza says Alicia is afraid of nothing, "except four-legged fur. And fathers" (32). Gradually, Esperanza comes to see that the pressure on women in Chicana families comes from a system she simply, though painfully, has to leave. This act reflects the life of Cisneros herself, who says she had to leave home in order to "write about those ghosts inside that haunt me" ("Notebook," 72-73).

Truly, all three books are wrought with violence, which the protagonists seem to forgive. Huck is abused by his father. On the river he watches whole families kill each other off, including his friend Buck, whose senseless death he mourns. Ultimately he witnesses the tar and leathering of the King and Duke, conmen for whom he feels "sorry" (216). Holden is also beaten several times once by his roommate Stradlater, whom he thinks is handsome and sexy, but who knocks Holden bloody for calling him on the way he treated Jane Gallagher (Holden's old girlfriend) in the back of his car. Holden feels "sorry" for most girls, including the prostitute, Sunny, with whom he would rather talk than have sex, whereupon her pimp Maurice socks him in the stomach to get his five bucks. Holden is also concerned about the suicide of a Pency student, James Castle, who after being humiliated by other boys for not taking something back, jumped out a window. Holden was touched when Mr. Antonelli, his English teacher, went down and picked him up, blood and all. This violent death is crucial for Holden, probably because he sees himself in Castle, and needs someone older to understand.

Esperanza also feels for the victims of violence. What is interesting is that she sometimes interprets violence in a broad sense as injustice, or something in society that keeps people homeless, or in shabby housing. In the attic of her new house she'll have, not "Rats," but "Bums" (87) because they need shelter. She has visions of the violence done to Geraldo, "another wetback," who rented "two-room flats and sleeping rooms" (66) while he sent money back to Mexico; killed one night by a hit-and-run driver, he (in the minds of his people) simply disappeared. That violence becomes worse when individuals are confined to their homes. Mamacita, the big woman across the street, is beautiful but cannot get out because she "No speak English" (78)—a phenomenon doubly tragic because her baby sings Pepsi commercials. But mostly Esperanza identifies with wives mistreated by men who confine them to their homes.

Raphaela is locked in because she is too beautiful for her jealous husband. Earl, a jukebox repairman, and Sire, who drinks beer, hold their wives tight lest they relate to anybody else. Things like this make Esperanza's "blood freeze" (73). She dreams of being held too hard. Once, after letting a man kiss her because he was "so old," she says he "grabs me by the face with both hands and kisses me on the mouth and doesn't let go" (55). So, like Holden and Huck, this girl cares for others because of the violence done to them (and herself) in all kinds of contexts.

All three protagonists have a favorite place to escape oppression. For Huck, it's the raft, where he gets to know Jim—who becomes both friend and "father." Twain catches the harmony of their relationship in a natural setting through the poetic (melodic and imagistic) voice of Huck:

> We had the sky up there, all speckled with stars, and we used to lay on our backs and look up at them, and discuss about whether they was made or only just happened; I judged it would have took too long to make so many. Jim said the moon could 'a' laid them. (111)

Holden finds his main refuge in Central Park where he watches the ducks in the lagoon, once naively asking a cab driver where they go in winter. At another time walking through the park he sees a boy with his family singing and humming "If a body catch a body, comin' through the rye." Here Holden, like Huck, voices in a poetic way his unconscious longing for community—and the setting is again in nature. Later, he tells us that he would like to be that "catcher" (173), as though one could save the innocent ones lost in the world of adults.

Ironically, Esperanza already has a family whom she loves, but that does not free her, for her father is gone and her mother stuck. She too longs for friends, talking first about a temporary friend Cathy who then moves away. Later, she takes some of her sister's money to buy a share in a bike with her neighbors Rachel and Lucy so she can play with them, but that is fleeting. As she matures and sees what is happening to people, she picks four trees, which like her have "skinny necks and pointy elbows" (74). Others, like Nenny, do not appreciate those trees, but for Esperanza, they "teach" (75), helping her to realize that like them she is here and yet does not belong. And like the trees Esperanza, who thinks in images, must continue to reach. Her goal, like that of Huck and Holden, is not to forget her "reason for being" and to grow "despite concrete" (75) so as to achieve a freedom that's not separate from togetherness.

All three protagonists have friends who fail them, usually in some kind of romantic context. Huck rejects his friend Tom Sawyer because of Tom's "A-rabs" and "elephants" (13), and in the end Huck gets impatient with Tom's excessive charades to free Jim. "What I want is my nigger" (230), says Huck. Holden's critique of romanticism has to do with girls. He gets disgusted with the abusive way his friends treat them. Ackley, for instance, is a "terrible personality," always raving about "giving it" (37) to some girl, but Ackley is just a talker. It is Stradlater who actually takes out Holden's friend Jane Gallagher and abuses her in the back of his car and then brags about it. Later, Holden recalls some beautiful moments with Jane, with whom he always felt "happy" (79), and of whom he never took advantage.

Esperanza's best friend Sally is also a kind of romantic. She paints her eyes like Cleopatra and likes to dream. In an autobiographical note, Cisneros says she "glamorized living" in shabby neighborhoods where "the best friend I was always waiting for never materialized" ("Notebook," 70). Tragically, it is Sally who betrays her friend and admirer in the monkey garden (an animal pen turned old car lot) where she trades the boys' kisses for her lost keys, while all concerned laugh at Esperanza for trying to defend her friend with a brick. Later, Sally leaves Esperanza alone at the fair next to the "red clowns" (at once comical and tragic figures) where she is molested because her romantic friend "lied" (100). Actually, the whole experience is a lie, given what she had been led to expect.

Still, all three have a moral center, a person they can count on, or should be able to. Huck, of course, comes to appreciate Jim, who has "an uncommon level head for a nigger" (71). Ultimately he will literally "go to hell" (200) for this man he has come to trust and love. Holden puts his trust in his English teacher, Mr. Antonelli, who invites the boy to his house overnight, listens and gives him sound advice. He tells Holden his father is really concerned, and that he's heading for a special kind of fall (187). In the end, however, Antonelli makes sexual advances toward Holden, so the boy leaves and consequently does have a breakdown. The one person Holden loves and trusts, of course, is his sister Phoebe, and his memories of the innocent fun they had together are touching. But she is too little to be a source of emotional help, and when she follows him out of the house, he puts her on a carousel at the zoo where she can play. It's that wonderful image of childhood that Holden cannot get beyond because of his acute sensitivity toward a world he sees as phony, but in which he feels he is going "down, down, down" (197).

Esperanza also has a little sister, Nenny, for whom she feels responsible. Nenny, however, is again too little. Esperanza often refers to her as "stupid" and in the chapter on "Hips," where Esperanza is becoming more aware of the sexual role of a woman's body, she says Nenny just "doesn't get it" (52). Her real hope comes in Aunt Lupe who is dying—"diseases have no eyes," says the young poet. In a game the girls invent, they make fun of Lupe, and for this Esperanza, like Huck, feels she will "go to hell" (59). Actually, it is Lupe who listens to the girl's poems and tells her to "keep writing" (61). That counsel becomes the basis of Esperanza's future apart from Mango Street.

It is important to recognize that the three novels contain religious language that at once seems to undercut traditional religion, and in the mouths of the young seems to say more than they realize. Huck, for instance, is supposedly an uneducated soul, and when Miss Watson talks about going to "the good place," he replies that if she's going there he "doesn't think he'll try for it" (2). This is not only humorous, but unknown to Huck juxtaposes for the reader the fact that Miss Watson does not seem to connect her practice of religion with ownership of slaves. Christianity has to do with compassion, and that Huck will put into practice in his friendship with Jim. Likewise, Holden might see religions and ministers as phony, and himself as an atheist, but in arguing with one of his school mates, he says that he has an attraction to Jesus, and does not like the Disciples because they let Jesus down. And he can't imagine Jesus sending even Judas to hell. For the reader, Jesus' compassion only parallels Holden's own life, where he feels so deeply for others, though so many fail him.

For Esperanza, religion is a cultural thing; in her Catholic world, God the father and Virgin Mother are household terms. But for this young poet, religion takes on mythic or poetic dimensions. She sees herself, for instance, as a red "balloon tied to an anchor" (9), as if to say she needs to transcend present conditions where mothers are trapped and fathers abusive. She even sees herself molested in a monkey garden (a modern Eden) among red clowns (bloodthirsty males). She appeals to Aunt Lupe (Guadalupe, after the Mexican Virgin Mother), who tells her to write, to create. In the end, when Esperanza meets three aunts, or sisters (her trinity), she in effect has a spiritual vision, one which she describes in concrete language. One is cat-eyed, another's hands are like marble, a third smells like Kleenex. The girl uses these sights, smells, and touches to envision poetically her future house. As with Huck and Holden, there is something she does not fully understand. What she knows is that through these comadres (co-mothers) she will give birth to something very new. Like the two male protagonists, she longs for a respect and compassion absent in her experiences on Mango Street, and these women are her spiritual inspiration.

The ending of Mango Street is also very significant in terms of literary continuity. Just prior to the end Esperanza meets the three aunts at the funeral of a sister of her friends Lucy and Rachel; they tell her she cannot forget who she is and that if she leaves she must come back. In the end the girl recognizes that she both belongs and does not belong to Mango street. Then she vows to return to the house because of the "ones who cannot" leave. One reason for this is her writing, which has made her strong. She plans to "put it down on paper and then the ghost does not ache so much" (110). What this means relative to other women's novels is that she reverses a trend. In Our Nig, Nig is dissipated in the end. The protagonist of Yellow Wallpaper goes crazy before literally crawling over her dominating husband's body. Edna in The Awakening swims to her death rather than face a culture that will not recognize her identity. Not so with Esperanza. She is strong (something Mexican women should not be), perfectly aware of the problems with a patriarchal culture, and because of her love for her people, albeit abused and dehumanized, vows to return, and it is the writing which gives her the strength.

Here is where Cisneros returns to Huck and Holden for her cue. Consciously or not, Huck has challenged the very basis of a pre-Civil War culture. In the last fifth of the novel, however, it's not clear whether he returns to the ways of Tom Sawyer in staging Jim's escape or whether he's come to a new level of consciousness where he confronts Tom in the name of Jim. In the end he lights out into the territory so, in his words, they won't "civilize me" (274). In this way he seems to reject the culture of slavery, even though in Tom Sawyer Among the Indians, written afterwards, Huck returns to that culture by adopting with Tom old romantic ways. In any case, the notion of going back, even to join an abusive culture, or not going back, is a key issue in Twain's handling of Huck in The Adventures of Huckleberry Finn.

Holden is slightly different. In the end he is recovering from the shock he received from living in a post-World War II world. It has devastated him. But in telling his story he seems to come back to normal, so that the very telling has the effect of giving him strength. Indeed, he says,

> I sort of miss everybody I told about. Even old Stradlater and Ackley, for instance. I think I even miss that goddam Maurice. (214)

It's not clear how Holden will relate to his phony world again, any more than it is with Huck, except that he consciously chooses it, perhaps because he needs people, no matter what they are like. But the fact is he's going back. Esperanza's choice has a different twist. Thoroughly aware of the abusive nature of her culture, she comes to the decision that though she does not want to come from Mango Street, and does not want to go back till somebody "makes it better" (107), she nevertheless chooses to return for the sake of the others. She is "strong" (110) and, in contrast to Huck, feels drawn back, not just because she needs people, like Holden, but because they need her.

There is one other way in which Cisneros seems to look to her predecessors for literary and cultural continuity, and that is the way she as an author comes into the text. Mark Twain, of course, creates in Huck the authentic voice of an illiterate river boy. At times, however, it is not clear whether it is Huck speaking, or Twain the satirist. When Huck tears up his letter to Miss Watson, for instance, he may think he's going to hell, but we know he's acted morally, indeed courageously. And sometimes Twain uses a tone and style quite different from Huck's, as in Col. Sherburn's lecture to the mob on cowardice after the killing of Boggs. Here Twain seems to be talking directly to his reader, and if we can connect the two incidents, the author may be directly lecturing us all on how cowardly we are compared to the growing, thinking, choosing Huck. In Catcher Holden speaks in the language of an immature adolescent, often using words like "sonofabitch" and "goddam," while in his own mind he's becoming a "madman" (134). Still, we sympathize with him as sensitive, perceptive, and highly moral. At times, however, Salinger seems to break through the text, as in the person of Antonelli, who tells Holden "you're not the first person who was ever confused and frightened and even sickened by human behavior." Then he continues, "You'll learn from them - if you want to. Just as someday if you have something to offer, someone will learn something from you" (171-72). It is as if Salinger is telling his audience to read Holden's story if you really want to know what is wrong with this age.

In Mango Street Cisneros has created the voice of a child, who is also a poet, a writer. For the most part that voice is consistent, but sometimes not. Once when Esperanza is playing an outside voice puts her friends and herself in perspective:

> Who's stupid?
>
> Rachel, Lucy, Esperanza and Nenny. (38)

In this case it is the author who seems to be speaking. And when Lupe is dying, and Esperanza helps lift her head, suddenly we are inside Lupe: "The water was warm and tasted like metal" (61). Here the author's presence is unmistakable. Perhaps Cisneros's most significant intrusion comes when Esperanza says that Mexican men do not "like their women strong" (10)—a comment that belongs more to an adult than a child, and it seems to underpin the whole novel. Shannon Sikes claims that Esperanza as writer plays with the narratorial voice throughout the book, so that it's difficult to distinguish between the younger and a later, older person who is both character and author (12-13).

So Cisneros, like Twain and Salinger, seems to enter the narrative to help define its ultimate meaning. Unlike the boys' quests, however, this novel is a collection of genres—essays, short stories, poems—put together in one way to show Esperanza's growth, but in another to imitate the part-by-part building of an edifice. Indeed, the house on Mango Street does not just refer to the place Esperanza is trying to leave, but to the novel itself as "a house" which Esperanza as character and Cisneros as author have built together. Huck may go out to the territory, rejecting civilization, and Holden may tell his story to gain the strength to return, but Esperanza through her writing has in fact redesigned society itself through a mythical house of her own.

In this regard, Lupe once told Esperanza to "keep writing," it will "keep you free" (61). At that time the girl did not know what she meant, but in the end Esperanza says "she sets me free" (110), so in a sense the house is already built - a monument to her people and her sex. Andrea O'Reilly Herrera says that Esperanza's house is an imaginative version of Mango Street "resurrected, reconstructed, and rendered through language" (4). Indeed, Esperanza is very different from the other women in the text. She has learned from them and not made their mistakes. So she is not trapped like her mother, Alicia, or Sally, or the others. Like Huck and Holden, she is the example for other Chicana women whom Cisneros would have us take to heart. Indeed, as the witch woman Elenita predicted earlier, Esperanza elects to build a "new house, a house made of heart" (64). And in the tradition of, but distinct from Huck and Holden, that is just what she has accomplished.

REFEENCES

Branch, Edgar. "Mark Twain and J.D. Salinger: A Study in Literary Continuity." *Salinger: A Critical and Personal Portrait*. Ed. Henry Anatole Grunwald. New York: Harper and Row, 1962. 226-40.

Chopin, Kate. *The Awakening*. New York: W.W. Norton, 1976. Originally published in 1899.

Cisneros, Sandra. "From a Writer's Notebook." *America's Review* 15:1 (1987), 69-73.

——. *The House on Mango Street*. New York: Vintage, 1989. Originally published by Arte Publico Press in a somewhat different form in 1984.

Gilman, Charlotte Perkins. *The Yellow Wallpaper*. New York: Feminist Press, 1973. Originally published in 1889.

Gonzalez-Berry, Erlinda, and Tey Diana Rebolledo. "Growing up Chicano: Tomas Rivera and Sandra Cisneros." *Revista Chicano-Riquena*, 13:3-4 (1985), 109-19.

Herrera, Andrea O'Reilly. "Sandra Cisneros & The Big House On Mango Street: The Development of Self." Unpublished essay.

McCracken, Ellen. "Sandra Cisneros' The House on Mango Street: Community-Oriented Introspection and the Demystification of Patriarchal Violence." *Breaking Borders*. Ed. Asuncion Horno-Delgado, et al. Amherst: University of Massachusetts, 1989. 62-71.

Rivera, Tomas. . . . *y no se lo Trago la Tierra*. Huston: Arte Publico Press, 1987.

Rocard, Marcienne. "The Remembering Voice in Chicana Literature." *America's Review*, 14:3-4 (1986), 150-59.

Salinger, J.D. *Catcher in the Rye*. Boston: Little, Brown, 1945.

Sikes, Shannon. 'Narratorial Slippages and Authorial Self-Construction in Sandra Cisneros' The House on Mango Street. Unpublished essay.

Twain, Mark. *The Adventures of Huckleberry Finn*. New York: Holt, Rinehart and Winston, 1948. Originally published in 1885.

——. *Tom Sawyer Among the Indians*. Berkeley: University of California, 1989.

8

Seven Recent Commentaries on Mark Twain

—Peter Schmidt

It seems like such a simple scene: two white boys and a black man whose name is Jim escape to a raft, but one of the white boys and the black man decide to stop their flight because the other boy has been wounded and needs a doctor. The passage has no Melvillean hieroglyphs or Jamesian secret codes. Surely late-twentieth-century literary criticism, with all its state-of-the-art sophistication and jargon, would be able to establish interpretive norms for a plausible reading-explaining why the characters behave as they do, and what it all means. Yet just the opposite is the case. Critics cannot even agree on why Jim says what he does, much less whether the whole scene is ironic or not, or what kinds of historical contexts should help us have a coherent conversation about it.

The book in question, of course, is Huckleberry Finn, and the scene the ending of chapter forty. Consider the following excerpts from recent books attempting to interpret this passage. Each is intelligently argued, but together they are about as mutually incompatible as two readings can possibly be:

> Vowing to risk his freedom for Tom, Jim asks, rhetorically: if Tom were being set free and "one er de boys wuz to git shot," would Tom say, "save me, nemmine `bout a doctor f'r to save dis one?" You can bet "mars Tom Sawyer" wouldn't. Having evoked his torturer as his model, Jim swears fidelity to him: "No, sah—I doan' budge a step out'n displace, 'dout a doctor; not ef it's forty year!" (chap. 40). That Jim identifies himself as "one er de boys" reveals a self-image acquired from the black image in the white mind. Once a man with plans to bring his wife and children out of slavery, he is now too young even to think of family. He is also young enough to assure the junior master forty more years of servitude. Bizarrely juvenilized, he is also grotesquely feminized. In a dress again when captured, he is praised by his captor, the doctor, for his faithfulness and exemplary nursing . . . [W]hile the slaveowners may believe blacks are encoding dangerous messages, the reader knows it is Tom who decides what Jim will say, blocks out the letters, and . . . leaves him "nothing to do but just follow the lines." (chap. 38)
>
> If one considers only the behavior of the whites during the ending, one might agree . . . that the ending "satirize[s] the principle and practice of white supremacy." In reality, though, it is impossible to satirize/subvert the myth of white supremacy while reiterating the myths of black gullibility, passivity, dependency, and so forth. (Mensh and Mensh 93-94, 97)

Their faith in Tom was properly placed, degrading though it was. In this respect, Tom accomplishes

> more than the region he represents accomplished as an integrated "new South."
>
> But Twain pushes us into a second reversal so rapidly that we race past this point. Tom has been injured, and Jim and Huck's rejoicing quickly ends. The pair turn their immediate attention and concern to Tom. How characteristic of these two, as we have come to know them! Opponents have asserted that it is not incumbent upon Jim to sacrifice here the very thing for which he has been questing since the narrative's beginning. Some critics, particularly African American parents, cite this scene as especially racist because Twain describes Jim as relinquishing his freedom for a white boy who really does not have his best interest at heart to begin with . . .
>
> But we must believe all that has happened in the novel up to this point. We have exhilarated with Jim's evolution in previous chapters. We believed Huck's ultimate sacrifice [in choosing to be damned for befriending Jim] . . . [W]e have seen intimately their loyalty, their faith, their honesty, their naivete, their fortitude, and their self-reliance. How could Jim have done anything but what he did? It is exactly what we expect of him as the man, the free man, the husband, and the father we know him to be . . . [I]t is Jim the fully rounded character who empowers himself to risk sacrificing his freedom for what he feels to be right. (Chadwick-Joshua 126-27)

Both these readings attempt to give us a clear and consistent way to interpret Jim's apparent willingness to give up his chance to escape. For the Menshes, all interpretation of Jim's behavior must be understood primarily in reference to white models of the "good nigger," in contrast to whites' views of rebellious slaves or postwar freemen arrogantly claiming their rights. If Jim's behavior appears to fit this historically verifiable "good" stereotype (and the Mensbes argue that it certainly does), then Twain cannot be challenging that stereotype, but reinforcing it. Even if Twain makes light of white fears (most clearly in chapter forty-one, where friends of the Phelpses make quite a "clack"—Huck's word-about crazy niggers scaring them to death). Even if Twain clearly has portrayed a different and more rebellious Jim elsewhere in the novel. Chadwick-Joshua, on the other hand, places the possibility of Jim's free will at the center of the scene, not Twain's or whites' stereotypes. She stresses the consistency of Jim's evolution as a free man throughout the novel, including in this final raft scene, highlighting the tension between his refusal to give up his dream of freedom and his caution and cunning—he will wear even the humiliating mask of deference when necessary. Jim's behavior, of course, is notoriously difficult to interpret as expressing an ever-present drive toward freedom; his actions often appear at odds with that goal, whether it be his passivity, or his superhuman patience during Tom's "Evasion" scenes late in the novel, or Jim's gushing to Huck much earlier that he didn't care any more what became of him or the raft after he lost Huck in the fog. In each case, Chadwick-Joshua deals with such anomalies in Jim's behavior by reading them either as cunning strategies to make whites treat him better, or signs of Jim's inner patience and goodness-inveterate strengths of character that she argues are not Uncle Tom-like but rather a kind of heroic stoicism analogous to Albert Murray's celebration of the blues hero. For Chadwick-Joshua, Jim's decision not to leave Tom behind in chapter forty is a principled act-the act of a truly free man-that transcends any historical context we might place it in and makes secondary any stereotypical behavior we might mistake it for. Jim knows he cannot pursue his freedom if his sound heart tells him he left behind a human being who might die; his decision to aid

Tom is not mere passivity but an active choice of great moral power, consistent with almost everything Jim has done in the novel.

In Chadwick-Joshua's eyes, the "Jim dilemma" for many of Twain's readers comes because, ultimately, they cannot fully grant Jim agency, even though they criticize Twain for not doing so. For such readers, as soon as Jim appears to be performing a stereotype, that becomes what Jim is, not just what he appears. Unlike the Menshes' model for Jim's portrait by Twain, in which stereotype will always trump the illusion of agency, for Chadwick-Joshua the opposite occurs: Jim's character evokes transcendent norms of moral behavior that will normally trump any stereotypes they may evoke. Chadwick-Joshua's defense of the novel also implies something else: when critics of any race attack the novel for its portrait of Jim, instead of exposing Twain's inadequacies what they most often reveal is their own reluctance to grant Jim freedom.

Another way to state this dilemma—which readings of Huckleberry Finn have exacerbated over the years rather than solved—is that two incompatible understandings of satire (and the function of literary genres in general) bedevil Twain criticism. The first (eloquently represented in its latest incarnation by the Menshes) holds that satire is always already historically situated; although it may criticize some assumptions of its world, it is ultimately enmeshed within it, valuable to us because it reproduces in narrative the contradictions within the society itself. Thus Twain may be "antitraditionalist" (96) in his satire of whites, but he grounds that satire on a black character whose behavior mostly conforms to whites' stereotypes of what "goodness" will look like. The second position is equally well represented by Chadwick-Joshua, and is in line with many earlier commentators who have read the novel as a satiric allegory of unfinished moral development. Such a reading of the novel assumes that a great work of art transcends its historical context and its culture's (and author's) limitations in certain very specific ways that it is the moral imperative of literary criticism to define. For Chadwick-Joshua, both Jim and the novel itself must be granted agency—a will to freedom (no lesser word will do)—that cannot be fully contained either by Tom's scripts to "rescue" Jim nor by readers' attempts to rescue the novel from its supposed faults. Art, in other words, can never be thoroughly imprisoned in the nightmare of history. Furthermore, the reason why Twain critics cannot agree on how to read the novel is because—despite the proliferation of "theory" in the twentieth century—they cannot agree on even the basic principles of how to identify and interpret irony and satire, much less the myriad other tonal and ideological complexities of a work of literature.

Neither the Menshes nor Chadwick-Joshua make such broad claims about literary interpretation as I have made here, but I believe one of the reasons why they come to such opposite conclusions studying the same evidence is that they are using entirely different models for what literature is and how to interpret it—models that I have tried to foreground here. Both books honorably extend the two main schools of Huckleberry Finn criticism, those critiquing the novel and those defending it, and both will prove indispensable for Twain criticism in broadening our discussion of the novel's engagement with genres (satire, "Southwest" and minstrel humor, ex-slave narratives, etc.) and their historical contexts. Ironically, these two books achieve forcefulness, in part, because they don't engage thoroughly enough with counterarguments to their own theses. This tendency makes both books consistent but also less dating than they might have been.

There is a deeper level of irony. The Menshes seek to question Twain's much—celebrated understanding of irony and satire. Yet in the passage excerpted above they do their own not wholly successful imitation of Twainian ventriloquism, merging their own critical voice with an imagined version of Jim responding to Tom ("You can bet `Mars Tom Sawyer wouldn't'"). They are drawn into this imitation of Jim even while they seek to alienate readers from succumbing to Jim's eloquence, as Huck does. Chadwick-Joshua, similarly, becomes caught in rhetorical strategies that are full of troubling ironies. Seeking to persuade readers to see strategy in Jim's argument rather than self-enslavement to Tom, she constructs an ideal interpretive community that has no dilemmas, only consensus ("we must believe," "we have exhilarated," etc.).

Huckleberry Finn is renowned for its pairing of scenes, where a later incident will thoroughly expand or revise, even undo, the meanings of an earlier one. So it should not be surprising that the novel generates the same patterns of paired opposition in its interpreters-particularly when the issue of racial stereotypes and American history are involved. This dilemma in Twain criticism—call it the Huck/Jim dilemma—is arguably the central difficulty facing all cultural analysis: how to strike the proper balance between free will and determinism.

Whatever doubts I feel about the Menshes' and Chadwick-Joshua's conclusions, it should be clear that the issues they raise and the friction and light their opposed ways of reading generate must be counted among the strengths of Twain criticism, not a sign of confusion regarding method or goals. It's pretty much true, after all, that the greater the writer, the more he or she generates opposing ways of reading. We can't imagine the kind of vigorous debates that bedevil and enlighten Twain studies in, say, Timrod criticism. (Though contemporary American studies could use some new readings of Timrod's Ethnogenesis!) Twain is "powerful" strong that way, as Huck might say.

Along with Shelley Fisher Fishkin's work, the Satire or Evasion? Black Perspectives on "Huckleberry Finn" anthology (ed. Leonard, Tenney, and Davis), and the essays collected in the Bedford/St. Martin "Case Study in Critical Controversy" edition of the novel edited by Graft and Phelan—to list just a few—these studies of Huckleberry Finn by the Menshes and Chadwick Joshua should be required reading for any one who has the responsibility of leading readers through Twain's novel and the troubled American history of racism that roils in its wake. Teachers must use articulate but opposing readings—even via brief photocopied excerpts or their own study questions—to help readers question their own assumptions, get beyond simplistic labeling, and explore new ways of interpreting our past. I think of it as the "Sankofa" principle of teaching, and Chadwick—Joshua and the Menshes (indeed, all of the authors whose books are considered here) are part of our necessary journey back in order to move forward.

The other commentaries on Twain under consideration here do not so neatly focus on the Huck and Jim dilemma.

Jonathan Arac seeks to become the Socratic gadfly of Twain criticism. In Huckleberry Finn as Idol and Target, Arac is incensed with how Twain's commentators have idealized Huck and Jim's relationship as they have made the case for the novel's canonization and its alleged embodiment of primary American values. Arac wittily uses Huck's being tormented by his "conscience," his culturally conditioned ways of evaluating good and bad, to suggest that such a shared cultural memory is "not necessarily a good thing" (216). That is, we need constantly to be skeptical about the ways we are reading both this novel and its engagement with American cultural history. Arac seeks a "contrapuntal" criticism, a countertradition to mainstream voices in Twain criticism primarily celebrating the ways in which the novel is subversive. (Arac rightly notes the tension here: the novel supposedly both embodies universal values and eternally questions them. His point is not that this is contradictory, but that this tension is too timidly explored by the majority of Twain's commentators.) After reading Arac, particularly the eloquent jeremiad of his introduction and opening chapter, Twain's readers should never again easily slip into the too-familiar ways in which the book has been praised. On this count alone, his book is invaluable.

I also found much to think about in a number of Arac's other central topics. To mention several, I would cite memorable set-pieces on Twain's reception by the French, the relevance of Uncle Tom's Cabin, critics' frequent use of the phrase "Nigger Jim" even though that phrase is never found in Twain's novel, and the importance of the popular Century Magazine for the boom in Twain's reputation that occurred in mid-career. (For a more thorough meditation on Twain's accommodations to the genteel tradition, however, see Leland Krauth's book discussed below.)

One of Arac's topics that has rightly received much attention is his critique of the connections between nationalism and the complex politics of canonization. Arac is correct, I believe, to argue that certain works are hypercanonized. That is, if what is canonized is equated with the proper shared "memory" that all Americans should have, hypercanonization means that a single book supposedly embodies the values of the entire canon itself—it becomes "quintessential," a kind of miniature memory-chip. Arac, of course, is hyperskeptical about such a process, both in general and in the particular case of Twain's Huck. He quite rightly links the pressure to hypercanonize certain texts with attempts to assert hegemony over contemporary crises about the USA's cultural identity and direction. Arac gives a provocative survey of over fifty years' worth of arguments that have been made for the centrality of Huckleberry Finn, including a skeptical look at those critics who themselves have been canonized within the mainstream of Twain studies, vs. those accorded more marginal status. In one of the book's strongest chapters, he undertakes a stimulating re-reading of Lionel Trilling's famous introduction to Huck Finn, placing the essay in the context of Cold War cultural politics.

Arac is helpful as well when it comes to evaluating the strengths and weaknesses of different classroom approaches to teaching Huck Finn. (In general, I think professional Twain critics need to take even more responsibility providing teachers of grades 8-12 and undergraduates with new approaches toward helping students understand the strong reactions the book provokes.) Perhaps too briefly, Arac gives critical assessments of a number of such guidebooks for teachers, including one published by the National Council of Teachers of English. Above all, Arac urges teachers of Twain to take seriously statements by some students and parents about the pain caused by the way Huckleberry Finn is taught in many classrooms—objections that are much too often glibly dismissed by "experts" as ignorance or censorship or racism. Here I could not agree more with Arac. A good teacher can turn anguish and rage about the book into a way to understand Huck's and Jim's emotions, not to mention re-evaluating how we ourselves make judgments, particularly about "race." Most good teachers have to learn how to "teach the conflicts" and show students what is excluded by a text; it doesn't come naturally. Complacent language about Huckleberry Finn's sound heart often shows more arrogance than insight. In many high school curriculums, Huck Finn may be the only book in which "race" is emphasized. This puts an impossible burden on the novel's teachers. If students came to the novel after reading (say) some Douglass or Jacobs or Swift, or if they read it in the context of contemporary narratives dealing with racial issues, they will become better readers of Twain. The antidote to hypercanonization is to broaden the company of authors read when students first encounter Twain.

That said, I must register many objections to individual points Arac makes, both about particular scenes in the novel and about the failures of Twain criticism as a whole. In general, Twain criticism is far more diverse and contentious than Arac admits; its "mainstream" may flow mostly one way (toward acknowledging Twain's centrality in the American literary landscape), but like the Mississippi it has many different currents and colors, and someone like Arac intent on plowing upstream against the flow needs to take more cues from Twain the riverboat pilot about how to avoid snags and tow-heads. Arac is often too dogmatic to steer his craft well—he bulls too straight ahead and, fixated on showing us the wrecks of other riverboat critics, smashes into some shallows himself.

Take, for instance, Arac's critique of Fishkin's now-famous thesis and evidence regarding Huck's use of black English (186-94). Arac makes a number of criticisms of Fishkin, but his attack on her use of linguistic evidence centers on the issue of whether particular words and phrases of Huck's are indeed black English, as Fishkin contends, or are widespread American usages not associated just with black speakers. Arac does show that this issue may be more complicated than Fishkin acknowledged in 1993, but Arac's own logic seems to me to be excessively narrow and thus flawed. To show that some whites (English as well as Americans) use words such as "powerful" as an adjective does not necessarily refute Fishkin's contention that this usage was characteristic of nineteenth-century black English and, even more importantly, recognized as such both by Twain and by nineteenth-century linguistic experts. Arac may quote a few citations from Shakespeare and Swift and the OED, but that can only reduce the valid scope of Fishkin's generalizations; it cannot refute the fact that Twain, the author of "Sociable Jimmy," his most extended portrait of a black story-teller, demonstrably associated many of these debated words and phrases with the expressive capabilities of black speakers and then used their linguistic creativity to help shape Huck's.

I also have space to take issue with certain elements (not the whole) of Arac's attack on what he feels are absurdly inflated claims about Huck's moral nobility in the famous "I'll go to hell" scene in chapter thirty-one (37-62). Arac justifiably warns readers against attempts to turn the novel into "a talisman of self-flattering American virtues" (62), but several of his central claims about chapter thirty-one are questionable. Arac castigates Huck (or rather his creator) for never acting publicly to express his support of Jim, thereby creating "no place that citizens can work together in resistance" (as if that should have been a major purpose of Twain's novel). He continues: "to keep pure a reader's sense of Huck's individual autonomy, Twain had to purge from Huck's consciousness the available alternative languages of value in post-Jacksonian America" (61). But this is a surprising claim to make, given that Arac dismisses Fishkin's suggestion that Huck's speech is inflected with black speech and, thus, not autonomous or pure. Furthermore, as we will see below, other Twain critics see important parallels that Arac is blind to between Huck's points and, say, Frederick Douglass's, surely one of the "alternative languages of value" to which Arac alludes. In addition, how many readers would agree with Arac's premise that Twain was determined to emphasize Huck's "autonomy"? Perhaps not even Arac himself, who admits elsewhere that, in chapter thirty-one, Huck displays "a mind, a style, open to the voices of others" (54). Arac's point about the deceptiveness of Twain's religious language in the "I'll go to hell" speech is an intriguing one (he says it encourages the illusion that Huck's moral choice is absolute and self-determined). However, many of Arac's other claims in this chapter and elsewhere are ill-conceived.

A discussion of the larger historical context of Huckleberry Finn should compare and contrast anti-slavery arguments that are different from Huck's, using the kind of research Arac presents and that Twain critics have long been providing. But when Arac suggests that in chapter thirty-one "the notion of justice is a culturally valued abstraction that could support Huck in his moment of need" (61), he reveals himself to be a critic with a deaf ear—not to mention one who refuses to accept Twain's epochal decision to write the novel from within Huck's consciousness and language, and to use irony as his primary mode. If Arac is so insistent on damning Huckleberry Finn for what it excludes, he should consider the results of applying such a critical method to other novels. How seriously, for instance, would he take a critique of Toni Morrison's Beloved that censured its author for focusing on the consequences of a girl's murder by her mother, rather than on the many available "positive" stories of the Underground Railroad's success, or the "culturally valued abstractions" from anti-slavery writings that could support Sethe in her moment of need? (Stanley Crouch grouched just this kind of unsound objection to the canonization of Beloved.) Arac dismisses with a wave of the hand Morrison's reading of "`Huck's ultimate act of love, in which he accepts the endangerment of his soul.'" Instead he offers the unimpressive conclusion that in chapter thirty-one "religious satire outweighs experiential pathos" (54).

In the end, Arac's mistakes do not invalidate his project of taking seriously "Bakhtin's idea of a `dialogue' among socially antagonistic languages as the basis for the form and accomplishment of Huckleberry Finn," as well as his goal of attending to what the novel does not do as well as to what it does. These approaches just need to be handled more subtly than Arac can manage. (For further assessment of Arac's critique of both the novel and its history in American culture, I especially recommend Margolis and

Wieck, both discussed below.) The central questions Arac dares to ask about chapter thirty-one still resonate profoundly: "if other voices can sound through [Huck's], why so limited a repertory? What were the social alternatives, even within slave society, that Twain excludes from this scene?" (54). But why not also ask how such absences (if we can hear them) contribute to the pathos of Huck's crisis?

Carl F. Wieck's Refiguring "Huckleberry Finn" contains a lifetime's worth of reflection about the novel condensed into eleven succinct, and often elegant, adventures in reading, from pondering the references to two's and doublings (all a pun on "twain"), to the list of items found in the floating house, to the influence on Twain of Jefferson, Lincoln, and Douglass. The best chapters are the ones on Douglass (chapter two); on the language of "right" and "rights" (chapter three); on references to the figure forty in the context of Reconstruction promises (chapter seven); "On Black and White in Huckleberry Finn" (chapter nine); a chapter on lying and truth-telling (10); and the concluding essay on "Knowledge and Knowing." Wieck in general positions his own close readings very well within and against the currents of Twain scholarship past and present; the notes are meticulous and generous, though he also will not back down from a fight when needed. Wieck's book is one of the first to take issue with Arac. He gives a detailed refutation of Arac's claim (54ff) that references to Fourth of July rhetoric are absent from Huck Finn; he focuses closely on the presence rather than absence of Douglass and Lincoln; and his chapter three may very well have been written to refute Arac's claim that "the only person in the book to use the language of 'rights' is Pap" (55).

Without stating so directly, Wieck makes a strong case for reading Douglass's Narrative and Twain's novel side-by-side; in his view, Douglass' influence on Twain's book "was stronger and more profound than has hitherto been understood" (39). Wieck shows how Douglass's analysis of arguments about spoiling slaves can help us read the early scene in which Jim is "most ruined as a servant" in Huck's eyes. He traces motifs of darkness and refuge in both texts, critiques of religion, and parallels between Master Thomas's advice to Douglass and Tom's advice to Jim. A number of critics have recently encouraged us to read skeptically Jim's supposed joy at Tom's gift of $40, but it is Wieck who draws attention to the relevance of Douglass's wry reflections on the "wages" he earned as a slave. The chapter on "rights" usefully opens with a discussion of pre-Civil War debates on civil rights and makes a provocative case for the influence of the Unitarian minister Theodore Parker on both Lincoln's Gettysburg address and Twain's Huck Finn. Wieck then turns to illuminating brief discussions of differing views of natural rights relevant to Pap, the King and the Duke, Huck's confusion over Jim's feelings toward his family, Huck's dilemma on the sinking Walter Scott, and Tom's appropriation of Jim's rights in the Evasion chapters.

In chapter seven, on why the number forty gets several notable references in the novel, Wieck well synthesizes and extends the work of Doyno, Light, Chadwick-Joshua and others to connect this reference to Twain's coded satire of the debacle of Reconstruction, especially the negated promise of forty acres and a mule for freed slave families. Wieck's reading is less original but more sound than Stacey Margolis's in the March 2001 PMLA. Margolis provides a fascinating discussion of postwar negligence and liability law and claims that Huck Finn, like tort law, argues for the necessity of assessing effects over intentions, a standard that would implicate both Tom and the nation as being collectively accountable for what is done to Jim. Wieck, however, never pushes for the kind of structuralist distinctions Margolis advocates when she dubiously argues that "the interest of the novel lies precisely in its attempt to think about the problem of American racism in structural rather than personal terms," or, even more simplistically, that Tom's $40 "looks instead like formal, legal recognition of [Jim's] personhood . . ." (340, 339). ("Looks" to whom? Would she also make such a statement about the $40 paid to Huck in the "smallpox" episode in chapter sixteen?) All those interested in Huck Finn and/or law and literature should ponder Margolis's article carefully, particularly her claim that it is "a novel in which your effects on other people rather than your feelings about them define what you have done and, more important, what you can be held accountable for" (334). But Wieck's chapters four and seven synthesize in a more reliable way much current critical thinking on the novel's ending as a veiled denunciation of America's postwar betrayal of black freedom and the government's constitutional and legal obligations.

The chapter "Black and White in Huckleberry Finn" would be a fine choice for teachers who needed to require their undergraduates read just fifteen pages or so of commentary Oh "race" and the novel. (In contrast, neither the Mensh nor Chadwick-Joshua arguments are so condensable, nor are other collections of recent views on the subject.) Wieck stresses Twain's repeated technique of irony, inversion, and omission when engaging with racist stereotypes, and like Frederick Crews, among others, Wieck makes a strong case for the validity of Twain's decision to attack racism indirectly, through humor and irony. He documents the low number of the usual demeaning physical descriptions of blacks; shows how whiteness is often portrayed as unclean and disturbing; soberly analyzes how the notorious minstrel-like details in the portrait of the slave Nat may be more complex than has been realized; and gives excellent suggestions for interpreting Huck's comment that Jim was "white" inside (on the last point, see also Chadwick-Joshua 128-29). Wieck reads the Sherburn episode as being full of reversals of the "normal" lynching scenario and justification, yet also revealing

Twain's ambivalence regarding the violent "manhood" that thwarts a mob's attempts at vigilante justice. I do wish there had been more focus in this chapter on Huck's own assertions of racial privilege (his whiteness), and also that Wieck had not been so ready to agree with Earl Briden's argument that the Kemble illustrations were accepted by Twain in order to make less threatening the disturbingly close relations between Huck and Jim.

Chapter ten, on lies and telling the truth "mainly," may be my favorite. It gives a superb overview of humor, irony, and paradox in the wily prefaces that Twain wrote throughout his career, from Prince and the Pauper, Life on the Mississippi, and Huck Finn through Connecticut Yankee, Pudd'nhead, Joan of Arc, and What is Man?—particularly how Twain delighted in satirizing popular nineteenth-century claims to truthfulness and sentimental fidelity. (Interestingly, the Tom Sawyer introduction is an exception to this pattern.) Wieck even demonstrates that the opening of The Gilded Age engages with Hawthorne's famous introduction to A Marble Faun lamenting about the lack of subjects the American scene provides for novelists. All of which is a preface to Wieck's shrewd and profound reflections in chapter ten on truth, lies, and consequences in Huck's story. Wieck's conclusion sees a prophecy of Twain's post-1885 development as a writer "cunningly cloaked in the fact that Huckleberry Finn, the novel in which Twain appears to have undertaken a major onslaught on the long-respected custom of pretending to deal frankly and truly with the reader, closes with the words, 'The end, yours truly Huck Finn'" (145-46).

Wieck's concluding chapter does not mention once the pretentious word epistemology, yet it gives a quite thought-provoking reading of the novel as a dramatization of different kinds of knowledge and ways of learning or refusing to learn. False assumptions or incomplete knowledge make for humor in many scenes, trauma in others. Sacrificing to others one's right to assert what one knows or guesses always has bad consequences. There are myriad characters who can't be knocked out of their comforting delusions, plus a precious few—most notably Huck and Jim, at least some of the time—who are much more flexible and open. Wieck quips that the book could be called The Education of Huck Finn (though Huck would never give it such a title himself), and he usefully points out that the more Huck learns, the more tolerant he becomes, not the reverse: Huck is generous far beyond the level acceptable to the social rules he knows and tries to respect.

The weakness of Wieck's short essays are related to their strengths. They can be too simplistic and too adept at making all details fit that chapter's thesis. I was initially prepared to dislike the book because (with the exception of a fine anecdote about Huck Finn's influence on a boy growing up with a Nazi father in the 1930s) its opening paean to a boy-hero speaking a "universally understood language" representing American freedom (19) reminded me all too well of Jonathan Arac's rightful warnings against such language. Wieck's opening passages seem in part written expressly to refute Arac and invoke both Jefferson and Lincoln as crucial muses for Twain. Wieck certainly makes a case for their relevance, but his brief reading of Lincoln's and Jefferson's lives and writings is too simplistic to provide an effective counterargument to Arac. Only in the second chapter in Wieck's book, the one on Douglass, does he really begin to hit his stride.

Another caveat I have is that Wieck proves more adept at stressing the coherence and consistency in Twain's portrait of Jim than he is at probing its contradictions. Ditto for his portrait of Huck, which adds yet one more voice to the many readers who have interpreted Huck's tale as a kind of halting pilgrim's progress away from racism. Such readings ignore too many of both Huck's contradictions and Twain's, and they make Twain's use of irony seem so controlled—and the "right" way to read the book so obvious—that they can't account for a reader's identification with Huck's and Jim's trauma and confusion (and that identification—indeed, that reenactment of trauma—is crucial). Nor can Wieck's defense of the best ways to "refigure" the novel really explain why the book has from the moment of publication been read in such painfully contradictory ways. It so touches American cultural insecurities and guilt that we keep trying to make it into an icon or a target, a dangerous lure or a pastoral hymn, a coolly calculated satire or a model of democracy in action—or even (cf. Margolis) a kind of legal brief concerned solely with effects, not intentions. Could it be that it is not just the "Jim dilemma" but Huck's crisis of whiteness that so provokes? An American dilemma indeed. It could also be that the novel poses dilemmas about freedom and determinism that are so unsettling commentators rush in to try to solve Twain's riddle.

If Wieck shows the virtues of many years of reflection on Twain, the author of Proper Mark Twain, Leland Krauth, well represents the new generation of Twain scholars who came of age in the 1990s. This generation had to face synthesizing deconstruction and the new historicism, intertextuality's dissolution of form vs. the "return to form," an emphasis on the aesthetic and ideological workings of genre and convention that characterized some of the most innovative American studies work of the last decade. One of the many younger scholars who have been inspired by (and had their books blurbed by) Louis J. Budd, Kranth has written a fine book that strives to give us a new synthesis of the whole of Mark Twain's career.

Krauth's thesis is relatively simple yet yields superbly nuanced discussions. He wrote his book to counter what he felt was an over-valuation of the transgressive Mark Twain. Rather, he argues, we must learn to see the proper vs. the improper Mark Twain as being mutually constitutive—the satiric sensibility that performs its social role by subverting social pieties, vs. the side of Twain drawn to sentimentality, melodrama, and the use of humor to reaffirm certain core values, domestic truths, and conventions. The first chapters test Krauth's thesis on Twain's earlier career in the West, when he rewrote his actual Western experiences into more respectable narratives (Roughing It), and on Twain's early travel books Innocents Abroad and A Tramp Abroad. The middle of the book offers readings of Life on the Mississippi and Twain's boy books. Kranth then turns to Twain's complex impersonation of a "Victorian Sage" in Connecticut Yankee, Pudd'nhead, and the "Mysterious Stranger" variants, and concludes with a close reading of selected late texts, including Following the Equator and the autobiography. He traces productive tensions in all of these texts, not just between the different social functions of humor, but also between standard vs. vernacular diction, melodrama vs. realism, sentimentality vs. satire, and didacticism vs. description with a minimum of commentary. Each chapter presents a balanced mix of close readings and broad historical and biographical scope. None of these are exactly new topics or approaches in Twain studies, but Krauth gives them an invigorating and succinct rethinking. And he is surely right that the "subversive" Twain has been too one-sidedly stressed. If one were teaching a course devoted to the whole of Twain's career and could assign students to buy just one secondary source, this slender, well-written volume would not be a bad choice.

Chapter two gives an immensely useful overview of the history of Western travel narratives from the Renaissance on, and places Twain's early work within the proper context of Victorian travel narratives that judged other cultures in terms of "progress, hygiene, women, morality, and religion" (55) in order to stabilize the self and assert the superiority of one's "home" culture. Krauth's readings are decently informed by developments in contemporary anthropology (such as Mary Louise Pratt) and postcolonial theory, as well as earlier consideration of these topics in Twain scholarship. He argues that Tramp Abroad is under-discussed, perhaps because it is more circumspect in judging other civilizations than Innocents and more domestic, with little wrestling with the large philosophical, religious, or cultural topics that often occupied "serious" Victorian travel writing. Krauth reads A Tramp as a comic anti-travel narrative in which all of Twain's announced goals (including hiking the Alps and learning German) are undone in favor of re-discovering the virtues of domesticity and gentility. There are compelling readings of the Knave of Bergen and "lost sock" episodes, plus a shrewd emphasis on the contrast between Twain's love of exterior incident vs. an inward journey reluctantly taken into hidden anxieties, especially about his own professional competence as a writer and cultural commentator.

Of Krauth's middle chapters, it makes most sense given the other works discussed in this omnibus review to focus on his reading of Huck Finn. In Life on the Mississippi and his pre-Huck boy books, Krauth claims, Twain affirmed sentimental values but was "uneasy about the aesthetic by which he represents them" (12). He found the solution in Huck, whose greatness derives from the ways in which the book's languages (emphasis on the plural) hold all of the dichotomies of Twain's aesthetic in productive tension. "Jim's dialect refashions the cliches it uses; Mary Jane's intensity squeezes the saccharine from her sentiments . . . and Huck's vernacular, with its incorrect grammar, odd phrasings, and poetic rhythms, vivifies his feelings. Different as Twain makes these characters ... in making them all susceptible to the heartfelt, he establishes the moral center of the novel" (183-84). Krauth's concentration on his thesis gives him much less to say about issues of "race" than the other books under discussion here, but when he does broach the subject he is astute. For example, consider his take on the last chapters:

> Although concern over the treatment of Jim has obscured it, the fact is that the Phelps household is presented—its tolerance of slavery notwithstanding—as a pretty good country place. Aunt Sally and Uncle Silas are good country people. The hypocrisy of Miss Watson, the brutality of Pap, and the pretension of the Orangerfords are all replaced here with honesty, kindness, and simplicity. (186)

In chapter seven, one of the best in the book, Krauth takes on Twain's impersonation of a Victorian "Sage"—the dispenser of bon mots, traditional morals, and reformist ideals in the midst of a money- and machinery—mad age via his public speeches and texts such as Connecticut Yankee and Pudd'nhead Wilson. Many commentators have focused on why the tension between vernacular and genteel languages is demonstrably less successful in Yankee than it is in Huck. Krauth's take on this issue argues that "Hank looks contemptuously at aristocrat and commoner alike, denouncing them with a cynicism that reflects Twain's own darkening views"; moreover, "style and value remain divided" throughout the tale, with Twain consistently resorting to fairly formal and proper diction "as the medium for Hank's pronouncements as Sage" (198). Satiric energy is canceled by overly genteel language handled without irony. Pudd'nhead is read as an attempt to solve this problem at the core of Connecticut Yankee. Pudd'nhead's Sage is cryptic, covert, ironical and misunderstood, the opposite of Hank, and the text's exploration of radically fragmented selfhood shifts from the farce of "Those Extraordinary Twins" to the darker implications of the published novel. Krauth makes sensible use of earlier studies of the novel and has fine things to say about the role of the epigrams and the tension between the dog joke at the beginning vs. the use of Wilson at the end to rationalize the status quo and apparently solve the identity questions the novel raises. Valid, too, is the observation that Pudd'nhead is Twain's most sustained work in an ironic mode—yet one that contains ironies lost on Twain himself, especially the text's latent sexism, racism, and elitism (cf. 207-08). Krauth also gives us a fine overview of textual and interpretive issues relating to the three "Mysterious Stranger" manuscripts, and wryly concludes: "Ironically, the ideas that Twain took so seriously, and thought shocking [humans as cruel and machine-like, etc.], are commonplace" enough to be found in the sermons of Victorian preachers (218). Krauth proves that his generation of scholars can shape a working synthesis between its impulse to stress transgression and its need to emphasize cultural boundedness. The one certain flaw in Krauth's study I saw after one reading is his odd treatment of Justin Kaplan. The thesis of Kaplan's 1966 biography Mr. Clemens and Mark Twain is in many ways parallel to Krauth's, though Krauth hardly personifies Twain's opposing personae so neatly, nor does he divide art and life as Kaplan does. Kaplan is cited in Krauth's bibliography but slighted in the text and footnotes, and the index omits him entirely. (For the record, the index should include Kaplan citations at least on pp. 190, 252, and 255-56; I may have missed other references.) Proper Mark Twain deserves to sell well and be reprinted, and when it is, this Oedipal slip should be properly corrected.

Ken Burns's four-hour television documentary Mark Twain (along with its obligatory coffee-table book) has, of course, recently raised the presence of this writer and celebrity in the public eye far more than any work of literary criticism could do. To some degree, Burns's approach to the meaning of Twain's life is a welcome diversion from the other way in which Twain has recently been in public consciousness, as a silent spectator to narrow and shrill debates about whether Huckleberry Finn is racist. In his documentary, Burns takes the same approach to Twain that he did for the history of jazz and baseball; that is, he emphasizes how aesthetic forms embody democratic values and undermine racism. The documentary achieves a decent amount of nuance and complexity when it involves Twain's life, especially the tension between his Samuel Clemens and Mark Twain personae. However, the only literary text of Twain's that is discussed beyond just a few sentences, Huckleberry Finn, is treated in an extremely simplistic way-as a satire against racism that straightforwardly celebrates the friendship between a white child and a Negro man. Burns's documentary claims that Jim is the first portrait in world literature of a "real" black person rather than a racist stereotype, one that will inevitably get readers to question their preconceptions about blacks in the same way that the book's action changes Huck. Tell that to Tom Sawyer.

The audacity and simple-mindedness of such a claim is simply staggering. Perhaps it is explainable as a covert attempt to do an end-run around much of the recent arguing over Huckleberry Finn—but it is hardly excusable. The work of Frederick Douglass, Harriett Jacobs, and William Wells Brown—to name only three-hardly needs to be insulted to make a case for Twain's Jim. Any summary of the book's virtues that downplays its dangerous satire and dodges the controversy over the ending is just simply irresponsible. This is an especially grievous fault because Burns is a film-maker with the skill to handle nuance and contradiction, even though he is mostly drawn to hagiography. The documentary does dramatize well the recent discoveries in Twain scholarship about Twain's debt to black voices in shaping his art, and indeed uses two of those scholars, Jocelyn Chadwick-Joshua and Shelley Fisher Fishkin, as prominent commentators. Its recreation of the standard interpretation of Huck's psychological drama in the "I'll go to hell scene" in chapter thirty-one is also superb. But in making Huck's story a simple pilgrim's progress away from racism Burns insults most recent Twain scholarship and misses the only chance that will come in the mass media in years for a truly democratic debate about the roles the novel has played and continues to play in U.S. race relations. Teachers who use the documentary in classes will now have to provide supplemental material. Early in Burns's documentary there is a brilliant discussion about how the call "mark twain" signified to a steamboat pilot not so much safe water as the dangerous boundary between deep water and dangerous shallows. It's too bad that, in dealing with Twain's masterpiece, Burns thought he could achieve safe passage by heading for the shallows. Twain loved controversy; why should his video biographer be shy of it?

Near the end of their swaggering and witty preface to The Gilded Age, Charles Dudley Warner and Mark Twain appear to be infinitely generous: "We do not even expect the critic will read the book before writing a notice of it." Of course, a deeper game is being played. The authors have just called their critics' bluff and planted the suggestion that both the negative and positive reviews of their book will contain a good number of stretchers. I don't dispute that we are living in a second gilded age, nor that (at least within the confines of academia) some are also enduring a second "age of criticism" even more "unusual" than the one Warner and Twain tweaked. Within and without academia, Americans are so proud of our decadence we would need several contemporary Mark Twains to take soundings of our delusions-beginning with how we define decadence as virtuous. At the risk of angering the ironic ghosts of The Gilded Age, I will set down for the record that I have indeed read all of the works that I here give "notice" of, and, even more scandalously, enjoyed them and intend to read and consult them again. I suspect I won't be the only one doing so, particularly those of us who are hired scouts leading students through Twain's landscape. And—contra Burns—I've also found that several different and conflicting points of reference are best if you want to mark twain. The six authors discussed here certainly give us that. The current state of Clemens commentary shows that the death of literary criticism has been somewhat exaggerated.

9

Gloom and Doom in Mark Twain's Connecticut Yankee, from Thomas Malory's Morte Darthur

—Betsy Bowden

Taylor Roberts' recovery of Mark Twain's own copy of Thomas Malory's Morte Darthur rekindles questions concerning Twain's process of composing A Connecticut Yankee in King Arthur's Court.[1] As a specialist in medieval English literature, I wish to document more minutely than have Americanists Twain's use of his direct source, purchased in 1884. This article will compare Twain's experience of reading the unabridged Morte Darthur to his expectations primarily based on its condensation as The Boy's King Arthur, which he had owned since 1880.

This comparison can help circumscribe the impact on American literary culture of idealizing Europe's past—that is, of the phenomenon now termed "medievalism."[2] Connecticut Yankee retains evidence of one significant moment in diachronic literary change, which seems so often to lurch onward just out of sight, like Malory's "questynge beeste." Our glimpse of that moment occurs at the oft-discussed disjunction between the first and second paragraphs of chapter 21 of Connecticut Yankee. I suggest that in 1887-88, at some point in between the two summers when he wrote those two paragraphs, Twain finally faced up to amoral nihilism in the real Morte Darthur and therefore, according to the best information then available to him, in the real Middle Ages.

A time frame is well established for the composition of Connecticut Yankee. Early in 1886 Twain wrote the opening frame and chapters 1-4; during the summer of 1887 chapters 5-9, 11-20, and the beginning of 21; then one year later the remainder.[3] After the first paragraph of chapter 21, the novel's plot and comic tone collapse. Thereafter loosely linked episodes writhe with inconsistent characterization, vacillating objects of mockery, and gratuitous bloodshed.

Scholars have documented external events that could have affected what Twain wrote during the summer of 1888: family illness, financial problems (notably overinvestment in the Paige type-setting machine), national or international politics, and his musings about capitalist industrialization, a trip downriver in 1882, or a visit to Hannibal in 1885. Scholars document also Twain's relevant reading, including History of European Morals from Augustus to Charlemagne, other historical and scientific works, fantasy stories by Max Adeler, an attack on America by Matthew Arnold, a magazine series on Russian atrocities, and pseudo-medieval fiction, notably that by Miguel de Cervantes (beloved by Twain) and Walter Scott (detested).[4]

In addition to these other factors, I propose, Twain during 1887-88 finally found time to finish reading the whole of Morte Darthur, in the mass-marketed Globe edition he purchased December 6, 1884.[5] The course of composition of Connecticut Yankee reflects not only outside events and readings but also Twain's escalating disillusionment with his primary source text. As one result to be discussed, his novel's Last Battle feels horrific even to readers familiar with its far gorier prototype: the civil war that destroyed legendary Camelot.

In its entirety, Malory's very long book came to confirm what Twain began to suspect while reading its opening chapters, on Sundays and trains during a lecture tour. Le Morte Darthur stands solid witness against any Golden Age of childlike innocence. From Malory Twain learned that the alleged glory days of British chivalry provide no admirable heroes, no moral or ethical standards, no inspirational ideals. Contrary to medievalism's rose-colored reconstruction of the Middle Ages, contrary to the pure-hearted world created in meticulous excerpts for The Boy's King Arthur, contrary to the Globe edition's effusive introduction, Twain discovered for himself that King Arthur and the Knights of the Round Table lie and cheat and steal and make solemn vows intending to break them. They casually commit rape and adultery, betray friends and feudal lords, seek blood revenge contrary to law, shrug aside the slaughter of women, children, kin, innocent bystanders, and each other. Twain could not have anticipated so. At his time, scholars of medieval literature were not yet analyzing how Morte Darthur reflects the fifteenth-century Wars of the Roses, during which Malory was adapting the prose narratives of thirteenth-century French monks in order to express his own concerns as a nobly born prisoner in an England in chaos.[6]

Those thirteenth-century monks had applied a Christian veneer to twelfth-century verse romances, which re-told earlier tales, and so on backward into unrecoverable oral tradition. Arthurian legendry, having no canonical text, has long stood as sounding board for reinterpretations that echo the suppositions of each sociocultural era in turn. Twain's preconceptions about the Middle Ages came from various sources, including Alfred Tennyson, but most specifically from The Boy's King Arthur. This article will explore Twain's responses to reading Malory entire after having read Malory excerpted. I suggest that the gaping chasm between expectation and realization helped to compel Twain's swerve, at chapter 21 of Connecticut Yankee, toward a dismal landscape devoid of yet another set of potential ideals.

Of his writings prior to Connecticut Yankee, Twain had explored British history most fully for The Prince and the Pauper. He completed a draft of the earlier novel on September 14, 1880, then sought feedback and made revisions until February 1, 1881, when he considered it ready for publication.[7] While rewriting, he was eager to read a newly published book relevant to his own. On November 18 and December 13, 1880, his household purchased two copies of The Boy's King Arthur: Malory's Morte Darthur as condensed, re-organized, re-spelled, glossed, and introduced by Sidney Lanier. A tour de force of well-wrought censorship, this Young Adult classic remains popular today.

In contrast to the complete Morte Darthur that Twain acquired four years afterward, The Boy's King Arthur does express ethical and educational values. To some extent this condensed version would have reinforced the idealized Middle Ages that Twain still associated "in his complex mind" with mythic dimensions of the Mississippi, the frontier, and the antebellum South: "His criticism of medievalism notwithstanding, Twain yearned at times to escape imaginatively into that very period, as into his own childhood."[8] Lanier's abridgment, however, predisposes Twain or actual boys to regard its chivalric tales more as worthwhile literature than as escapist romance. The introduction assumes readers' knowledge of Shakespeare's plays and British history, their interest in thirteenth-century French and fifteenth-century English, their ability to follow a long passage in the earliest Middle English with interlinear translation. Lanier directs attention to morality as firmly as to linguistic and literary history, declaring decisive distinctions between good and evil:

> Into the fine fellowship, then, of lordly Sir Launcelot, of generous Sir Tristram, of stainless Sir Galahad . . . of dolorous Sir Balin and Sir Balan, of persevering Sir la Cote Mal Taile, of hilarious Sir Dinadan, and of a hundred more,—as well, alas! as into the ungentle company of cowardly King Mark, of traitorous Sir Mordred, and of wicked Morgan le Fay,—I commit you.[9]

The editor emphasizes that "every word in the book . . . is Malory's, unchanged except that the spelling is modernized." Bracketed insertions supply Lanier's own "connective clauses . . . to preserve the thread of a story which could not be given entire." Knowing these to be excerpts, Twain could guess that Lanier had cut out scenes with sexual overtones as implied by Tennyson's Idylls of the King, which is loosely derived from Le Morte Darthur.10 In Lanier's introduction and bracketed connectives, however, nothing divulges the massive extent of excision. About two-thirds of the original is gone. Entire books of Le Morte Darthur are seamlessly cut from The Boy's King Arthur, besides very many chapters, paragraphs, sentences, phrases, and individual words. A chapter count allows approximate comparison: the twenty-one books of Le Morte Darthur encompass 502 chapters total, whereas the six reorganized books of The Boy's King Arthur include only 173 of those chapters, most of them truncated.

Twain, however, would justifiably assume that the Malory text purchased on December 6, 1884, differed little from his children's version at home. The two books are similar in length: 403 pages for the condensation, 487 for the whole. Moreover, layout and paper stock and print font and illustrations make The Boy's King Arthur larger and much heavier than the Globe Morte Darthur, a small volume printed on thin paper in double columns of tiny typeface.

On that rainy Saturday in a Rochester bookstore, Twain's companion George W. Cable told him that the book in hand was "Sir Thomas Malory's Morte d'Arthur . . . you will never lay it down until you have read it from cover to cover." Twain's journal confirms the acquisition; his copy of the book supplies further substantiation, in the form of notes about that lecture tour jotted on endpapers. A quarter century afterward, in eulogy, Cable mentioned that his colleague finished Morte Darthur in a day or two. Previous commentators therefore assume that Twain read the entire unabridged Malory before he even began to think about a novel based on it.[11] I propose that he did not.

This is a very long book in Late Middle English. A university-trained medievalist could not read it cover to cover in a day or two. Even in modernized orthography, Le Morte Darthur moves ponderously because of repetition, convoluted syntax, an immense cast of characters, and a numbing succession of incidents that differed for Malory in details no longer discernible. Through the first half of Connecticut Yankee, notably in Sandy's tale in chapter 15, Twain implies amusement at his own snail-like progress through Malory's narrative obfuscation. In an 1886 letter, he expects to be writing his novel at the rate of three chapters per summer for the next thirty years.[12] Is he joking about the time needed just to finish reading the medieval prose that had inspired his conception?

At the hotel in Rochester, anticipating no such longterm commitment to a pocket-sized book, Twain could first have used its index to seek out favorite passages. In an 1883 letter he had mentioned "Sir Kay in Sir Launcelot's armor," an episode that he knew from book II, chapter 8 of The Boy's King Arthur (BKA II.8). He could find it in Morte Darthur as book VI, chapter 11 (MD VI.11), indexed as "Launcelot de Lake, Sir . . . slays two giants."[13] Twain was to reproduce this passage, with its resonant images of disguise and shifting identity, in his "Word of Explanation" prefacing Connecticut Yankee (CY, 48-50).

The second passage that Twain quotes early in his novel, as Merlin's soporific story, occurs likewise in both expurgated and unexpurgated Malory: chapter 1.6 in The Boy's King Arthur equals Morte Darthur 1.23125].[14] If Twain sought out Arthur's acquisition of Excalibur, on December 7, 1884 or thereafter, a chapter title across the page may well have caught his eye and given him pause. The Boy's King Arthur retains no trace of Morte Darthur 1.25[27], entitled "How all the children were sent for that were born on May-day, and how Mordred was saved." Saved from what? Neither Lanier nor Tennyson lets slip a hint that, because "Merlin told king Arthur that he that should destroy him should be born on May-day . . . many lords' sons , . . were sent unto the king . . . and all were put in a ship to the sea, and some were four weeks old, and some less." The ship sinks; only Mordred is cast ashore, to be raised as a foundling. Already the Last Battle looms: "Many lords and barons of this realm were displeased, for their children were so lost, and many put the blame on Merlin more than on Arthur; so what for dread and for love they held their peace."

Thus ends the first of twenty-one books in the Globe edition. Unlike book I of the version for boys, this book I begins with a blow-by-blow account of the problematic engendering of Arthur. Even if Twain supposed that Lanier had bowdlerized, he would not have foreseen so many explicit details nor such a matter-of-fact tone. Likewise, perhaps he anticipated more random violence than Lanier's version allows. It would nevertheless seem excessive that, only forty pages into the action, Arthur is attacking eleven legitimate kings' armies with such enthusiasm that "their horses went in blood up to the fetlocks."[15]

Other excised elements would have come as complete surprises. Skimming the Globe "Table or Rubrysshe of the Content of Chapters," for example, a reader easily notices Morte Darthur X.24: "How Sir Lamorak visited king Lot's wife, and how Sir Gaheris slew her which was his own mother."

Matricide in Camelot? In The Prince and the Pauper, maternal love conquers all. Surely a Knight of the Round Table who slays his own mother—accidentally, of course—endures agonies of guilt that make Orestes seem calm, and surely swift punishment follows. A reader of Tennyson or Lanier would suppose so. Quite otherwise, this chapter tells how Arthur's nephews conspire to murder not their widowed mother herself but instead her suitor favored by Arthur, Sir Lamorak. They mistakenly believe that Lamorak's father killed their father, and have never bothered to ask. Sir Gaheris ambushes the lovers in bed together. Slapping his forehead, presumably, he realizes that Lamorak is therefore not clad for battle. Rather than challenge an unarmed knight, Gaheris "suddenly gat his mother by the hair, and strake off her head." Now that I have your undivided attention, he tells a "dismayed" Lamorak, "in what place I may get thee I shall slay thee; and now my mother is quit of thee." Although matricide per se is no crime, the dead mother in question is sister to the King. Therefore Arthur, "passing wroth," orders Gaheris "to go out of his court." Sir Gawaine is wroth as well, because his brother let Lamorak escape instead of slaying him unarmed. Sir Launcelot and other Knights of the Round Table fret lest the embarrassing incident deter Sir Tristram from coming to court.

A Connecticut Yankee makes no direct reference to guilt-free, mildly scolded mother-slayers. To set bounds around this account of Malory's influence on Connecticut Yankee, I will let stand that chapter plus the mass infanticide as my sole examples of multitudinous elements that Twain would not have anticipated in Morte Darthur but that he does not mention as such on paper. Nor will I posit an origin in Malory for any detail that merely occurs in both narratives, without corroborating evidence as to its source. A cave or prison or tower in Connecticut Yankee, that is, need owe no debt to a cave or prison or tower in Morte Darthur. 'Twere to consider too curiously to consider so. Parallel ideas and images may come from everyday life or from Twain's other reading, especially that credited in his own notes.[16]

The two episodes just described exemplify ones that, if noticed early on, could have sparked Twain's determination to read carefully the whole of Morte Darthur before passing judgment on any such episode taken out of context. Thereupon he set out in quest of what he never did find: basic human values in medieval literature. During his progress through Malory, Twain's reading and his life experiences coalesced more and more to convince him that mechanistic, amoral forces shaped earthly events. Any apparent humankindness meant no more than did the scraps left behind by Lanier's editorial scissors.

"See Morte Darthur" concludes the earliest notebook entry that blossomed into Connecticut Yankee. Although Malory offers no runny-nosed knight who "can't get at handkerchief, can't use iron sleeve" (N & J3, 78), the novel does directly rework the Globe edition in various ways substantiated by the author's handwritten notes. During the three-year course of its composition Twain methodically read Morte Darthur from beginning to end, chapter after tedious chapter. Simultaneously he was using the index, chapter titles, and running heads to locate passages that he recalled from The Boy's King Arthur or that otherwise interested him.

Thus the opening of Connecticut Yankee echoes Twain s response to the opening of Morte Darthur, notably to the sex and violence that Lanier had eliminated from Malory's book I. The second segment written of Connecticut Yankee, from chapter 5 through the first paragraph of chapter 21, reflects Twain's bemusement at the prolixity of Malory's books II-XII, replete with aimless wandering and fighting and smiting and betraying and celebrating. In Twain's own copy of Morte Darthur, also, the last few books of this second segment contain the preponderance of evidence for his study of Malory's language qua language. The novelist underlines archaic phrases, about half of which are defined in the index, and he notes in a margin that "certain expressions come suddenly in and become frequent thereafter."[17]

At Malory's book XIII, however, commences a continuous narrative familiar from The Boy's King Arthur: the Quest for the Holy Grail. Some underlining continues; however, for this final segment Twain has cause to shift attention away from language, toward content. To investigate ethical dimensions of Malory entire, Twain would want to peruse with extra care the account of the Grail quest, which segues into the great civil war that destroys Arthur, Mordred, and vast armies of followers. Within Morte Darthur's books XIII-XXI also occurs the Launcelot-Guenever affair so trumpeted by Tennyson but shushed by Lanier.

Sometime between autumn 1887 and summer 1888, I suggest, Twain finally finished reading every word of Morte Darthur. There was no ethical dimension after all. Between July 1888 and March 1889, having found in Malory no trace of chivalric values or inborn human goodness, Twain had to create a consistent conclusion for this novel long promised to his publisher. Although a consistently unsettling conclusion did emerge from his pen, a genial glow left his writing—and left it, many readers feel, never quite to return.

It was not any one gruesome, amoral passage somewhere in Morte Darthur that induced tonal disjunction between the first two paragraphs of Connecticut Yankee's chapter 21. Opprobrious incidents abound even in Malory's book I, which Twain read before he began to write the novel. Instead, the accumulation of such passages kept raising higher and higher his anticipation for the eventual emergence of the countervalent value system implied by The Boy's King Arthur. I will document that process of accumulation by comparing Connecticut Yankee to Morte Darthur segment by segment, drawing attention to passages not present in The Boy's King Arthur and also to Twain's handwritten notes in the manuscript and elsewhere.

The segment of Connecticut Yankee written first, in early 1886, exemplifies Twain's continuing use of the Globe edition's apparatus, including its seventeen-page index, which gives references for both content and vocabulary. Hank Morgan's exchange with the undercook, for instance, comes straight from the index: "Let to, hinder from" (CY, 61).

In addition, the novel's opening chapters contain evidence that Twain had read thoroughly at least book I of Morte Darthur. Conveniently, a contemporaneous guide to English literature summarizes precisely those passages of book I that Lanier eliminates from The Boy's King Arthur. Arthur

> was a child of shamefulness—not begotten in lawful wedlock. His father, Uther Pendragon, was transformed by the art of the magician, Merlin, into the likeness of Ygerne's husband, and Arthur

> was the issue of this illicit love and supernatural delusion of a faithful wife [whose husband Uther had treacherously slain]. Again, the Arthur of the old story was not stainless in the sense of loving one woman and cleaving to her. When he was a young squire, and before his origin was known either to himself or to the public, he lay with Morgause (or Bellicent), the wife of Lot, his half-sister; and in that unwittingly incestuous connection begat Mordred, who became afterwards his fatal enemy. After the battle with the eleven kings at Bredigan, he gratified, by the help of Merlin (who would not seem to have been scrupulous about playing the pander), a passing fancy for Lionors [who bore his child] . . . Finally, as regards his [alleged] singleness of purpose in driving out the heathen . . . Arthur of the old story . . . made great war for the common selfish purpose of "getting all England into his hand;" and did not scruple to try to secure his power by committing to the mercy of the waves all children born on Mayday.[18]

Within Connecticut Yankee the blunt sexuality of Malory's book I transmutes into the naked children of chapter 1, and thereafter into the peeled Yankee discussed as if cabbage (CY, 56-57, 80). Its unprincipled war-mongering appears in Connecticut Yankee chapter 2 as knights who tell "of blood and suffering with a guileless relish that made me almost forget to shudder" (CY, 66). Chapter 3 opens with further note of the belligerence that permeates Morte Darthur book I, but not The Boy's King Arthur book I; then Sir Kay concludes the exchange-of-armor episode quoted in the "Word of Explanation." Knowing the outcome from The Boy's King Arthur II.12, Twain could review it in Morte Darthur VI. 18 under the same title, "How Sir Launcelot came to king Arthur's court, and how there were recounted all his noble feats and acts." Enter Merlin, droning about obtaining Excalibur, an episode that occurs in each version's book I. So does the preceding chapter, the title of which inspired Twain's use of the story: "How Merlin saved Arthur's life, and threw an enchantment upon king Pellinore, and made him to sleep."[19] Everybody sleeps at court, except the Connecticut Yankee, until roused by Sir Dinadan's prank. Sleuthing for exploits of the "hilarious Sir Dinadan" that he recalled from Lanier's version, Twain would have found in the Globe index a dozen scattered page references and, as one of two subheads, Dinadan "forced into woman's garment." This enticing reference intensified Twain's conception of Knights of the Round Table as "big boobies . . . great simple-hearted creatures" lacking only brains.[20] Like other episodes in Malory, this one involves disguise and status and questioned identity, all themes of the novel in progress as well. In Morte Darthur X.49 (but not in The Boy's King Arthur) Launcelot dons female clothing to defeat Dinadan jousting, then forces him to wear like garments to court. At the sight of Dinadan in drag, Guenever "laughed that she fell down, and so did all that were there." In Connecticut Yankee chapter 4, similarly, the frenzied dog is forced to wear mugs, and everyone laughs until tears flow "and some fell out of their chairs and wallowed on the floor in ecstasy" (CY, 76). Additional matter-of-fact sexuality closes Twain's chapter 4.

Prurient matters appear less often in books II-XII, the corpse-strewn stretch of Morte Darthur through which a meticulous reader next must trudge. Lanier did bowdlerize what was there, Twain learned. For example, The Boy's King Arthur chooses his bride on account of true love, enhanced by a relevant dowry: the Round Table, which Guenever's father had seized from his father. Lanier omits Merlin's direct warning to Arthur "that Guenever was not wholesome for him to take to wife, for . . . Launcelot should love her, and she him."[21]

This is but one of many passages from which Lanier excises not only sexuality but also, or instead, Merlin. Until the magician dies "assotted . . . on one of the ladies of the lake,"[22] Merlin appears much oftener than he does in The Boy's King Arthur, and wields far greater, more malevolent power. That more substantial role in Morte Darthur caused the novelist to change his initial conception of Merlin. Sometime between early 1886 and mid-1887, Twain decided to transmute the tedious old fool of Connecticut Yankee chapter 3 into Hank Morgan's chief adversary.

Besides altering Merlin's character, while writing the second segment of his novel, Twain was familiarizing himself with Malory's language in order to incorporate it as both object and weapon of mockery. As indicated by underlining, especially in Morte Darthur books XXII, his careful scrutiny enabled him to compose exuberant dialogue in Late Middle English, such as Clarence's in chapters 5 and 6. Twain furthermore draws attention to the older language's beauty compared to sports journalism, in chapter 9, and compared to American slang in several passages.[23] Nods to tedium occur also, of course. In chapter 15 Hank Morgan keeps dozing off and losing track of Sandy's tale just as Twain would catch himself doing with Malory's intertwining, interchangeable adventures in flyspeck-sized print.

Within this second segment of his novel, written during the summer of 1887, Twain quotes two lengthy passages that are both eliminated from The Boy's King Arthur. Their presence testifies to Twain's methodical reading of the entire Morte Darthur, rather than just recalling and reviewing familiar episodes. The knightly adventures retold by Sandy occur midway through a very long stretch of Malory that Lanier drops without a trace: The Boy's King Arthur skips all fifty-three chapters in between Morte Darthur III.2 and VI.1. Twain had no prior reading experience, therefore, as guide through the convoluted quests of Sirs Marhaus, Gawaine, and Ewain with three damsels aged fifteen, thirty, and threescore.[24]

With the other verbatim quotation, Twain draws attention to the missing context for Lanier's excerpts. The sports report of Connecticut Yankee chapter 9 occurs within an eight-chapter description of a tournament, left out of the narrative sequences that Lanier reformulated in order to glorify Sir Gareth. "I struck out of my priest's report," notes sports editor Hank Morgan, "an unpleasant little episode that day." In events following the chapter quoted, Gareth twice defies tournament regulations by attacking his own kin. "O brother, said Sir Gawaine" the second time, "I wend ye would not have stricken me."[25]

Twain was beginning to see how seldom Malory's supposed paragons of chivalry recognize any code at all in combat games, much less in combat, much less in life. Nonetheless, still considering broken rules potentially comic, in his notebook he contemplated having Hank Morgan cheat at a "Competition of bards" by pretending that Tennyson's work was his own. Such an episode would, however, have compromised the narrator's verbal integrity. In the completed novel the Boss conquers Camelot using visual delusion, such as fireworks, but he refrains from lying outright.[26]

"There never was such a country for wandering liars," though, and therewith enters the Demoiselle Alisande la Carteloise (CY, 134). Sandy's appeal for aid resembles those by two maidens in parallel stories left nearly intact by Lanier. In one sequence the damsel Linet sets out reluctantly with a presumed kitchen knave. He endures her insults, proves his worth, reveals himself as Sir Gareth, and marries her; at the same ceremony, two of his brothers marry her convenient sister and niece. An equally perfunctory wedding concludes the adventure of Sir La

Cote Male Taile and the damsel Maledisant, who rides along insulting his clothing more than his social rank.[27] Both stories contribute to Hank Morgan's marital obligation toward his talkative protegee. In addition, these two sequences from Morte Darthur books II-XII both include details that Twain reworked for Connecticut Yankee chapters 5-20. It is Linet who refuses to eat with a supposed commoner, as Sandy refuses to eat with the freemen. It is Maledisant who brings her assigned champion to the castle Orgulous, which becomes the ogres' castle sought with Sandy.[28]

By themselves such parallels would not prove that Twain resolutely, in the course of time, read every single chapter of Morte Darthur. His quotation of two passages purged by Lanier, with attention drawn to the monotony of one and the environs of the other, does imply such thoroughness. His handwritten notes, preserved in several places, provide corroboration. As one instance, the part of Twain's manuscript written during summer of 1887 retains marginal mention of two nobles' names (CY, 642-43). "Sir Madok de la Montaine, 222" has just that one page reference in the Globe index, referring to Morte Darthur IX. (not in BKA). Here Twain makes note of a new-met knight with a mouth-filling moniker and with deeds in Camelot easily summarized, to whom he can assign toothbrush merchandising in Connecticut Yankee chapter 20.

At chapter 16 of his manuscript, Twain needed a soap salesman. He considered "Sir Griflet Le Fise de Dieu," who appears early in both versions.[29] Finding index references to Griflet scattered through the whole of Morte Darthur, he decided instead upon La Cote Male Taile, whose more concise adventures feature the "evil-shapen coat" that Twain transmutes to a signboard, soon to be fashionable attire.[30] He does keep in mind his euphonious first choice, however. When Clarence names the dead in chapter 42, the Globe edition's "Sir Griflet" becomes "Sir Griflet le Fils de Dieu."[31]

A notation that likewise implies esteem for Malory's mellifluous language, despite its density, is pencilled onto a discarded manuscript page. The alliterative, almost onomatopoetic "I saw nothing but the waters wap and the waves wan" occurs near the end of both Malory versions. The sentence is Sir Bedivere's second bald-faced, self-serving lie to King Arthur, before finally obeying his liege lord's deathbed command to return his sword to the lake whence it came. Twain copied it from the Globe edition, as The Boy's King Arthur has instead "water wap . . . waves wane."[32] In addition to an entry "Excalibur (Cut-Steel) . . . is thrown into the water," the Globe index glosses the archaic phrase itself with a unique, therefore conspicuous, reference to Idylls of the King: "Wap, strike, move quickly . . . Mr. Tennyson renders 'Wap and wan' by 'lapping on the crag.'" Perhaps Twain meant to compare translations of a phrase still problematic for philologists, which a footnote to The Boy's King Arthur defines in yet a third sense as "water lap and waves ebb." While examining Bedivere's deceitful claim, however, the novelist was confronting ethical as well as linguistic problems left unresolved at the end of Malory's narrative—problems that Tennyson and Lanier had manipulated in order to resolve their two works in ways as divergent as their respective modernizations of "wap" and "wan."

Other handwritten evidence even more directly discloses Twain's thoughts about concluding his novel so that its civil warfare and ethical irresolution would echo the legendary last days of Arthur. Papers separate from the manuscript, datable to summer of 1887, preserve his ruminations on religious factors in the dissolution of Camelot. From The Boy's King Arthur, amplified by Tennyson, Twain would recall that news of the Holy Grail evokes Arthur's outright lament: "ye have bereft me of the fairest fellowship and the truest of knighthood that ever were seen together in any realm of the world . . . It shall grieve me right sore the departing of this fellowship."[33] In Twain's plottings not incorporated into the novel, the Grail would have arrived and affected the kingdom in that conventional manner:

> The Grail appears, covered. Galahad swears to go seek it a year & a day. Whereupon the whole tribe resolve to go grailing, & Arthur is grieved. Is here my chance to push a RR [railroad] along, while they are out of my way?[34]

While musing upon the token of religion that tilts Arthur's kingdom toward its downfall, Twain used Globe apparatus to locate a relevant detail retained by Lanier: "Ch VII, p. 352. This is one of the beautiful chapters. Launcelot & his son Galahad descended from Christ. In what way? A curious tradition; Christ left no offspring."[35] Despite Twain's hope for clarification, the full-length Morte Darthur provides no insight into this or any other theological question. Page 352 is one of only three references to "Christ, Lord Jesus" in the index. Of the others, one half-sentence recounts the Holy Grail's origin, and another specifies a year A.D. "Church" has only two index references: an edifice in London, an element in allegory.[36] The index is not exhaustive. Nonetheless, the "Christ" and "Church" entries well represent the proportion of attention devoted to religion throughout Morte Darthur. Malory's knights move through a Roman Catholic world, but they encounter no trace of some omnipotent religious establishment poised to challenge the kingdom.

The dread Interdict, therefore, is a major plot element imported by Twain to devastate the Boss's power base just as the Holy Grail destroys that of the legendary Arthur. No "Interdict" appears in the Globe index, which has just three entries for "Pope of Rome." First, a jealous knight who beheads his faithful wife must convey her to Rome, sleeping nights with both corpse parts; there the Pope permits burial. Second, King Mark counterfeits letters from the Pope that do not fool Tristram. Third, the war incited between Launcelot and Arthur "was noised through all Christendom, and at the last it was noised afore the Pope," who charges Arthur "upon pain of interdicting of all England, that he take his queen dame Guenever unto him again, and accord with Sir Launcelot." Arthur obeys one papal injunction and tries hard to obey the second. No punishment ensues. Rather than from Malory's passing mention, Twain learned about another era's Interdict from at least two sources, which he credits.[37]

Twain first read all three "Pope of Rome" passages after 1884. In Lanier's version the Knights of the Round Table emulate nineteenth-century Protestants: on their own recognizance they behave properly. Indeed, the Roman Catholic Church stands helpless in one memorable incident just before the Last Battle. Briefly, ineffectually, the Bishop of Canterbury scolds Mordred for treason: "Is not King Arthur your uncle, no further but your mother's brother? Leave this opinion, or else I shall curse you with book, and bell, and candle." Mordred brushes him aside—"Peace, thou false priest . . . for, and thou chafe me any more, I shall make strike off thy head"—and England's highest ecclesiastic flees into hiding (BKA VI.27). Over his shoulder, as it were, he tosses a curse never again mentioned. After re-emerging as humble hermit to comfort and bury major figures, in both Malory versions, he finally regains his bishopric by grace of Arthur's cousin Constantine, the new King.[38]

While considering for his novel the role of the Church in general, and specifically that of a papal Interdict, Twain would have sought out the Bishop's futile curse in Morte Darthur. There he discovered one of Lanier's predictable expurgations. In the quotation above, in between "mother's brother" and "Leave this opinion," the Bishop continues, "and are ye not his son, therefore how may ye wed your father's wife?" (MD XXI.1) Elsewhere Lanier inserts a bracketed substitute for every word "father" referring to Arthur: "I know well that my [uncle] will be avenged upon me," says Mordred, and at the death-blow "right so he smote [the king] with his sword holden in both his hands" (BKA VI.30).

The latter quotation occurs within the war correspondent's report in chapter 42 of Connecticut Yankee, where Twain leaves incest intact: "he smote his father Arthur with his sword."[39] Very unlike Tennyson, however, Twain blames irregular sexuality not at all for the ruin wrought within his own imaginative kingdom based loosely on Malory's work. His love-smitten Launcelot means well; and marriage transforms Sandy from hog-worshipping chatterbox into "flawless wife and mother" (CY, 448, 452).

Love as a valued bond, like religion as a force for social control, comes to Connecticut Yankee from the author's experiences and readings exclusive of Malory. The Boy's King Arthur retains but distant murmurs of family matters. In Morte Darthur itself, after book I, sporadic acts of sexual intercourse function as means to various ends that enhance male status. La Beale Isoud is only a pawn in Tristram's power game. The gentler, more enigmatic affairs of twelfth-century verse romance had disappeared beneath the hands of the thirteenth-century Cistercian monks whose prose vulgate cycle Malory was translating. And the "knyght presoner" assuredly added no love interest to his military chronicle, meant to document civil wars of devastation prior to those swirling outside his prison cell. Long ago one famous King died along with most of his retainers, demonstrates Sir Thomas Malory. But monarchy and aristocracy, as great British institutions, survived the cataclysm.

And survive they did, for centuries more, to Twain's disgust. As Howard Baetzhold proves, though, both before and after the Connecticut Yankee years the author held mellower attitudes toward the nobly born.[40] Any thoughtful reader of Morte Darthur might well wonder whether its political system deserves another chance under Constantine the silent cousin, Bedivere the blatant liar, and the disloyal gentry who fled with Launcelot to France. Mark Twain, as author in charge, wielded his power to slay the lot.

Readers appalled by the Battle of the Sand-Belt, and shocked by Hank Morgan's gleeful slaughter of his erstwhile comrades, might attend more closely to correlations between it and the conclusion to Morte Darthur.[41] Body count, for example, is comparatively low: a mere twenty-five thousand British aristocrats (CY, 486). From The' Boy's King Arthur Twain knew that Camelot collapses in the aftermath of complexities that lead to two armies poised in mutual mistrust. An unthinking knight draws his sword to slay an adder. Battle rages until "an hundred thousand laid dead upon the down" (BKA VI.30).

During the course of composition Twain came to clarify his ideas about an Armageddon to conclude his novel, a no-holds-barred battle sparked by mistrust and miscommunication between two factions of a disintegrating nation. With the recent U.S. war in mind, he contemplated ways to avoid or mitigate a conflict like the legendary one that obliterated Camelot. However, he had not yet articulated to himself one necessary feature of the Connecticut Yankee's realm: it must leave no trace on subsequent British history. Without clear precedent at his time, Twain confronted a dilemma now made explicit by writers of science fiction, to wit, that a credible time traveller to the past must not change the course of history. Thus the novel could not retain a conclusion that Twain entertained but discarded, whereby sensibly clad knights would seek the Northwest Passage in lieu of the Grail, from their seats at the Round Table turned stock board.[42]

Instead, Twain followed through on his initial idea of a Last Battle that differs from its prototype in military technology, but that echoes loud and clear its futility and gore. In 1886 he lauded in a letter Malory's "last battle—the Battle of the Broken Hearts, it might be called." Nearly two years earlier, he had jotted in his notebook an idea that he was to incorporate into Connecticut Yankee: "Have a battle between a modern army . . . & Prince de Joinville's Middle Age Crusaders." Recalling Lanier's scenario, he could readily find its equivalent in the Globe edition, which even provides an index entry for "Adder stings and produces a war."[43] While thinking about his novel as a whole, but before he finished reading Malory cover to cover, Twain would want to refresh his memory about civil war in Camelot. What would have surprised him about Morte Darthur book XXI, which coincides approximately with the ten closing chapters of The Boy's King Arthur book VI?

Here as elsewhere, most of Lanier's deletions defy detection. Perhaps, though, some readers have puzzled at a narrative gap in one section, The Boy's King Arthur VI.29-30. The night before the battle, Gawaine's ghost tells Arthur not to fight Mordred yet, because Launcelot is en route from France with support troops. Why do two armies and one adder nonetheless assemble on Salisbury Plain the next morning, and why do Arthur and Mordred drink wine before witnesses as a legally binding pledge?

Whether or not Twain had noticed a gap, he found disheartening details at this point in Morte Darthur (XXI.3-4). In the passage excised by Lanier, King Arthur gives his sworn oath on a treaty that he fully intends to break. "God hath sent me to you," says Gawaine's unabridged ghost, to tell you to "take a treaty for a month day; and proffer you largely, so as to-mom to be put in a delay. For within a month shall come Sir Launcelot, with all his noble knights, and rescue you worshipfully," albeit not on bicycles (cf. CY, 425-26). The next morning Arthur sends two noblemen and two bishops to make fraudulent offers: "And spare not, proffer him lands and goods . . . and at the last Sir Mordred was agreed for to have Cornwall and Kent . . . [and] after, all England, after the days of king Arthur." Lying under oath, certain of Launcelot's aid in regaining his kingdom by force, a smugly treacherous Arthur lifts his wineglass to seal the deal. The adder then strikes at random. Perhaps, indeed, feline or porcine or ursine or simian royalty would set higher ethical standards than does the Once and Future King.[44]

It is probable that Twain first read this passage, and noted with alarm King Arthur's false oath, before the period in 1887-88 during which his comic vision took such a marked turn toward black humor. Like the matricide or baby-massacre chapter read in isolation, this passage would have increased Twain's determination to refrain from judgment until he had put all such disturbing incidents into the broadest, most legitimate historical context available at his time: that of the definitive account from medieval Britain of the allegedly illustrious King Arthur and his presumably heroic Knights of the Round Table. Therefore, he read it all.

Besides Idylls of the King and The Boy's King Arthur, where else had Twain acquired preconceptions that a genuinely medieval King Arthur might provide a role model transcending time? Remnants of his prior suppositions sometimes resurface in the novel, notably at the smallpox hut where Arthur demonstrates "heroism at its last and loftiest possibility ... challenging death in the open field unarmed" (CY, 331). More subtly, in chapter 42 Twain revises chronology before the Last Baffle in order to protect his own Arthur's integrity. As Clarence reports the situation, first had come "talk of peace" and a sworn treaty between Arthur and Mordred. Only afterward did Gawaine's ghost advise the King "to refrain from conflict for a month" for no given reason (CY, 461-62). To avoid denigrating the novel's King Arthur, that is, Twain distorts the troubling elements that he first encountered in the full-length Morte Darthur. Into the vacuum left by suppression of the legendary King's dishonor steps a villain, a deus ex machina indeed: the Church. Enforced morality equals immorality, as a way to end the novel. William Blake would have applauded. But Twain had once expected otherwise from Malory's Morte Darthur.

It is far beyond the scope of this article to reconstruct Twain's entire horizon of expectations regarding Malory and regarding, ultimately, any possibility that childlike innocence of a preindustrial age might provide counterweight to the determinism of a universe governed only by laws of physical motion. Besides The Boy's King Arthur, though, one certain source merits special mention: the introduction to the Globe edition itself. There Edward Strachey quotes selectively from fiction and chronicles, from England and the Continent, from several centuries other than the fifteenth, in order to generate awe for this actual medieval author's treatment of chivalry, sparkling and flashing everywhere as it runs through that great complicated tissue of human life which we call modern civilisation . . . chivalry, the humaniser of society . . . Chivalry . . . no longer comes to us with the outward symbols of war-horse, and armour, and noble birth, and strength of arm, and high-flown protestations of love and gallantry; yet we never fail to know and feel its presence. We recognise the lady and the gentleman not less surely now than they did in old times; and we acknowledge their rights and their power over us now no less than then . . . Let us then look back to those times when chivalry had an outward, visible form, and was embodied in its own proper institutions, with orders, and statutes, and courts of its own jurisdiction, and rituals, and customs, like those of other great social institutions. (MD, xix)

Twain or any reader may search Malory in vain for outward, visible forms of any such concept. Orders and statutes and courts and institutions are absent from Camelot, or powerless, or maintained by unscrupulous brute strength. Principles of human conduct figure only insofar as a Knight of the Round Table can gain status by ignoring, bending, or breaking them. In ways that cry out for full-scale examination by specialists in late-nineteenth-century literature and society, Sir Edward Strachey's preface to Sir Thomas Malory's work is a false but persuasively eloquent validation of their mutual honorific "Sir." Further study can reveal more also about Mark Twain's hopes, prior to 1888, that "nobility" might describe some innate quality within every human soul—something that children lose gradually, and perhaps not altogether—instead of describing just the monied, landed social class overthrown in the French and American Revolutions but surviving in insidious forms, especially in the South, and still functioning in England. The boy from Missouri anticipated finding in Malory what he saw lacking in nineteenth-century remnants of the class system: honor, faith, charity, selfless virtue, deserved nobility, essential human values that transcend time and place. He found nothing of the sort. But his long, long quest through the whole Morte Darthur warmed up his pen in hell.[45]

NOTES

1. Taylor Roberts, "The Recovery of Mark Twain's Copy of Morte Darthur," *Resources for American Literary Study* 23 (1997), 166-80.

2. For the concept, see the journal *Studies in Medievalism* (1979-). In reference to Twain the fullest discussion is Kim Moreland, *The Medievalist Impulse in American Literature: Twain, Adams, Fitzgerald, and Hemingway* (Charlottesville: Univ. Press of Virginia, 1966), 28-76.

Predecessors include S.B. Liljegren, *The Revolt against Romanticism in American Literature as Evidenced in the Works of S.L. Clemens* (1945; New York: Haskell House, 1970); Paul L. Kegel, "Henry Adams and Mark Twain: Two Views of Medievalism," *Mark Twain Journal* 15.3 (1970-71), 11-21; T.J. Jackson Lears, *No Place of Grace: Antimodernism and the Transformation of American Culture, 1880-1920* (New York: Pantheon, 1981), esp. 97-181; Stephen Knight, *Arthurian Literature and Society* (New York: St. Martin's Press, 1983), 187-202; and Clara Bartocci, "A Connecticut Yankee in King Arthur's Court," in *Medieval and Pseudo-Medieval Literature: The J.A.W. Bennett Memorial Lectures*, Perugia, 1982-1983, ed. Piero Boitani and Ann Torti (Tubgingen: G. Narr; Cambridge: D.S. Brewer, 1984), 161-80. For bibliography on the Arthurian context see Debra N. Mancoff, *The Return of King Arthur: The Legend through Victorian Eyes* (New York: Harry N. Abrams, 1995), 166-69.

3. For stages of composition see Henry Nash Smith's introduction to the standard edition of *Mark Twain, A Connecticut Yankee in King Arthur's Court*, ed. Bernard L. Stein (Berkeley: Univ. of California Press, 1979), 1-13, hereafter cited parenthetically as CY with page numbers only (continuous through text and editorial apparatus). Among studies cited by Smith, see especially Howard G. Baetzhold, *Mark Twain and John Bull: The British Connection* (Bloomington: Indiana Univ. Press, 1970), 102-61. Also see Everett Emerson, *The Authentic Mark Twain: A Literary Biography of Samuel L. Clemens* (Philadelphia: Univ. of Pennsylvania Press, 1985), 154-68. For a summary of twentieth-century criticism on the novel, see Howard G. Baetzhold, "A Connecticut Yankee in King Arthur's Court," in *The Mark Twain Encyclopedia*, ed. J.R. LeMaster and James D. Wilson (New York: Garland, 1993).

4. Most commentators posit combined causes. Of the biographical factors listed, the last three are described respectively by Henry Nash Smith, *Mark Twain's Fable of Progres: Political and Economic Ideas in "A Connecticut Yankee"* (New Brunswick: Rutgers Univ. Press, 1964), 36-66; Sherwood Cummings, *Mark Twain and Science:*

Adventures of a Mind (Baton Rouge: Louisiana State Univ. Press, 1988), 141-44, 160-61; and Justin Kaplan, *Mr. Clemens and Mark Twain: A Biography* (1966; New York: Simon & Schuster, 1983), 293-301. Concerning W.E.H. Lecky's History of European Morals (1869), see Harold Aspiz, "Lecky's Influence on Mark Twain," *Science and Society* 26 (1962), 15-25; Rodney O. Rogers, "Twain, Taine, and Lecky: The Genesis of a Passage in A Connecticut Yankee," *Modern Language Quarterly* 34 (1973), 436-47; and Baetzhold, *Mark Twain and John Bull*, 134-43. For other readings in history see Roger B. Salomon, *Twain and the Image of History* (New Haven: Yale Univ. Press, 1961); James D. Williams, "The Use of History in Mark Twain's A Connecticut Yankee," *PMLA* 80 (1965), 102-10; and Baetzhold, *Mark Twain and John Bull*, 111-15 and passim. For scientific readings see Cummings, *Mark Twain and Science*; and Thomas D. Zlatic, "Mark Twain's View of the Universe," *Papers on Language and Literature* 27 (1991), 338-55. Adeler's influence is emphasized by David Ketterer in two articles, "'Professor Baffin's Adventures' by Max Adeler: The Inspiration for A Connecticut Yankee in King Arthur's Court?" *Mark Twain Journal* 24, no. 1 (1986), 24-33, and "'The Fortunate Island' by Max Adeler: Its Publication History and A Connecticut Yankee," *Mark Twain Journal* 29, no. 2 (1991), 28-32; and by Horst H. Kruse, "Mark Twain's A Connecticut Yankee: Reconsiderations and Revisions," *American Literature* 62 (1990), 464-83. For Arnold's impact see John B. Hoben, "Mark Twain's A Connecticut Yankee: A Genetic Study," *American Literature* 18 (1946-47), 197-218; for the Russian atrocities Howard G. Baetzhold, "The Course of Composition of A Connecticut Yankee: A Reinterpretation," *American Literature* 33 (1961-62), 195-214.

5. Properly speaking the Globe Morte Darthur is a modernization, not an edition. Its 1883 printing, Le Morte Darthur: Sir Thomas Maloo's Book of King Arthur and of his Noble Knights of the Round Table, glossary and introd. Edward Strachey (London: Macmillan, 1883) is hereafter cited parenthetically as MD followed by book and chapter number. I lack access to the 1879 printing

owned by Twain; however, I find no discrepancies comparing the quotations and references in this article to the printings of 1868, 1876, and 1889. (I thank Melanie Wisner of the Houghton Reading Room, Harvard University, for assistance with spot-checking.) Each of the first two Globe printings (both 1868) includes a four-page glossary with page references, which was intercalated into the index beginning in 1869. With almost no other changes, the unabridged Malory continued to reach a ready market. It had been reprinted at least twenty-five times by 1931, when Eugene Vinaver began preparing his critical edition of Malory; in 1934, as his work was ongoing, a fifteenth-century manuscript of Malory was found in the Fellows' Library of Winchester College. Vinaver's attention to the 1934 discovery, detailed in his Introduction to *The Works of Sir Thomas Malory*, ed. Eugene Vinaver, rev. P.J.C. Field, 3rd ed., 3 vols. (Oxford: Clarendon, 1990), viii-ix, both transformed Malory scholarship and created practical problems in citation; see note 14 below. Prior to Roberts, "Recovery of Mark Twain's Copy," the novelist's use of the Globe edition was established by Robert H. Wilson, "Malory in the Connecticut Yankee," *Studies in English* 27 (1948), 186-87n4, and reinforced by editor Bernard L. Stein, CY, 612n90. Also see Alan Gribben, comp., *Mark Twain's Library: A Reconstruction*, 2 vols. (Boston: G.K. Hall, 1980), 447-48.

6. Besides the French prose vulgate cycle mentioned, Malory in some sections adapts shorter works, including the Middle English Alliterative Morte DArthure. For his sociohistoric context see Vinaver's introduction to *Works of Malory*, xix-xxxiv. Malory's writings do contain some positive values, detectable by present-day scholars using data previously unavailable.

7. On the process of composition see Mark Twain, *The Prince and the Pauper*, ed. Victor Fischer and Lin Salamo, assisted by Mary Jane Jones (Berkeley: Univ. of California Press, 1979), 7-8. Also see 351-64 for Twain's list of "Middle-Age phrases for a historical story," taken mostly from Shakespeare and Scott.

8. Moreland, *Medievalist Impulse in American Literature*, 75.

9. The Boy's King Arthur, Being Sir Thomas Malory's History of King Arthur and his Knights' of the Round Table, ed. and introd. Sidney Lanier (New York: Charles Scribner's Sons, 1880), xxii, hereafter cited parenthetically as BKA followed by book and chapter number. Lanier's Boy's King Arthur was further condensed in 1917, and republished with illustrations by Andrew Wyeth. Its continuing popularity is attested by two copies of a 1952 reprint of the 1917 revision in active circulation at the Free Library of Philadelphia, Children's Department, which also holds (in Special Collections) the 1880 edition here cited. Lanier's was one among many versions of Malory prepared for young people. For an overview see Mancoff, Return of King Arthur, 111-17.

10. BKA, xxii. Twain's attitudes toward Tennyson require treatment separate from this article on Malory, especially because Schleiner finds "no explicit reference to [Idylls of the King] before the Yankee planning notes." "Romance Motifs in Three Novels," 347n24. Concerning Tennyson see CY, 552; Gribben, *Mark Twain's Library*, 692-94; Baetzhold, *Mark Twain and John Bull*, 148-49, 348n27, and passim; and *Mark Twain's Notebooks and Journals*, Volume III (1883-1891), ed. Robert Pack Browning, Michael B. Frank., and Lin Salamo (Berkeley: Univ. of California Press, 1979), 420, hereafter cited as N & J3.

11. Quotation from *Mark Twain and George W. Cable: The Record of a Literary Friendship*, ed. Arlin Turner (East Lansing: Michigan State Univ. Press, 1960), 135; also see 96. For Twain's confirmation see N & J3, 79; also see sources summarized at CY, 1-3. Roberts quotes a lecture-tour list from the book's endpapers ("Recovery of Mark Twain's Copy," 172). Twain's use of Malory has been discussed by Wilson, "Malory in the Connecticut Yankee"; James Russell, "The Genesis, Sources, and Reputation of Mark Twain's A Connecticut Yankee in King Arthur's Court (Ph.D. diss., Univ. of Chicago, 1966); Baetzhold, *Mark Twain and John Bull*, 105-6, 131-33, 34546nn2-4, 352n40; Alan Gribben, "'The Master Hand

of Old Malory': Mark Twain's Acquaintance with Le Morte d'Arthur," English Language Notes 16 (1978), 32-40; Lesley C. Kordecki, "Twain's Critique of Malory's Romance: Forma Tractandi and A Connecticut Yankee," *Nineteenth Century Fiction* 41 (1986), 329-48; Carey McWilliams, "Malory, Sir Thomas," in *Mark Twain Encyclopedia*; Moreland, *Medievalist Impulse in American Literature*, 57-58; and Richard Kaeuper, "Telling It Like It Was? Mark Twain's Rereading of Chivalry in Malory's Morte Darthur," in *Retelling Tales: Essays in Honor of Russell Peck*, ed. Thomas Hahn and Alan Lupack (Rochester: D. S. Brewer, 1997), 179-90.

12. *Mark Twain to Mrs. Fairbanks*, ed. Dixon Wecter (San Marino: Huntington Library, 1949), 258.

13. Twain's letter to Mrs. Cincinnatus A. Taft, August 14, 1883, is partially reproduced in Susy and Mark Twain: Family Dialogues, ed. Edith Colgate Salsbury (New York: Harper & Row, 1965), 170.

14. For Merlin see CY, 72-74. Bracketed arabic numerals in some citations of Morte Darthur refer to printer William Caxton's chapter numbers as reproduced in Vinaver's Works of Malory. The Globe Morte Darthur assigns consecutive numbers to some chapters that are combined in Caxton's 1485 edition, therefore also in Vinaver's Works of Malory. Vinaver supplies Caxton's book and chapter numbers only as marginalia, however, because the manuscript found in 1934 (see note 5 above) has a different organizational framework. Caxton's helpful guideposts are eliminated by well-intentioned recent scholars, such as R.M. Lumiansky re-modernizing Morte Darthur a century later for the Globe edition's publisher (New York: Collier Macmillan, 1982).

15. MD 1.15[17]; not in BKA.

16. Twain abandoned a plan to provide an appendix, parallel to his "Notes" for The Prince and the Pauper, giving sources for historical information incorporated into Connecticut Yankee. See CY 515 Group D; and N & J3, 351,501-6. For other relevant reading see CY, 517, 549-68; and N & J3, 167-68, 216, 384, 398-402, 413-20, 475.

17. Roberts, "Recovery of Mark Twain's Copy," 173.
18. William Minto, *Characteristics of English Poets from Chaucer to Shirley* (Boston, 1874), quoted from 1889 edition in *Malory: The Critical Heritage*, ed. Marylyn Jackson Parins (London: Routledge, 1988), 200-201. Twain did not own this book, according to Gribben, *Mark Twain's Library*.
19. MD 1.22-23[24-25]; BKA 1.5-6.
20. CY, 68-69. For Dinadan see BKA, xxii, and (e.g.) IV.40-45; cf. MD X.55-60.
21. MD III. 1; cf. BKA 1.24.
22. MD IV. 1; not in BKA.
23. For Clarence's language see CY, 86-87, 91-92; for attention from Twain's narrator CY, 121, 172-73, 257-59. In "Master Hand," Gribben documents Twain's praise of Malory's language outside the novel as well.
24. CE 173-80, 221-23; MD IV.16-18[19], 24-25[25-26]; not in BKA.
25. CY, 121-22; MD VII.28-30[29-31]; cf. BKA III. 18.
26. N & J3, 420. Regarding this visual/verbal matrix, Thomas D. Zlatic usefully analyzes this novel as "a critique of an oral culture expressed from a literate perspective at the dawn of electronic communication," in "Language Technologies in A Connecticut Yankee," *Nineteenth-Century Literature* 45 (1990-91), 453-77, 456.
27. For Linet see MD VII.1-35, BKA III. 1-19; for Maledisant MD IX1-9, BKA IV. 21-29.
28. For Linet see MD VII.5, cf. CY, 155; for Maledisant MD IX.3 ff., cf. CY, 138 ff.
29. E.g., MD 1.20[22]; BKA 1.4.
30. CY, 185; MD IX.1-9.
31. CY, 460; MD XX.8; not in BKA.
32. CY, 633; MD XX1.5; BKA VI.31.

33. BKA V.3; cf. MD XIII.7.

34. CY, 513; cf. CY, 124.

35. CY, 513; MD XIII.7; BKA V.3.

36. For "Christ" see MD II.16, XVII.4; for "Church" MD 1.3[3, 4, 5], XVII.5.

37. For the bisected wife see MD VI. 17; for Mark MD X.51; for Arthur's obedience MD XX.13-14, cf. CY, 461. For Interdict sources see N & J3, 167, 504, 506; also see CY, 512, and N & J3, 414-15. Further ridcule of established religion includes N & J3, 45, 265-66, 410-13, 416-19, 540.

38. MD XXI. 13; BKA VI.37.

39. CY, 463; MD XXI.4.

40. Among many attacks on monarchy and aristocracy see CY, 208-9, 236-37, 284-96, 316-18, 540, 591; N & J3, 392, 398-403, 406-25, 431, 435, 470, 475, 520-21, 525, 539-41,606, 609, 635; and others discussed by Baetzhold, *Mark Twain and John Bull*, 102-61.

41. For a summary of critics' responses to the Battle of the Sand Belt see Susan K. Hams, *Mark Twain's Escape from Time: A Study of Patterns and Images* (Columbia: Univ. of Missouri Press, 1982), 53n3.

42. CY, 502, 506, 510; cf. CY, 124. For the point about science fiction I thank Matthew Appleton. I wish to thank all other students who have joined me in juxtaposing Morte Darthur and Connecticut Yankee in two courses, *Literature of Travel and Arthurania*, in Fall 1993 and Spring 1995 respectively. I also appreciate the interest generated by Realm of the Isles (the Rutgers/Camden chapter of Markland Medieval Militia) and input from Kimberly Adams, Carol Singley, and other colleagues.

43. For the letter see Mark Twain to Mrs. Fairbanks, 258; for the note N & J3, 86; for the scene MD XXI.4, BKA VI.30.

44. For animal nobility see CY, 445-46, 229-40; N & J3, 402, 419.

45. Paraphrased from Twain's letter to William Dean Howells, September 22, 1889, reproduced in Mark Twain-Howells Letters: The Correspondence of Samuel L. Clemens and William D. Howells, 1872-1910, ed. Henry Nash Smith and William M. Gibson, assisted by Frederick Anderson, 2 vols. (Cambridge: Harvard Univ. Press, 1960), 613; partially repr. in CY, 29.

10

What's Funny about Huckleberry Finn

—Sacvan Bercovitch

What's funny about *Huckleberry Finn* is that it's a humorous story. This sounds like a tautology and it is, but in a special sense. The story is humorous because it's told by the quintessential American Boy, Huck Finn, and according to *the* American humorist, Mark Twain, the humorous story is quintessentially American. Here is how Twain explains it, in a late essay entitled *"How To Tell A Story"*:

> The humorous story is American, the comic story is English, the witty story is French. The humorous story depends for its effect on the *manner* of the telling; the comic story and the witty story upon the *matter* . . . The humorous story bubbles gently along, the others burst.
>
> The humorous story is strictly a work of art—high and delicate art—and only an artist can tell it; but no art is necessary in telling the comic and the witty story; anybody can do it.

> The humorous story is told gravely; the teller does his best to conceal the fact that he even dimly suspects that there is anything funny about it; but the teller of the comic story tells you beforehand that it is one of the funniest things he has ever heard, then tells it with an eager delight, and is the first person to laugh when he gets through.
>
> Very often . . . [the] humorous story finishes with a nub, point, snapper, or whatever you like to call it. Then the listener must be alert, for in many cases the teller will divert attention from the nub by dropping it in a carefully casual and indifferent way, with the pretense that he does not know it is a nub.[1]

The present essay is about the nubs or snappers in *Huckleberry Finn*, and by extension about a distinctive and (according to Twain) a uniquely American mode of being funny—a Trickster's mode with an American slant. I refer to deadpan, of course, the comic form familiar to Americans through a wide range of folklore, from Yankee Peddler to Riverboat Con Man, and particularly the Western Tall Tale. The joke is told "gravely," the teller is straight-faced—he recounts in earnest detail how Davy Crockett at six years of age killed the biggest bear in Arkansas or how you can get the Brooklyn Bridge dirtcheap—and what's funny is the listener who believes and marvels at the story. In Twain's case, the joke often reflects the peculiar historical conditions of the Southwestern frontier. These conditions have often been commented on, but their bearing upon Trickster behavior is so striking—they so clearly provide the setting for Twain's notorious Tricksterism—that they are worth rehearsing at some length:

> "Tall humor," Henry B. Wonham observes, "is American not because it is incongruous—all humor is that—but because it articulates incongruities that are embedded in the American experience. A country

> founded, settled, and closely observed by men and women with extraordinary expectations, both exalted and depraved, could not help but appreciate the distance that separated the ideal from the real, the 'language of culture' from the 'language of sweat,' the democratic dream from the social and economic reality of the early American republic."

The "gap" between culture and sweat found in frontier experiences—which characteristically included Indian wars, slave-dealing, *herrenvolk* white racial solidarity, endemic violence, economic instability, fluidity, humbuggery, and speculative fantasy—cultivated a vernacular humor of extremes, along with pleasure in horror and depravity (an outgrowth of urban contact zones, as well) . . . "Tall" humor was a form of initiation and survival in response to the radical physical and social uncertainties on the edge of settler—colonial expansion. This humor thrived at the borderland of displacement, migration, and violence, finding much of its pleasure in dethroning the condescension of gentility at the thickly settled Eastern core, while at the same time reproducing the radical incongruities and discrepancies at the root of all American experience.[2]

This setting—a new capitalist nation in the violent process of emergence—is a Trickster paradise. Its social and psychological uncertainties, its physical turbulence and shifting borders, make for a world that's not only ripe for but conducive to all manner of Trickster wiles: transgressing boundaries, defying taboos, mocking rules and regulations. And its "radical incongruities" provide ample scope for Trickster fun in what (according to the *Oxford English Dictionary*) are the three basic meanings of the word: (1) *Funny* as in "just plain fun," with the innocence of Young Hermes or Baby Brahma—the child-like humor we designate as "kidding around." (2) *Funny* in its antiquated meaning of "befool," as in "playing a hoax on someone," with the cruel edge of con games associated with Coyote—a cunning humor that thrives on "humbuggery and speculative fantasy" and that often issues as satire, since the hoax that thrives upon the hypocrisies of everyday life—the joke that highlights the "distance separat[ing] the ideal from the real"—serves to reinforce social norms *as ideals.* (3) *Funny* as in "odd or curious," the chilling sense of some sinister hidden meaning, as when we say there's "something funny" about Trickster Fox; he might be a killer. This last layer of humor tends towards "horror and depravity." It's the kind of humor we associate with sick jokes and the absurd.

Usually deadpan artists specialize in one or another of these ways of being funny-let us call them innocent, satirical, and sinister—but the humor reaches its highest pitch, the finest turn of its "high and delicate art," when the joke reverberates with all three layers of fun, from (cheerfully) "that's *funny*" to (suspiciously) "*that's* funny."

Mark Twain's deadpan is Trickster fun at its best, and *Huckleberry Finn* is his funniest book, in all three senses of the term. What makes it distinctive, however—what separates it from generic deadpan—is Twain's deliberate and sustained use of the third, sinister, "odd or curious" sense of funny. Without submerging the cheerful and satirical layers of fun—indeed, while drawing these out to their limit—his humor involves a drastic turnabout in deadpan effect, virtually a *reversal* of conventional techniques. The novel is a great example of child-like, fun-filled wonder and a great work of social satire whose comic mode overturns the very tradition of deadpan it builds upon. Ostensibly that tradition belongs to the narrator-hero. Huck speaks "gravely" and often plays the Trickster; but the funny thing is, he's not a humorist, not even when he's putting someone on (as he does Aunt Sally, when he pretends to be Tom Sawyer). In fact, he rarely has fun; characteristically he's in a sweat, and on the rare occasion when he does try to kid around (as when he tells Jim that the two of them were not separated in the fog), the joke turns back on itself to humiliate him. Huck has a stylized deadpan; his voice may sound comic to the comically disposed listener, but actually it's troubled, earnest. The nub or snapper behind that stylization, the humorous intent of *Huckleberry Finn*, the unusual twist to the joke—is directed against Huck's apparent deadpan. For of course the "teller" is really Mark Twain, the Comic Writer, and *this* deadpan artist is not straight-faced (as Huck is), but smiling. He wears the Mask of Comedy. Officially, he's telling a very amusing, sometimes hilarious story, and having a wonderful time at every point. His "story bubbles gently along," he's laughing through it all; and so are we.

So here's the Trickster set-up, American-style, of *Huckleberry Finn*: the deadpan artist is Mark Twain, wearing the Comic Mask, doing his best to conceal the fact that he even dimly suspects that there's anything grave, let alone sinister, about his story-and he succeeds famously. Then, as we laugh, or after we've laughed, we may realize, if we're alert, that there's something we've overlooked. We haven't seen what's funny about the fact that we've found it all so funny. This Trickster has conned us, somehow diverted our attention away from the real point, and we have to go back over the story in order to recognize its nub.

Recognition in this sense begins with two general premises of Trickster humor. The first is that what's funny works as a connective. The joke interweaves the different aspects (innocent, satirical, and sinister) of Trickster fun—it makes these volatile, interchangeable. What's a harmless prank as far as Huck is concerned (e.g., Tom's coin trick at the start) may be a hoax on Twain's part. And what seems a hoax to Huck (e.g., the tricks played at the end upon Jim) may have something sinister about it for Twain.

In all these instances, satire mingles with brutality and brutality flows into "just plain fun."

The second general premise of Trickster humor involves the connectives between the joke and its cultural contexts. The linguistic play of deadpan calls up diverse situations, social, personal, and historical, and by joining these the humor points us towards connections within the culture. The joke may be said to bridge various aspects of life: institutions, practices, beliefs, customs. All humor works in this way more or less, but there's something distinctive (here as elsewhere) about Tricksters. They tend to direct their jokes *against* the very cultural connections that their humor invokes. In a recent overview of the Trickster Figure, Lewis Hyde describes this technique in physiological terms, as an assault upon the vulnerable parts of the social body. He points out that Tricksters work best in the intersections of culture, the intricate, delicate links between different social practices and institutions. Home, job, school, church-these variant spheres are connected by joints, which are in fact anatomical weak-points. Thus the fragility of the knees (where "the shin-bone's connected to the thigh-bone"), becomes an image for Hyde of cultural weak-points, where (say) official religion jars with official politics, or where variant conventions and rules of behavior (residual, dominant, emergent) may overlap and clash. At these junctures, traditionally, the Trickster comes most vividly to life—unsettling the system, upsetting its rhythms, exposing conflicts and contradictions.[3]

Mark Twain's Trickster trademark is the shock to the funny-bone. Imagine a culture like the antebellum frontier (or for that matter the Reconstructionist Southwest), which is both racist and egalitarian, and where that contradiction is the sign not just of hypocrisy (ideal versus real) but of separate, deep-rooted traditions, each involving its own disparities between "culture and sweat," its own configuration of realities and ideals. The minstrel show was a genre born out of precisely these conditions. So think now of this Trickster's minstrel act: the audience hears a long funny story about a "nigger" and they laugh along. The nub of course is that they're being laughed at; they've been taken in and made the butt of a joke. Once they see that, they understand what's funny about the story, and *they're* free to laugh at themselves for having laughed in the first place. That freedom, I'm suggesting, comes with the shock to the funnybone. It's a complex sensation, like the odd "tingling vibration" you feel when you're hit on the funny-bone. A light touch might mean no more than a bit of healthy fun-say, the cheerful wake-up call of social satire (the N-joke reminds you of your egalitarian principles). A sharp touch might be unnerving—a bitter protest directed against the system at large (you recognize that you are part and parcel of a deeply racist society). A direct and vicious cut would be painful, a sensation of pure violence, as in the sinister sense of "funny" (you realize that egalitarianism itself is a joke, you're a sucker for having believed in it at all).

Twain's deadpan spans all of these forms. The light touch marks his early career. His tales of the Wild West and Innocents Abroad are sometimes savage in their exposure of pretense, but their manner and tone emphasize the ebullient Pan in the *deadpan*. Twain's late career shifts the emphasis to the nihilistic undercurrent in deadpan: the deadly laughter of *The Mysterious Stranger*, the doomsday humor of *A Connecticut Yankee*, the absurdist stories collected in *The Great Dark*. *Huckleberry Finn* might be described as early-middle-but-especially-late Twain. It's the apotheosis of American deadpan, a carefully coordinated synthesis of all three layers I've sketched of the meaning of *funny*. Twain's mode of coordination—the dialectic behind his synthesis-is the drastic reversal of effect I spoke of: the Trickster with the Comic Mask. And the nubs or snappers he delivers constitute the most severe set of shocks in the literature to the American funny-bone.

The first shock is that the novel is funny at all. The slave-hunt serves as both metaphor and metonymy for the world it portrays: *Huckleberry Finn* describes a slave-hunt undertaken literally, collectively, by an enslaved society, a culture in bondage to all the Seven Deadly Sins (in addition to the sin of chattel-slavery), and accordingly characterized by violence, mean-spiritedness, ignorance, and deceit. A fair embodiment of this world is Pikesville, a "nondescript" shanty-town somewhere along the river:

> All the streets and lanes was just mud; they warn't nothing else *but* mud—mud as black as tar and nigh about a foot deep in some places, and two or three inches deep in *all* the places. The hogs loafed and grunted around everywheres. You'd see a muddy sow and a litter of pigs come lazying along the street and whollop herself right down in the way, where folks had to walk around her, and she'd stretch out and shut her eyes and wave her cars whilst the pigs was milking her, and look as happy as if she was on salary. And pretty soon you'd hear a loafer sing out, "Hi! *so* boy! sick him, Tige!" and away the sow would go, squealing most horrible, with a dog or two swinging to each ear, and three or four dozen more a-coming; and then you would see all the loafers get up and watch the thing out of sight, and laugh at the fun and look grateful for the noise. Then they'd settle back again till there was a dogfight. There couldn't anything wake them up all over, and make them happy all over, like a dogfight—unless it might be putting turpentine on a stray dog and setting fire to him, or tying a tin pan to his tail and see him run himself to death. (p. 183)

Readers of the novel tend to remember Pikeville not for that bit of "fun" (though that's the town's main source of laughter), but for the Shakespearean soliloquy delivered there by the Duke and the King:

> To be or not to be; that is the bare bodkin
> That makes calamity of so long life . . .
> 'Tis a consummation devoutly to be wished.
> But soft you now, the fair Ophelia,
> Ope not thy ponderous and marble jaws. (p. 179)[4]

That's what we laugh at, as we should, but consider the image of the dog running himself to death. And now think of the nub concealed within the Shakespearean parody: the Duke and the King are debased men, the townspeople are debased, and debasement in both cases is a metonym for the slave code. The stray dog is Jim on the run, Huck hounded by "sivilization." The animal kingdom parades before us as in a Trickster's Eden-utopia: pigs, "tigers," dogs, and people mingling happily in the "two or three feet deep" mud (the sow "happy as if she was on salary," the loafers "laugh[ing] at the fun"); and the joke lies in the calamity we humans make of so long life. Clearly, this is the world of the late "dark Twain," the author of *The Damned Human Race* who tells us that his religion is "Calvinism without God," and who, in his Satanic *Letters from the Earth*, explains why man, the lowest of all animals, "is first and last and always a sarcasm."

> Question: What's funny about *Huckleberry Finn*?
> Answer: the teller of this Tall Tale has persuaded us that he's a Comic Writer.

I mean to explore his method of persuasion through three typical jokes. The first is *his* first: Twain familiar opening "Notice to Readers" (p. iv):

> Persons attempting to find a motive in this narrative will be prosecuted; persons attempting to find a

moral in it will be banished; persons attempting to find a plot in it will be shot.

BY ORDER OF THE AUTHOR, Per G.G., Chief of Ordnance

This is a crucial point of the story. It introduces the reader to the text and connects Mark Twain ("THE AUTHOR") with Huck Finn, who has written "this narrative." The deadpan connective, "G.G.," links all the above (narrative, reader, author, and protagonist), and the Notice itself is a directive concerning interpretation. A directive *against* interpretation, to be sure, but a deadpan directive, which therefore requires interpretation. For obviously the Notice is a form of kidding around, a prank of sorts; and then, too, there's a satirical side to it, a subversive laughter in the "order" that ridicules authority. And finally there's the violence alongside and around the subversive tone—think of the penalties for trespassing (prosecution, banishment, death), and the deadly pun that reinforces them: "ordnance" is not (just) a colloquial misspelling; technically it means "cannon or artillery"; a "Chief of Ordnance" is an officer ready to blow you to pieces.

All this makes for an especially funny situation with regard to the act of interpretation. For the narrative itself—the book that's the subject of the directive against interpretation—*demands* interpretation all the time. We can't get any of its jokes without figuring out motive and plot, and we can't possibly do *that* without assuming a moral position. Take even the simplest joke: say, the story that Huck tells Jim about Solomon and the disputed child (pp. 94-96). No reader has failed to laugh at the incident and none can fail to notice that it concerns key structures of the culture-fatherhood, the Bible, schools, and civil authority—which are also key themes of the novel. It's perfectly natural, then, for Huck to "slide" from Solomon to kings in general. He tells Jim about European ex-kings who migrate to America and teach French; he then proceeds to explain why people need to know different languages (humans are different from one another, as dogs are different from pigs, pigs from horses, etc.); and Jim counters by pointing out that all people are alike (all people, universally, are different from dogs, horses, pigs, etc.). If he's a man, Jim declares, "*Well*, den! Dad blame it, why doan he *talk* like a man?" This is a parody of social pretension: Huck, the master of the colloquial style is celebrating the language of the elite, as French then was. And in turn the parody is a sick joke about Southern history: Jim, the victim of chattel-slavery (the example of man-reduced-to-beast-of-burden), is speaking "the language of culture" (Jefferson's language) *in* "the language of sweat" about the self-evident truths of human equality. How can we *not* interpret? And our interpretation is prodded, if we need prodding, by Huck's concluding response: "You can't learn a nigger to argue. So I quit." Huck doesn't see the fun in all this; he's simply frustrated. We do see the fun because we know we're hearing a comic tale (by Mark Twain, humorist); but in order to take that step we have to interpret. In short, we interpret because Huck doesn't.

Now let me recapitulate what's funny about the Notice. There's a joke here that involves us in a contradiction: the official order prohibits interpretation but the narrative demands interpretation. The nub or snapper is that the Notice is *calling attention* to interpretation. It's reminding us of our tendency to look for plot, moral, and motive, and then the narrative itself does the rest of the work: it virtually forces us to interpret. Having recognized that much, we should feel uneasy. There's something funny about this invitation to interpret—it's a Trickster's invitation. What's *his* motive? What's the *plot*?

To begin to explore the issue I turn to my second example, the last joke in the novel. I refer to what is surely Huck's best-known line—his decision to light out for the territory. Our general impression of the scene is that Huck leaves because he seeks freedom: "Aunt Sally she's going to adopt me, and sivilize me, and I can't stand it. I been there before" (p. 362). And no doubt Huck does want his freedom; but there's another layer of meaning in the text:

> . . . then Tom he talked along and talked along, and says, le's all three slide out of here one of these nights and get an outfit, and go for howling adventures amongst the Injuns, over in the territory, for a couple of weeks or two; and I says, all right, that suits me . . . (p. 361)

So Huck decides to light out "ahead of the rest," and the nub is: *he's just kidding around*. He plans to get an "outfit" and leave for a while ("a couple of weeks or two"), which we interpret as the flight to freedom—and then (if we follow critical tradition) we proceed to allegorize it as the freedom of the spirit. Over the past century that allegory has established itself as a staple cultural/counter-cultural icon: Huck Finn, the representative rebel (or rebel representative) hero of human potential and self-definition (and making it) and the open road.

It's a grand flight of interpretation on our part, but there's something funny about it. Our allegory of this child's-prank depends upon a series of exclusions. Consider the deadpan connection in the episode itself between African Americans and Native Americans: Jim "dressed up for howling adventures amongst the Injuns"! It's a joke akin to the Duke and King's, when they parade Jim through town dressed as a "*Sick Arab*—but harmless when not out of his head" (p. 203). Twain's Trickster play here should alert us to the intricate narrative joint we're in. Huck is about to light out from the Phelps for the territory: this liminal moment joins two crucial dimensions of the social body. First, the dimension of space: the "settlements," as defined by the Nword, are being linked to the "territory," as defined by the I-word. Then, there's the dimension of time: "Injun" is a clue to the cultural connections implicit in the novel's double time-frame. The fictional time, the period of Huck's adventures, is the antebellum South, the slavery era; the authorial time was the era of Indian-killing. Between 1876 and 1885, when the novel was written and published, the territories provided the setting for the final wars (under the notorious banner, "the only good Indian is a dead Indian") against the Native Americans.

Huck's "escape to freedom" is a Tall Tale which suggests how much can be excluded or concealed in the act of interpretation. And it suggests further what this kind of exclusion makes room for. I refer to the cultural icon ("lighting out") that draws its force from a powerful set of commonplaces: the notion that "the territory" in the United States means (and always meant) freedom; the familiar interpretations of "open land" as promise, opportunity, and possibility. The nub that ends *Huckleberry Finn* is that interpretation may be a trap of culture. I mean interpretation now in its institutional sense, as a process developed, nourished, and sanctioned by society—the official hermeneutic, as it were, by which we confirm our beliefs in what our culture has taught us to believe, and through which (according to this snapper) we conceal the unsavory realities of history. In this case, the incongruity between those realities (slavery, genocide) and those beliefs (freedom, innocence) is funny: funny enough, in the sinister sense, to provide the *finale* to the greatest deadpan act in the tradition of American humor.

Interpretation may be a trap of culture: Twain's snapper is especially striking in the context of Trickster fun-and-games. I said before, following Lewis Hyde, that the joints of the social body are cultural weak-points. Hyde adds that Tricksters instinctively fasten on those weak-points through strategies of interpretation; their hermenuetics of invention and surprise, of inversion and perversion, is a kind of endless arsenal of cultural resistance. Thus the Trickster becomes for Hyde a figure across time and place, from Greek Hermes to Allen Ginsberg, for the Artist as Subversive. And of course that archetype extends by implication to the discerning critic of Art. The impression it conveys of the powers of interpretation is as familiar as it is comforting. Conversely, Twain's joke about Huck's "flight to freedom" is as discomforting—as shocking and deflating—as it is surprising. The misfit it reveals between the text and the meaning we give it calls attention to the snares of interpretation. Among other things it reminds us that Tricksters steal their weapons of ludic resistance (puns, parodies, inversions) from social institutions—institutions of interpretation which are first and foremost centers of social control. Tricksters know where the status quo is most vulnerable, but so does the dominant culture. Historically, across time and place, the social body has defended itself *precisely at its joints* by means of interpretation. Society works through civic mechanisms and economic networks; culture works through the circulation of meaningful artifacts and stories—symbols, emblems, icons, myths. These constitute the moral and spiritual life-blood of the social body, and its heart is the process of interpretation. Chairman Mao was wrong about the basis of state power. Guns merely force us to submit; interpretation gets us to consent. The effect of a sound cultural heart in a healthy social body is that the body's very joints become a source of strength and revitalization, especially the joints that connect our capacities for creative play with our need for meaning—for purpose, identity, and ideals. Interpretation (so conceived, understood historically, in its institutional context) works by directing that deep and abiding need towards socialization. It turns our world, imaginatively, into a system; it organizes our fantasies and visions in ways that make sense of things as they are; it forges the foundational links between subjectivity and society.

This conservative, cooptive power is what Twain's deadpan compels us to recognize. The joke is aimed not just against ideology, and not just against organized myth. Its target is the adversarial interpreter. Ideology and organized myth are satirized through the figure of Tom Sawyer. That satire has long provided an attractive focus of adversarial criticism, but if we focus on Tom we're being diverted from Twain's deapan point. His joke centers on Huck, and he means by this (by alerting us to our very impulse to focus on Tom) to identify us as adversarial critics—readers for whom interpretation is the road to free and independent thought (the conceptual equivalent for the "open territory")—*within* the institutions from which we claim to light out. We end trapped in the very joints of culture through which we had hoped to escape. It makes for an unnerving shock to the funny-bone, but we owe it to ourselves, and to Twain's art, to account for our laughter.

His snapper has the authority of history behind it. One need only consider the fantastic conservative-cooptive force of the four-fold method of medievalist exegesis, with its levels of meaning ascending in a Jacob's-ladder from earth to heaven, from literal and political to moral and mystical. It is hardly too much to say that for a millennium in the Christian West interpretation thus fortified every social juncture-linked the king's "two bodies" to the relation between men and women, gender dualisms to the metaphysics of mind and body, and that binary in turn to the double visible-spiritual structure of the cosmos. In America, of course (Twain's and ours), the case is altogether different. Officially our interpretative modes are secular, antielitist, based on the separation of church and state, and insofar as the legacy of Christian hermeneutics persists—as indeed it does (that legacy is a major butt of Twain's humor)-it is a Protestant mode: basically individualist, geared towards subjectivity, centered in personal conscience rather than in church tradition and papal bull. But the results are no less binding and systemic. The success of society in the United States is due in no small part to the fact that the culture developed a distinctive network of moral-spiritual meanings (iconic, mythic, symbolic) together with a complex set of interpretive techniques appropriate to the civic institutions and economic modes of *this* society.

Huckleberry Finn is a deadpan exposé of those techniques—an anatomy of the official hermenuetic of nineteenth-century America as this developed from the Jacksonian era through the Gilded Age. As Huck tells the story, the cultural trap of interpretation is most conspicuously marked by conscience. It's conscience that makes him a racist-conscience that leads him astray at every moral juncture—and we interpret his conscience, properly, as an indictment of the values of the antebellum Southwest. But I believe Mark Twain had another culture in mind. There was no need in 1885 to indict slave society. Primarily, Twain's deadpan is directed against his readership, then and later (and perhaps still today). I refer to the conscience-driven forms of American liberal interpretation, and to its particular modes of socialization as these flowered during the last decades of the nineteenth century, the age of "the incorporation of America."[5] No work of art is more revealing of that process. As a Tall Tale, *Huckleberry Finn* draws upon an earlier period, the "free and open" Jacksonian Southwest where the joints of the nation's emergent social body seemed weakest, most vulnerable to the blatant "gap between the culture and sweat found in frontier experiences . . . Indian wars, slave dealing, *herrenvolk* white racial solidarity, endemic violence, economic instability, fluidity, humbuggery, and speculative fantasy." As a Trickster's deadpan, the novel turns the Tall Tale (at our expense) into a commentary on the process by which that gap was made a self-revitalizing source of cultural incorporation.

In my first two examples I tried to outline the scope of Twain's design in this regard. Now to specify his technique (the dynamics of his mock-interpretive nub or snapper), I turn to my third and main example. The passage comes at the end of Huck's adventures on the river. He lands at the Phelps Plantation, where he meets Sally Phelps, who mistakes him for her nephew Tom Sawyer. Huck instinctively goes along with his new identity, but gets confused in accounting for what now turns out to be his late arrival: Tom had been expected by steamboat some time before. Huck at first explains that the boat had been grounded, then can't think of *which* grounding—but I struck an idea, and fetched it out: "It warn't the grounding—that didn't keep us back but a little. We blowed out a cylinder head."

> "Good gracious! anybody hurt?"
>
> "No'm. Killed a nigger."
>
> "Well, it's lucky; because sometimes people do get hurt. Two years ago last Christmas your uncle Silas was coming up from Newrleans on the old Lally Rook, and she blowed out a cylinder head and crippled a man. And I think he died afterwards. He was a Baptist." (p. 279)

Again, we're at a key joint of the narrative. The arrival at the Phelps Plantation unites all three sections of the novel (Hannibal, where Tom figures prominently; the journey down the river; and Huck's adventures at the Phelps); and it connects all three layers of Trickster fun (innocent, satirical, and sinister). It also demonstrates Twain's hermeneutical imperative—we *must* interpret this scene (its humor leaves us no alternative)—while offering a striking example of what's funny about our habits of interpretation. I take the joke to lie in the (in)famous one-liner "No'm. Killed a nigger." We are then diverted from its nub by Aunt Sally's story of the Lally Rook. To recall Twain's instruction: when the joke comes, "the listener must be alert, for . . . the teller will divert attention from the nub by dropping it in a carefully casual or indifferent way, with the pretense that he does not know it is a nub." The Baptist is a decoy; it allows the story to bubble gently along. The nub is encoded in Huck's throwaway line: "No'm. Killed a nigger." In what follows I mean to decode Twain's deadpan by outlining seven points about Huck's response to which we should be alert.

First, his use of "nigger" is profoundly racist. We can't say (as too many critics have done) that it's just slang—a poor ignorant boy's way of saying African American. What Huck *means* is far worse than what a bigot means by "wop" or "mick." Huck is saying that a "nigger" is a *no one* (that's the "joke" in response to the straight-man query, "anybody hurt?"). If we're alert, the negational form ("No'm") serves to *highlight* the positive charge of "Killed," especially because of the pause indicated by the sentence break.

Second, Huck's response is gratuitous. As again we're reminded by the sentence break ("No'm. Killed . . ."), Huck could just as well have stopped at "No'm." And be it noted that that kind of gratuitous remark, in all its racist implications, is typical of Huck. The *casual* N-word is fundamental to his vocabulary. As critics over the past three decades have pointed out, the word "nigger" occurs on virtually every page of the novel; and it's worth emphasizing that it took three generations of readers *before them* to take offense. *Huckleberry Finn* was always controversial, but the first debates centered on issues of class, not race. The complaints had to do with Huck's delinquency, bad habits, and poor grammar. The N-word went unnoticed until the 1960s, and I believe that the not-noticing was basic to Twain's deadpan. Part of the joke is that the word was woven into the very fabric of

Twain's democratic culture. The N-word was at once unexamined and ubiquitous—unexamined because ubiquitous, and ubiquitous because unexamined—and never more so than in the era of Reconstruction, when the minstrel show was the most popular American form of humor. Huck's response is entirely appropriate to him and his readership alike.

It's also appropriate to the plot of the novel. That's the third point to make about Huck's remark. His joke concerns a dead person and death is a main narrative thread-death in the deadpan mode, gilded over by humor. A fair example of the gilding process comes in the early passages concerning Tom's gang:

> Tom got out a sheet of paper that he had wrote the oath on, and read it. It swore every boy to stick to the band, and never tell any of the secrets; and if anybody done anything to any boy in the band, whichever boy was ordered to kill that person . . . must do it . . . And if anybody that belonged to the band told the secrets, he must have his throat cut, and then have his carcass burnt up and the ashes scattered all around, and his name blotted off the list with blood . . . Everybody said it was a real beautiful oath . . .

Some thought it would be good to kill the *families* of boys that told the secrets. Tom said it was a good idea, so he took a pencil and wrote it in. Then Ben Rogers says:

> "Here's Huck Finn, he hain't got no family; what you going to do 'bout him?"
>
> "Well, hain't he got a father?" says Tom Sawyer.
>
> "Yes, he's got a father, but you can't never find him these days. He used to lay drunk with the

hogs in the tanyard, but he hain't been seen in these parts for a year or more."

They talked it over, and they was going to rule me out, because they said every boy must have a family or somebody to kill, or else it wouldn't be fair and square for the others. Well nobody could think of anything to do—everybody was stumped, and set still. I was most ready to cry; but all at once, I thought of a way, and so I offered them Miss Watson—they could kill her. Everybody said:

"Oh, she'll do. That's all fight. Huck can come in." (pp. 9-10)

This is funny, although not to Huck (he's "most ready to cry"). It's Tom who's having fun, along with us. But Twain the Trickster has a different point in mind. And (as in the case of Huck's response to Aunt Sally) his point is rather obvious once we're on to his method. Indeed, it's a point that's basic to deadpan technique, as Twain describes it: the humor "depends for its effect upon the *manner* of the telling . . . [as distinct from] the *matter*." Once we look as it were through the narrative manner to its matter the snapper to the gang-oath is as plain as the ubiquity of the N-word. Death and violence are writ large throughout the novel. The blood-bond that Tom invents is a mirror-reflection of the world of *Huckleberry Finn*. It foreshadows the death-hoax that Huck invents when he leaves for the river ("I pulled out some of my hair, and blooded the ax good" and made a track so that they'd look "to find the robbers that killed me") and the horrific scene earlier, when his blind-drunk father chases him around the shack with a "clasp knife," cursing and roaring (and laughing with "*such* a screechy laugh") that Huck is the Angel of Death, "saying he would kill me and then I couldn't come for him no more" (pp. 41, 36). These fantasies come to life, as it were, in the Boggs murder, in scenes of lynching and tar-and-feathering, in the Grangerford-Shepherdson clan massacre. According to Twain scholars, there are thirty-three corpses in *Huckleberry Finn*, and that does not include the section Twain omitted, surely one of the most vivid and most morbid he ever wrote, describing Pap's dead body. It's not too much to say that dead bodies, real and imagined, are the anatomical links of Huck's story. It's appropriate that G.G.'s "ordnance" (the Notice authorized by a Chief of Cannon and Artillery) should warn that anyone seeking a plot would be shot. Getting killed is a key to the novel's plot-line.

The fourth point to make about Huck's "joke" concerns the cause of death. On the river he travels, explosions are a common experience. Aunt Sally confirms this in the case of the poor Baptist, and we can find many other examples in the novel (steamboats grounded, blown up, cutting rafts in two). The point is: this river is dangerous. Critics have tended to sentimentalize the "natural setting" in *Huckleberry Finn* ("the rivergod" called the Mississippi), and to be sure the sentiment is invited by its comic author. But Twain the Trickster makes it plain that the river is a constant threat. "Nature," Satan reports in *Letters from the Earth*, "is a killer,"[6] and *Huckleberry Finn* might have been his proof-text. The river here is the source of storms and water-snakes; it calls up the fog that keeps Huck and Jim from reaching Cairo; its currents and counter-currents, twists and turns, carry the raft ever deeper into slave territory; it is ubiquitously "troublesome" to those who live in its vicinity:

> the houses was sticking out over the bank, and they was bowed and bent, and about ready to tumble in . . . People lived in them yet, but it was dangersome, because sometimes a strip of land as wide as a house caves in at a time. Sometimes a belt of land a quarter of a mile deep will start in and cave along till it all caves into the river in one summer . . . the river's always gnawing at it. (p. 183)

This river affords Huck and Jim some wonderful moments together; and to underscore their "idyll" critics have often quoted Huck's description of life on the raft: "what you want, above all things, on a raft, is for everybody to be satisfied, and feel right and kind towards the others" (p. 165). But the interpreters have generally failed to add that that's how Huck *rationalizes* allowing the King and Duke to have their way ("it warn't no use to tell Jim")—and they have generally failed to note that *for much of the river journey* (more than half of it) life on the raft is controlled and directed by those "scoundrels" (as Huck charitably calls them [p. 268]).[7] Huck and Jim may be in flight on the Mississippi, but the Mississippi is the natural habitat of the Duke and King, just as it is naturally the cause of mud-slides. In this book the river is emphatically not an emblem of Nature's Nation; it belongs to the world of Hobbes and Darwin, not of Rousseau and Emerson. Nothing is more natural about Huck, nothing more clearly shows how close he is to the river, than does his spontaneous invention of the exploding cylinder that (only) "Killed a nigger."

Not that Huck needs the river to prompt his invention; he always thinks in terms of death and disaster. That's the fifth point to note about Huck's casual response. It alerts us to the fact that he's a morbid, haunted young boy. I'm referring now to the general way he thinks and imagines rather than to his particular experiences. Twain provides two clues to Huck's inner world: the lies that Huck tells and the images that he conjures up when he's alone—in other words, the reality that Huck himself makes up, for others and for himself. In both cases, it's the reality of the grotesque. The stories he invents for strangers are a series of horror-tales: families dead, dying, or diseased. And his solitary musings take exactly the same form, except that the dead return as ghosts. One such moment occurs on his arrival at the Phelps Plantation:

> When I got there it was all still and Sunday-like, and hot and sunshiny; the hands was gone to the fields; and there was them kind of faint dronings of bugs and flies in the air that makes it seem so lonesome and like everybody's dead and gone; and if a breeze fans along and quivers the leaves it makes you feel mournful, because you feel like it's spirits whispering—spirits that's been dead ever so many years—and you always think they're talking about *you*. As a general thing it makes a body wish *he* was dead, too, and done with it all. (p. 276)

What's funny about this description—in both the fun sense of the term and in its "odd or curious" implication—is that actually it's a lovely Sunday morning; there's no reason for Huck to think this way, except that that's the way he thinks. One more example must suffice. I take this from the first chapter, Huck alone in his room at night, conjuring up the world out there in what may be read as an introduction to his general angle of vision:

> I went up to my room with a piece of candle, and put it on the table. Then I set down in a chair by the window and tried to think of something cheerful, but it warn't no use. I felt so lonesome I most wished I was dead. The stars were shining, and the leaves rustled in the woods ever so mournful; and I heard an owl, away off, who-whooing about somebody that was dead, and a whippo-will and a dog crying about somebody that was going to die; and the wind was trying to whisper something to me, and I couldn't make out what it was, and so it made the cold shivers run over me. (p. 4.)

What I termed Huck's casual response—his spontaneous invention of a dead person (or non-person)—is in fact perfectly characteristic, a typical product of his "mournful" fantasy life.

But of course it's not pure fantasy when he invents the cylinder explosion; this time Huck is not alone; on the contrary, he's trying hard to please someone else. He's being led on by Aunt Sally, who prods him about the grounding. He knows what she'd like to hear, and he knows she'll think a "nigger" is "no one," just as he knows she wants him to be like Tom. And naturally he complies. That's the sixth point to note about his response. Huck *wants* to conform. More precisely, he's a conformist who can't make it. Huck would like to please everyone, even Miss Watson. He would even like to live with Pap, if Pap would let him live; he tries as best he can to "satisfy" the Duke and King; he'd certainly like to join the Grangerfords (at the expense of abandoning Jim) and no doubt the Phelps as well; and he'd *love* to be Tom Sawyer—but he can't. Huck Finn is Woody Allen's Zelig in reverse: a deadpan artist's Zelig. Zelig may not want to be a Chinese chef or a Nazi, but he can't help becoming just like whoever he's with. Huck's dilemma is just the opposite: he can't help being different. Certainly, we sympathize with his difference, we applaud it, but the nub remains. Huck's desire to fit in is underscored by his inability to do so. And he wants to fit in because he believes in society and its values. He believes in racism, class hierarchy, Southern aristocracy, Sunday School religion. Why else would he be so disappointed in Tom's plan to "steal" Jim?

Well, one thing was dead sure, and that was that Tom Sawyer was in earnest, and was actuly going to help steal that nigger out of slavery. That was the thing that was too many for me. Here was a boy that was respectable and well brung up; and had a character to lose; and folks at home that had characters; and he was bright and not leather-headed; and knowing and not ignorant; and not mean, but kind; and yet here he was, without any more pride, or rightness, or feeling, than to stoop to this business, and make himself a shame, and his family a shame, before everybody. I *couldn't* understand it no way at all. It was outrageous. (pp. 292-293)

If this were a children's book called *Tom Sawyer*, we could read this passage as a healthy piece of social satire. The white-trash boy is at once denouncing (when he shouldn't) and looking up to (when he needn't) the respectable head-of-the-gang. But *Huckleberry Finn* is something else altogether (as Huck himself notes at the start): it's a complex, sophisticated narrative about a black-white relationship—to recall Twain's phrase, a work "of high and delicate art . . . [as] only an artist can tell it"—in which an African American takes on extraordinary human force. Jim, we learn, is the noblest person in Huck's life, the novel's wisest, deepest, and most sympathetic adult figure, the father Huck deserves and never had. Can it be funny that Huck thinks like *this* after their long experience together on the river? After all he has seen of Jim—having actually acknowledged, however reluctantly, Jim's goodness, intelligence (he "was most always right") and caring (he'd "do everything he could think of for me")—can he believe that it would be "ignorant," "leather-headed," and "mean" for Tom to "stoop to this business"(p. 270)?

In order to explain this nub we need to rehearse its context. The last narrative section (the Phelps adventures, occupying about a third of the novel) has become a familiar critical crux. Twain scholars have debated its merits ever since Hemingway advised readers to skip it altogether. Tom's tricks at the Phelps's place amount to a series of minstrel-show send-ups: Jim locked in a wood-shack, following the silly-cruel instructions of a couple of adolescent pranksters, who "smuggle" spiders into the shack, instruct him to write messages in blood, and feed him a corn pone with a candlestick hidden in it ("it most mashed all his teeth out"). "Jim he couldn't make no sense in most of it,"

Huck comments, "but he allowed we was white folks and knowed better than him; so he was satisfied" (p. 309). Tom's higher knowledge in this case comes from the romances of Alexandre Dumas; he names his scheme the Great Evasion; and the joke, it turns out, is that Jim has already been freed. Miss Watson (who earlier had intended to sell him down the river for $800) set him free on her death-bed (after his escape), so that Tom's games are a hoax, as *in effect* were Huck's efforts all along to help Jim escape. If we carry the logic of this hoax to its absurd end, we could say Jim was *lucky* he didn't get to Cairo and the North, since he would then never have known he was a free man.

Evidently Tom's games did amuse the minstrel-show audience of the 1880s and 1890s, but by the 1920s (as Hemingway's remark indicates) they had become troublesome for readers, and over the past half century critics have roundly denounced them and all that they imply. It's now safe to say (T. S. Eliot and Lionel Trilling to the contrary notwithstanding) that the last third section of *Huckleberry Finn* is a grand sarcasm on Twain's part directed against Tom Sawyer. But it's essential to recognize that this is a Trickster's sarcasm. The satire of the Good Bad Boy (whose mischiefby-the-book we see through and, accordingly, to whom we feel superior) is a Great Evasion to divert us from the nub. What's really funny about the hoax is that Huck goes along with it. He has the same respect for Tom at the end that he does at the start. Fundamentally, "Tom Sawyer's Comrade" (as the novel's subtitle funnily puts it) *is* the same Huck at the end that he was before he set out on his adventures. That's what makes it appropriate for him to respond to Aunt Sally as he does, in spite of all he has learned about Jim. Or rather, *because* of all he has *not* learned, for (as his gratuitous "No'm" should remind us) Huck never develops. He speaks and thinks and feels at the Phelps's pretty much as he does at Miss Watson's. There's a technical reason for this:

Huckleberry Finn is Huck's autobiographical retrospective, and if he had realized what we'd like him to have realized—if his Devil's Pact on the river had had any enduring positive value; if it had come to signal a genuine conversion *to* Jim's humanity, rather than just one more confirmation of his own fatalistic low self-esteem (his sense of being damned anyway, in a wonderfully grim-funny display of what Twain meant by "Calvinism without God")—then Huck would have written an entirely different book. He would have felt differently not only about Jim but about Tom and all others, including himself. The boy who might have emerged as critics have told us he did would never have said early in his river-journey that "you can't learn a nigger to argue"; he would have expressed *some* regret about having abandoned Jim to live with the Grangerfords; and certainly he would not have expected Jim to join him and Tom in the territory. That is to say, if Huck Finn had really grown morally, Twain the Trickster could not gull us into thinking that he does. There would be no point or snapper to his story. Humorously speaking, his Tall Tale would be un-American.

Huck doesn't develop so that we can be conned into believing he does: in this case, there's something funny about the nub itself. The joke suggests it's a good thing that Huck doesn't change. It reminds us that what we believe in ultimately is Huck's integrity. He has the same fantastic innocence from start to finish. He's always the same lovable boy with the "sound heart"; from the outset his innate decency is set in contrast to society's "deformed conscience"; we come to see in Huck a kind of essentialist Romantic-natural opposition to "sivilization." What's *funny* here (in the con man sense of the term) is that it's Huck's unchanging quality which makes him admirable. And to draw out this con game, it's precisely that admirable aspect of him—the potential we discern *within* Huck's transparent innocence—which invites us to interpret his narrative. As I noted earlier, Twain's hermeneutical imperative turns on the snapper that we engage in interpretation because our hero Huck doesn't. Which is to say: Huck doesn't develop, therefore we do it for him. We know him better than he knows himself. Indeed, we know him as he *cannot* know himself, since his naiveté, his *unfulfilled* potential, *is* what we know about him, and what we cherish.

The deadpan this involves posits two contrary responses on our part: first, our distance from Huck and our superiority to him; and second, our love of Huck and our identification with him. The link between these responses—the joke's nub—lies in Twain's directive for interpretation. I said earlier that the deadpan Notice invites us to seek moral, motive, and plot; the Trickster's point is to guide us into a certain mode of exegesis. We might call it a comic mode in the classic sense of the term. Its purpose is to resolve contradiction and restore order. The snapper this entails is dramatically illustrated in the scene that critics have rendered the *locus classicus* of Huck's moral progress. It comes at the point when Huck learns that the Duke and the King have disclosed Jim's whereabouts. Dismayed that Jim may be "sold down the river . . . amongst strangers," Huck decides it would be preferable to return him instead to Miss Watson, "his true and proper owner," so that he can "be a slave at home where his family was." Then Huck succumbs to conscience-stricken memories of how he himself has been responsible, directly or indirectly, for helping this "runaway nigger":

> I tried the best I could to kinder soften it up somehow for myself by saying I was brung up wicked, and so I warn't much to blame: but something inside of me kept saying, "There was the Sunday school, you could a' gone to it; and if you'd 'a done it they'd a' learn't you there that people that acts as I'd been acting about that nigger goes to everlasting fire."

It made me shiver. And I about made up my mind to pray, and see if I couldn't try to quit being the kind of a boy I was and be better. So I kneeled down. But the words wouldn't come . . . You can't pray a lie—I found that out . . . At last I had an idea: and I says, I'll go and write the letter—and then see if I can pray . . . So I got a piece of paper and a pencil, all glad and excited, and set down, and wrote:

> Miss Watson, your runaway nigger Jim is down here two mile below Pikesville, and Mr. Phelps has got him and he will give him up for the reward if you send.
>
> **HUCK FINN**

I felt good and all washed clean of sin for the first time I had ever felt so in my life, and I knowed I could pray now. But I didn't do it straight off, but laid the paper down and set there thinking . . . [and went on thinking] and then I happened to look around and see that paper.

It was a close place. I took it up, and held it in my hand. I was a-trembling. . . . I studied a minute, . . . and then says to myself:

"All right then, I'll go to hell"—and tore it up.

It was awful thoughts and awful words, but they was said. And I let them stay said and never thought no more about reformin. . . . (pp. 269-271)

What's funny about this scene is that it's: (1) playful—it's a mock-conversion that turns into a Devil's Pact; (2) satirical—it's a sweeping indictment of the ravages of Southern Evangelical Calvinism; and (3) odd, curious, and sinister—it's a savage mockery of our relation to the text. For in order to "get the joke" we *have* to interpret and yet we feel sure that our interpretation is voluntary; the meaning we find seems wholly subjective, a meaning "from the heart," and yet it's entirely predictable, a meaning directed step by step by Trickster deadpan. To begin with, we're led to interpret in a *consistent* pattern of inversions. Huck says "conscience" meaning the Right Thing to Do, and we think "source of evil"; he says "wicked" and we think "kind"; Huck laments that he was "brung up wrong" and we're glad that he has held fast to his virtues; he tells us he shivered with fear and we think he's brave and independent; he says, trembling, "I'll go to hell" and we think "he's saved!" This pattern of inversion is an act of protection. That's the second step of interpretation. Whether or not we're aware of it, we're reading between the lines in order to save the "true" Huck from everyone around him, from Tom and Miss Watson and the Grangerfords and the Phelps family. And our act of protection is in turn a claim to ownership. This third and triumphant final step of interpretation makes Huck *ours*. The opening gang-oath is worth recalling in this regard. The question that Tom raises about family hostages expands into a much larger question: to whom does Huck belong? The narrative plays out a series of options—Pap, Tom's gang, Jim—until it becomes obvious (or should) that Huck finally belongs only to *us*. We adopt him, take him into *our* True American family, into our hearts; we interpret him into our likeness; hermeneutically, we recreate Huck as the child-in-us.

Now, all of this (to repeat) is predictable, an interpretive design forced upon by the humor itself. That is, it's a design carefully elicited from us—with all the Trickster's "casual" airs and sly diversions (just "bubbling along")—by Mark Twain, Humorist.

Let us consider the snappers hidden in this narrative situation. First, there's the issue of "manner" (Twain's key to the deadpan relation between form and content):

Huck Finn is a great writer; his grammar and spelling are faulty, but that only accentuates the beauty of his style, which is extraordinarily simple, spontaneous, and open. And yet we have to protect him all the time from his own text. We have to explain away his words, to redefine the emotions he records, to reverse the convictions he sets out. Huck is a master of the literal statement; he writes with unfailing directness, lucidity, and vivid effect; he's the prime example (as Hemingway noted) of the American plain style. And yet we have to save Huck at every turn from his own plain meanings. We have no choice, as it were, but to recast "shiver" (when Huck says "it made me shiver") into *something* positive, to deny the import *for Huck* (the stated effect) of his decision to choose damnation, to white out not only his numerous N-words but the "no one" by which he glosses the word, at the Phelps's and elsewhere. Once we've done all that, we can laugh along *with* Huck, *our* Huck, the uncorrupted child in us who (we're certain) does *not* believe, would never *really* think, that "you can't learn a nigger to argue." To paraphrase Jim: we're sophisticated folks, and so we know better, and can smile contentedly and be satisfied.

Still, we should be suspicious by this point about the process we're engaged in. Our interpretation has led us step by logical step from protection to adoption to identification; and at the end our laughter expresses the child-in-us—who is *us*? The answer, I've suggested, is the liberal white reader of 1885, and beyond. For the term "liberal white" here refers to a social-symbolic system, an official hermeneutic, an institution of interpretation designed to fortify a certain way of life. "Liberal" so understood is a code word that can stretch to accommodate a wide range of positions, from (say) communitarian to libertarian, from left Democrat to right Republican. And "white" in this configuration can stretch accordingly to include a liberal rainbow-gamut of colors (black, brown, red, yellow). *Huckleberry Finn* has always been controversial, and many case-books have documented the polemical zigzags evident in its reception. Nevertheless, a consistent liberal theme dominates the discourse, a critical main-current that runs through virtually all sides of the argument (provided that the critic does not dogmatically, illiberally, condemn the book for being merely trashy or utterly racist). I refer to what Jonathan Arac has recently labeled the "hypercanonization" of Huck Finn. To judge from a century of Twain experts, Huck is "the individual in nature," "independent," "self-reliant," "the spirit of youth," "the spirit of adventure and expansion," the soul of "mobility," "enterprise," "unboundedness," and "exploration." More than that: Huck and Jim on the raft have been taken as a kind of communitarian utopia, the emblem of the "ideal society." In contrast to the restrictive possibilities associated with settlements, together they are seen represent the "spiritual values" of "voluntary association," "personal freedom" in a context of "true brotherhood," "responsibility and equality entwined." Critics have applied these abstractions as universals, but clearly they are universals within a distinctive historical frame, a configuration of beliefs and ideals that make up a singular cultural vision. As Norman Podhoretz, editor of the neo-conservative journal *Commentary*, has written: "Sooner or later, all discussions of *Huckleberry Finn* turn into discussions of America." Or in the words of the late Irving Howe, writing in his left-wing journal *Dissent*, "Huck is not only the most American boy in our own literature, he is also the character with whom most American readers have most deeply identified." Or once again, in the words of the Americanist scholar Eric Sundquist: *Huckleberry Finn* is "an autobiographical journey into the past" that tells "the story of a nation."[5]

Twain's Trickster humor stands out brilliantly *against* the background of this liberal consensus-in-dissent. The nub or snapper of our interpretation of *Huckleberry Fin-* both of the narrative and of its "autobiographical" hero—

is that what begins as our subjective assessment, and often our oppositional perspective (against "sivilization"), leads us happily, inexorably, *into* the institutions of culture. Thus it was all but inevitable that in our multicultural era, Huck should be discovered to be (in addition to everything else that's now identified as positively American) multicultural. This is not the place to discuss Huck's "blackness," but it's pertinent here as elsewhere to recall Twain's warning that interpretation may be a trap of culture. *Huckleberry Finn* is a journey into deadpan, towards a devastating nub. The plot is a river-story, the style is a flow of humor, and our interpretation is a raft that promises protection (from conscience, from Tom's games, from social enslavement, from racism and ethnocentrism, from all the slings and arrows of outrageous adulthood). But the river keeps returning us again and again to the settlements, the raft proves to be a very insecure haven, and on this "raft of trouble," on this river that betrays (and kills), we're left with two mock-symbolic figures. One is Huck Finn, bond-slave to society, mostly scared to death, speaking a language we don't trust, and (as Pap puts it, in his one drunken flash of insight) an Angel of Death. The other is Jim, the fugitive Black who need never have run off, who leads Huck into a Devil's Pact, and who, in doing so, ironically enacts his own version of the official hermeneutic: "Dey's two angels hoverin' round 'bout [every person]. One uv 'em is white en shiny, en t'other one is black. De white one gits him to go right a little while, den de black one sail in en bust it all up. A body can't tell yit which one gwyne to fetch him at the las'" (p. 27). So the nub is: the Angel of Death and the Black Angel, on a Trickster's raft-to-freedom, drifting deeper and deeper into slaveterritory. It makes for a savagely funny obituary to the American-myth.

I mean *funny* now in the manner of the late Twain, the comic nihilist who wrote that "only laughter can blow history to rags and tatters at a blast," the "laughing mortician" (as one of his heirs, Nathanael West, put it) who felt "quite sure that (bar one) I have no race prejudices nor color prejudices nor creed prejudices. Indeed I know it. I can stand any society. All that I care to know is that man is a human being-that is enough for me—he can't be any worse." For that deadpan artist, humor was a systematic exposé of the abstractions that held together what looked like an enlightened view of history. He states the rules of the game in "How To Tell A Story," and he shows how they work explicitly (exposes the nub itself) in *The Mysterious Stranger*. Here Satan, the divine Trickster, pairs up with a poor-white, innocent, sound-hearted little boy, a boy not unlike Huck—befiends him and conjures up for him a variety of alluring spectacles and promises, only to reveal, at the end, the absurdity of each one of them. "You perceive *now*," Satan declares, that it "is all a Dream, a grotesque and foolish dream." And then the boy's epiphany: "He vanished, and left me appalled; for I knew, and realized, that all that he had said was true."[9] That's the "humorous" *terminus ad quem* of *Huckleberry Finn*, the seventh and bleakest nub of the joke I've been discussing. "No'm. Killed a nigger" foreshadows the appalling post-snapper insight reserved for all enlightened close readers, those of us who finally "get it"-those who see (*through* the innocent fun and the social satire) the savagery of this most American of all Tall Tales. The exhilerating flight to freedom we'd marvelled at-black and white together, the individual regenerated by nature—was all a dream, a grotesque and foolish dream. Then, if we have the integrity, we may venture to laugh at ourselves for having been caught in the cultural hermeneutic by which we've remade Huck, laughingly, as *ours*.

Where does that leave the problem of interpretation? At best, I think, at the ethical juncture which Emmanuel Levinas describes as the connective between self and Other.[10] *Huckleberry Finn* leads us into something like an absurdist impasse—we must interpret (to get the joke), but we can't interpret (without making a joke of ourselves)—a comic position that leaves us without the traditional sustaining devices of comedy: bereft of the social norms embedded in satire, devoid of the moral or philosophical alternatives implicit in irony and parody, stripped even of the immemorial "liberating magic" of the folk-tale [11] (the deadpan exposes liberation in this sense as the storyteller's magic *trick*). What remains, then, is the sheer volatility of the fun that Twain sets loose in this novel. Considered as a Trickster's monologue, Huck's story has a certain brilliantlycontrolled authorial point-to-it-all; as humor, however, its layers of meaning are not only different but contradictory—cheerful, satiric, sinister—and yet they coexist, interpenetrate, modify, and undermine one another. I've called them layers to distinguish the relationship between them from what we traditionally mean by levels of meaning. Levels usually lead to a unifying, bottom-line interpretation, as in the medieval fourfold method, or in our deep interpretation of Huck's innocence (or his radicalism or his multicultural representativeness). By contrast, layers of meaning are mobile, shift shape like a kaleidoscope. It depends which way you turn them; and they are by definition always subject to another turn or series of turns. Thus what's funny about West's image of the laughing mortician (or about my my description of *Huckleberry Finn* as a "savagely funny obituary") is that "mortician" (like "obituary") is apocalyptic, the mark of an ending, whereas to laugh at something "funny" signals a different perspective on the matter: the possibility of another, different, and/or contradictory layer of interpretation.

That comic perspective follows from the *intentionality* of humor in *Huckleberry Finn* (as distinct from Mark Twain's intention), and it turns our laughter against any form of systemic, bottom-line interpretation, *including deadpan*. For of course deadpan is itself a model of the systemic. We're asked to get the snapper, *the* realization that explains (even as it undoes) everything that has come before. So the Levinasian joke (if 1 may call it so) is that the humor of *Huckleberry Finn* undoes the deadpan. Twain's nubs and snappers remain the key to the fantastic artistry by which he takes us in; with which he then guides us, if we're alert, to perceive the traps of culture, and through which he offers us the opportunity to have a good laugh at ourselves, good enough perhaps to blow history to rags and tatters. However, those nubs and snappers are dependent on the extraordinary creative power of Huck's story-telling. They leave us, that is, within the world of Huck's monologue—a world where Huck is alive and well, buoyant, on the go, enhanced (for us) by the satire we see *through* his straight-faced observations and nourished by the cheerful flow of jokes by which Twain ensnares us into wonder and belief. The dynamic this entails may be pictured as continuous, fluctuating, myth-making/myth-mocking negotiation between perceptions that tear meaning apart and protective revisions that build up meaning. It yields up a Huck we can't really know because we can't fix into categories: a Huck who's neither merely what he says he is nor merely a version of the American Boy we project nor (again) merely the butt of a Trickster's deadpan; who's therefore at least partly beyond our understanding or control, but to whose subjectivity we respond even though he's not *ours*—even though he gets us to laugh at our very urge to appropriate him. So interpreted, what's "finally" funny about *Huckleberry Finn* is that this Trickster's savage obituary to the traps of culture turns out to be a lifebuoy (a coffin-lifebuoy) keeping us in sight of the possibilities of an ethical life.

NOTES

1. Mark Twain, "How To Tell A Story" (1897), in *How To Tell A Story and Other Essays*, ed. Shelley Fisher Fishkind (Oxford University Press: New York, 1966), pp. 3-4.
2. Hilton Manfred Obenzinger, *American Palestine: Melville, Twain, and the Holy Land Mania*, forthcoming from

Princeton University Press, 1999. I take this to be not an argument for American exceptionalism but a picture of certain distinctive conditions in the unruly formation of a certain modern culture.

3. Lewis Hyde, *Trickster Makes This World* (Farrar, Straus and Giroux: New York, 1998).

4. Mark Twain, *Adventures of Huckleberry Finn*, ed. Walter Blair and Victor Fischer (University of California Press: Berkeley, 1988), pp. 183, 179 [page numbers indicated in the present essay all refer to this edition]; *The Damned Human Race*, ed. Janet Smith (Hill and Wang: New York, 1962), p. 62; and *Letters from the Earth*, ed. Benard DeVoto (New York: Harper and Row, 1962), p. 7.

5. Alan Trachtenberg, *The Incorporation of America* (New York: Hill and Wang, 1982), passim.

6. Mark Twain, *Letters from the Earth*, p. 6.

7. Huck and Jim spend eleven days together on the raft (chapters 11-16 and 18); the Duke and the Ying invade the raft in chapter 19 and remain for at least fifteen days—until chapter 31, when the raft lands at the Phelps Plantation.

8. Jonathan Arac, *Huckleberry Finn as Idol and Target* (University of Wisconsin Press: Madison, 1997), p. 3. For critical comments on Huck see Arac, passim, and the essays collected in Gerald Graff and James Phelan, *Mark Twain, Adventures of Huckleberry Finn: A Case Study in Critical Controversy* (Bedford Books: Boston, 1995).

9. Nathanael West, *Novels and Other Writings*, ed. Sacvan Bercovitch (Library of America: New York, 1997), p. 770; Mark Twain, "Concerning the Jews," in *Mark Twain: Collected Tales, Sketches, and Essays*, ed. Louis J. Budd (Library of America: New York, 1992), p. 355; and *The Mysterious Stranger*, ed. William M. Gibson (University of California Press: Berkeley, 1969), p. 405.

10. On the issue of ethics and aesthetics from this perspective, see for example *Otherwise Than Being, or Beyond Essence*,

trans. Alphonso Lingis (Martinez Nijhoff: The Hague, 1981), pp. 199 ff.

11. Walter Benjamin, "The Storyteller," in *Illuminations. Essays and Reflections*, ed. Hannah Arendt , trans. Harry Zohn (Schocken: New York, 1969), p. 102; that magic, writes Benjamin, leads back to "the earliest arrangements that mankind made to shake off the nightmare which history had placed upon its chest." Twain's distinctive use of deadpan is highlighted by comparison with the techniques of the Russian skaz: see for example Mikhail Bakhtin, *Problems of Dostoevsky's Poetics*, trans. R. W. Rotsel (Ardis: New York, 1973), pp. 153-163 (the three types of skaz that are defined here correspond provocatively to the three layers of "funny" I describe) and Donald Fanger's analysis of the skaz as a send-up of its readers (a monologue that "parodically mirrors the larger text of which it is a part," so that in laughing at the townspeople who listen to the story we laugh at "our own proxies") in *The Creation of Nikolai Gogol* (Harvard University Press: Cambridge, MA, 1979), pp. 102 ff., 178. Still another rich source of comparison (and contrast) in this respect would be Huck Finn vis-àvis the great monologue-figures of Sholem Aleichem.

11

Tom Sawyer's Games of Death

—Harold Aspiz

The Adventures of Tom Sawyer is constructed on a loose framework whose major elements include games of death and games of resurrection. (Both meanings of resurrection apply here: resurrection as grave robbing and resurrection as return to life from apparent death.) Indeed, the world of Tom Sawyer—Mark Twain's remembered and reinvented world of childhood—appears to be piquant and sweet largely because it is seen in chiaroscuro—a bright world set off by the shadowy terrors of danger, death and conformity. Young Tom—and obliquely through him the self-recreated young Sam Clemens—seems to exist on the manic edge beyond which lurks the menace of destruction and the unknown. Tom is a manchild continually living at risk in this child's world where the adults often appear to be custom-bound conformists with whom Tom has no quarrel provided they do not threaten him or interfere too much with the hijinks he shares with his juvenile companions. Inevitably, however, he is nourished by the values of this adult world.[1]

Young Tom is no budding John Keats, but his romantic soul is titillated by the bittersweet thought of his own death. Twain delightfully captures those emotional moments in a child's life when the thought of one's own demise seems to loom like a dark cloud - moments upon which the adult self may look back in bemused fascination. And true romantic that he is, Tom relishes these moments. On the Saturday evening following his triumphant ploy in persuading his young friends to whitewash his Aunt Polly's fence and his subsequent feeling "that it was not such a hollow world, after all," he becomes depressed and sulky because his aunt has wrongfully blamed him rather than his pampered kid brother Sid for breaking a cookie jar.[2] Recognizing her look of tearful contrition when she realizes her error, Tom bolsters his male ego by playing a consoling and satisfying game of death, imagining that he is "lying sick unto death" and not speaking a word to his grieving and repentant aunt. "Ah, how would she feel then?" he fantasizes. To vary the fantasy, he also imagines that he has been brought home after he has drowned in the river, "a poor little sufferer, whose griefs were at an end," and imagines that his grief-stricken aunt lies ill, broken with anguish over her mistreatment of him. So satisfying is this game of nursing his self-mourning that rather than risking its disruption by cheerful thoughts he runs off (like a nineteenth-century romantic poet cultivating his Waldeinsamkeit) to be alone with his tremors of mortality. This "agony of pleasurable" suffering is augmented when he imagines that Becky Thatcher (the pretty classmate on whom he has developed a crush) is grieving for him (pp. 54-55).

But the outside world proves less satisfying than his private fantasies. Tom's euphoria of pleasurable grief is dispelled when, standing under the window of his "adored Unknown," he is doused by a "deluge of water" thrown from the beloved's second story window by the Thatcher housemaid (pp. 55-56). On the blue Monday following an exciting weekend, and in a ruse to ditch school, Tom again pretends to be dying, upsetting his brother Sid and his

Aunt Polly, but he backs off when the old lady threatens to pull one of his loose teeth (pp. 71-73). Later, surreptitiously playing with a tick at school, he taunts his buddy Joe Harper with the prospect of his own death: "He's my tick and I'll do what I blame please with him, or die" (p. 82). Still later that day, disappointed over his estrangement with Becky Thatcher, he again reverts to the game of imagining himself dead, so that she will be sorry for cruelly spurning him: "Ah, if he could only die, temporarily," he is supposed to have thought (p. 87), thus sounding the keynote for the sort of resurrection game that the author will twice develop and dramatize in the course of the novel to form its most exciting episodes and which he, Twain, will one day introduce into his autobiography, imagining himself enjoying a post mortem tete-a-tete with his future readers long after his own death.

At midnight of that same Monday—to the ominous sounds of a cricket and a deathwatch beetle - Tom sneaks out of the house and goes with Huck Finn to the decaying Baptist graveyard. Frightened to be among the spirits of the dead, they watch in terror as three would-be resurrectionists—Dr. Robinson, Injun Joe, and Muff Potter (respectively a young physician, an arch-villain, and a slow-witted drunkard)—prepare to snatch the body of Horse Williams from its grave. In the darkness, Injun Joe picks a quarrel with Dr. Robinson and murders him, then puts the blame on Muff Potter (pp. 92-97). Thus the game of death that had been enjoyable as long as Tom could invent his own scenario with himself as the imaginary tragic hero turns horrifying and grim when objectified in the "real" world. And Tom's sense of guilt for hiding the fact that Muff Potter is innocent of Dr. Robinson's death, suppressed because of his fear of Injun Joe, almost devours him during the following weeks as he internalizes what he has witnessed. By way of contrast, his schoolmates, playing a pleasant childhood game of death, hold mock "inquests on dead cats" (p. 108).

The episode of grave robbery, of course, is the stuff of melodrama and, as Walter Blair suggests, Mark Twain may have borrowed the incident from Dickens's A Tale of Two Cities wherein a lad gets out of bed at night, goes to a graveyard, and sees three men rob a grave. In Our Mutual Friend, a book that Twain knew well, Dickens had used the theme of body snatching as both horror and comedy. But one might wonder why, unless Dr. Robinson was engaged in a little extracurricular anatomizing, the grave robbery occurs in the area of St. Petersburg, for no such incident is known to have happened in Hannibal, and there was no medical college closer than St. Louis.[3] In fact, Mark Twain recorded the information that a close relative of his, Jim Lampton, had attended the Missouri Medical College in St. Louis, whose chief, Dr. Joseph Nash McDowell, like the directors of so many medical schools, apparently procured corpses for dissection from suspect sources.[4] Throughout the last century, the stealing of corpses was a common source of bodies for dissection. Before the English Parliament passed the Anatomy Act in 1832, grave robbery was almost the universal source of corpses for medical research in Great Britain.[5] Similarly, as the supply of bodies of dead paupers and prisoners became inadequate to meet the needs of medical students in the American Midwest, three-man crews of grave robbers, usually working stealthily and rapidly by night, and accurately represented in the novel's grave-robbing scene, procured and delivered freshly disinterred corpses to anatomists before putrefaction set in. Favorite targets were village cemeteries located not far from a medical school.[6]

When paupers' graves could not be found, the robbers—frequently members of criminal gangs - looted the graves of respectable citizens (like the novel's Horse Williams). One such grave robbery of a distinguished person, that of Alexander T. Stewart, the retailing tycoon, formed part of the basis of Mark Twain's "The Stolen White Elephant," the original version composed in 1878.[7] The face of the "resurrected" corpse in The Adventures of Tom Sawyer is said to be "pallid"; Horse Williams was a white man. But many vandalized cemeteries, especially in Eastern urban centers, were the final resting places of Blacks. Thus in Chapter 15 of Twain's first novel The Gilded Age (a chapter attributed to Charles Dudley Warner) the young Quaker medical student Ruth Bolton arrives one night at a woman's medical college in Philadelphia, terrified to find on the dissecting table a dead black man whose face "seemed to defy the pallor of death, and asserted an angry life-likeness that was frightful" and appeared to cry out: "Haven't you yet done with the outcast, persecuted black man, but you must now haul him from his grave, and send even your women to dismember his body?"[8] Prior to the passage of the Pennsylvania Anatomy Act in 1882, Philadelphia medical colleges systematically purchased bodies "from the superintendent of the Lebanon Cemetery, a burial ground for Negroes in the lower part of the city." This type of clandestine activity had been going on for at least ten years.[9] Grave robbing had become a national scandal, and thus it may have helped to nourish the rich complex of ideas that underlay the scene of graveyard desecration in The Adventures of Tom Sawyer.

St. Petersburg/Hannibal was too far removed from any medical school to make Dr. Robinson's body snatching efforts plausible, but Mark Twain transferred the practice to St. Petersburg in order to provide Tom, Huck, and the townspeople with an eerie and somber variant of the game of death. Besides, Twain's novels, travel books, sketches, and notebook jottings reveal an abiding fascination with corpses and with corpse humor.[10] Twain's depiction of the grave robbery appears to be rapidly sketched, and more important for Tom's and Huck's reaction to it than as a violation of civic morality. Oddly enough, although the murder of Dr. Robinson, and particularly the secret of the true murderer, continues to haunt Tom for a long while, neither he, the townspeople, nor the author seems troubled by the act of grave robbing itself; there is no expression of shock or outrage concerning that matter. And Dr. Robinson, resurrectionist and murder victim, appears to be of little further interest to the novelist.

As Mark Twain fumbled for a method to organize and develop the novel, he must have realized the potential of games of death as major structural devices. Indeed, the two climactic episodes of the remainder of the novel involve Tom in games of resurrection—the first one played out as sentimental and idyllic comedy, the second as terror-filled melodrama. As Frank Baldanza has pointed out, "the situation of being thought dead" is an "organizational device" in both The Adventures of Torn Sawyer and The Adventures of Huckleberry Finn.[11] The first of these resurrection game episodes is the idyll of Jackson's Island, where three boys—Tom, Huck Finn, and Joe Harper—have secretly escaped from the adult world to the carefree place where, for a while, time stands still and adults seem powerless to interfere. Seated by the campfire on the deserted island, which to their young minds is an earthly paradise, Tom wonders, "What would the boys say if they could see us?" To which Joe Harper's reply suggests that the thought of death is never far away: "Say? Well, they'd just die to be here" (p. 118). Earthly bliss, it would appear, is only understandable against a background of death—a concept that would pervade Mark Twain's later writings. And when the boys observe the boat that is searching the river for their presumably dead bodies, they relish the idea of being thought dead and grieved for by their families and friends. Thus is acted out a much grander version of the game that Tom had played in his moments of moping and mock-grief for his "dead" self. As Mark Twain phrases the feeling:

> They felt like heroes in an instant. Here was a gorgeous triumph; they were missed; they were mourned; hearts were breaking on their account;

> tears were being shed; accusing memories of unkindnesses to these poor lost lads were rising up, and unavailing regrets and remorse were being indulged; and best of all, the departed were the talk of the whole town, and the envy of all the boys, as far as this dazzling notoriety was concerned. (pp. 124-25)

Twain's series of breathless independent clauses catches the sheer excitement of this game of death played in the sequestered, if ephemeral, paradise of Jackson's Island.

Eventually tiring of being away from the adult world and stricken by a conscience that was formed by that same adult world, Tom sneaks back home at night, hides beneath a bed, and has the perverse pleasure of hearing his Aunt Polly, his cousin Mary, Joe Harper's mother, and even his pesky kid brother Sid linger over his merits and mourn his supposedly dead self. Tom, too, is silently bathed in tears when he hears his aunt praying for him. As evidence of his presence there, after leaving his hiding place under the bed, he kisses the lips of his sleeping aunt. And to cap off this exhilarating phase of this game of death, he returns to the island in time for breakfast! (pp. 127-30). Apparently on Saturday, the fifth day of the Jackson's Island idyll (and in rather cavalier shifting of the novel's point of view), we see Tom's little inamorata Becky Thatcher grieve and cry over the apparent loss of her young hero (p. 139). And village folk young and old ascribe to Tom and his companions the sort of virtues that one might expect to hear in a eulogy. But Tom, in his own right, is an incomparable showman. Like P.T. Barnum, whose work Mark Twain admired,[12] and like Mark Twain's later fictional heroes Hank Morgan and Young Satan, who combined the spectacles of their own resurrection with dazzling and fiery showmanship, Tom cannot resist climaxing this game of death with the spectacle of his own resurrection.

Thus, on the last day of this game of death, on Sunday, in the village church nearly hushed in funereal gloom and despair, with Tom's and Joe's families dressed in mourning, and the church packed with mourners, the game reaches its triumphant climax. Following a stirring hymn the minister, taking as his text "I am the Resurrection and the Life," preaches a moving sermon glorifying the "lost" boys. As the "transfixed" minister looks upward to the church balcony he sees the three boys who have stealthily entered the church and "hid in the unused gallery listening to their own funeral sermon!" Then in a magnificent outburst of theatricality, the general ecstatic rejoicing over the resurrection of these presumably lost children becomes a vast community drama as the entire congregation sings "Praise God from whom all blessings flow" (pp. 140-41). At this point Mark Twain may have been taunting his readers. Indeed, unless he had chosen to commit brazen sacrilege by setting the scene on Easter Sunday, he has carried this resurrection game about as far as he could without overtly mocking the Christian doctrine of resurrection. The episode is filled with tension, sentimentality, and suggestiveness.

But we must not forget that the game is Tom's game. For our budding young Barnum, "this was the proudest moment of his life." And using one of his favorite words, Mark Twain acknowledges that the adults of the town were "sold"—duped, deceived, made to look "almost . . . ridiculous" by this mock-resurrection with its flaunted irreverence toward Christian religious views and village decorum. (The community might have felt a momentary twinge of shame or outrage or may have been tempted to question its value system, but the thrill of hearing the congregation sing "Old Hundred" outweighed any impulse to self-analysis.) The town exists largely as a setting for Tom's adventures, and in his eyes the wave of adulation among the townsfolk and children crested until "the very summit of glory was reached"—or almost reached as Becky, ignoring him, cast a faint shadow of death over him: "it maddened him to see, as he thought he saw, that Becky Thatcher never once suspected that he was in the land of the living." Nevertheless, Tom thought, "he would live for glory" (pp. 141-47). "This long episode," says Everett Emerson, "ends with Tom's pleasure at what many have wished for and few achieved—a triumphant return to his own funeral."[13] But soon the St. Petersburg adults are disabused, the escapade is forgotten, and the game is over. It was, after all, a glorious capstone to all those little private games in which Tom wished himself dead but still able to hang around to relish the grief and mourning of his loved ones. And although the reader might expect this resurrection to linger in Tom's—and Mark Twain's—mind, nevertheless, after a chapter or so, the author and his hero seem to forget about it and it is not mentioned again as they move on to other episodes.

A game is not a game without an adversary—in this instance the supposedly unimaginative, sentimental, and vulnerable adults of St. Petersburg. And the game of resurrection requires an artificial playing field—in this case the illusion of a homogeneous white society untainted by slavery (a black child assists briefly in the fence painting)—a classless, cohesive, reverent society of child-loving, rather obtuse adults and their ingenious children. And the game's the thing: the Sunday resurrection in the village church is ultimately an inspired bit of chicanery akin to Tom's tricking the village boys to whitewash his Aunt Polly's fence and enjoy their work. "In fact," says Forrest Robinson,

> Tom Sawyer successfully conveys the illusion that all experience is ultimately reducible to entertainment. Murder, grave-robbing, the withholding of life-saving evidence, impulses to suicide, simulated disasters, numerous close brushes with death, the violation of sanguinary oaths,

> wrenching fear and guilt, and numberless suppressions of the truth and miscarriages of justice are all transformed, through masterful orchestration and narrative control, into entertainment.[14]

But of all the novel's entertainments the game of death is the most impressive and, perhaps, the most fun. Moreover, only when Mark Twain finally concentrates on death games does the novel acquire a measure of cohesive structure. Toward the novel's end, the death games become very complex and intense; in fact, Mark Twain stages two death games at once, thus achieving a notable level of structural sophistication.

Apparently intrigued by this game of comic resurrection, Mark Twain might have concluded that anything worth doing well is worth doing twice. Thus in a subplot of his unperformed play "Cap'n Simon Wheeler, the Amateur Detective. A Light Tragedy," completed the year after the appearance of The Adventures of Tom Sawyer, he burlesques the game of resurrection. To offset the play's main plot about the blundering detective Simon Wheeler who sets out to solve a murder that never occurred, Mark Twain has young Hugh Burnside exchange garments with a "deceased" tramp (in reality a villain) whose body he hides under a bed. Hugh then pretends to be mute. Ever fond of corpse humor, Mark Twain has Hugh declare in an aside to the audience: "It's pretty warm weather, but I reckon he'll keep." In a varïant of Tom Sawyer's resurrection game, Hugh, now disguised as the tramp, enjoys watching his friends weep and mourn over the body they presume to be his. Touching his eyes with a rag in a gesture of mock grief and sounding rather like Tom Sawyer, Hugh remarks: "It's delicious to be grieved for like this." And although Tom Sawyer was never able to witness Becky Thatcher's grief, Hugh is able to observe the lamentations of his beloved. Rocking in mock-agony, Hugh is so delighted with the spectacle of his own funeral that he says in an aside: "I don't want to live—I'm glad I'm murdered"; later he muses: "I wish I could have such a funeral every day of my life." Like Tom Sawyer he is able to enjoy his own funeral sermon. (Twenty-five years later, Mark Twain—who despite his skepticism concerning immortality liked to toy with the idea of his own immortality - would encourage some literary friends to compose some mock post-mortems for him so that he could enjoy them while he was still alive.[15]) Shuffling as with suppressed sobs, Hugh remarks in another aside:

> "There warn't a dry eye in the house. I wouldn't missed my funeral for a gold mine. I never, never heard such a moving sermon in my life. Ah, it's a big day for me—a mighty big day . . . I'll never forget my funeral, till I have another. How they cried! How she cried! Darling! Such a sermon! Why I never began to imagine I had so many virtues."

The play ends when Hugh slips off his disguise and proves to be very much alive. As Simon Wheeler concludes in a Tom Sawyerish vein: "To track out a murderer ain't much but to track out a lost corpse and fetch him home alive and good as new takes genius."[16]

What we have here, then, is an extension into farce of Tom Sawyer's triumphant return from Jackson's Island. Tom's game of death had mocked the believers in Christian resurrection but cushioned its mockery in childish game play and comic sentimentality, however, Hugh's "resurrection" game in this rickety farce is too redolent of black comedy and sacrilege to have suited the sensibilities of a Victorian audience.

Because The Adventures of Tom Sawyer was composed in a desultory and episodic manner, Twain follows the Jackson's Island episode with lesser happenings. The murder in the graveyard surfaces again, and Tom and

Huck are filled with suppressed terror of the murderous Injun Joe and compassion for the falsely accused Muff Potter. The suppressed painful and "dreadful secret of the murder was a chronic misery" to Tom, explains Mark Twain (p. 165). But Tom once again emerges as "a glittering hero" (p. 173) when he testifies in court about the murder in the graveyard. Later, in a seeming variant of the grave robbery motif, Tom and Huck dig for buried treasure near a haunted house, wherein Injun Joe comes close to discovering and killing them. Perhaps the most important element in this frightening episode is Huck's emergence as a strong colloquial character, thus enabling Mark Twain, for the first time in his fiction-writing career, to develop a double (simultaneous) plot with both suspenseful elements centered on death games. Concurrent with Tom's and Becky's confrontation with death in McDougal's Cave, Huck has his own heroic adventure.

Injun Joe, nursing a deep-seated sense of vengeance against the Widow Douglas (her late husband Judge Douglas had ordered him horsewhipped and jailed as a vagabond) plans to deform the widow. In this novel (unlike The Adventures of Huckleberry Finn) the widow is still a handsome woman. Joe plans to "go for her looks," to "slit her nostrils" and "notch her ears like a sow's," then "tie her to the bed. If she bleeds to death, is that my fault?" Mark Twain is generally circumspect in treating the deaths and mutilations of females. They may be beaten, they may die of hunger, disease, or immolation, but they are not sexually violated. However, there can be little doubt that Injun Joe's planned mutilation of the Widow Douglas has undertones of deadly rape, for he plans to violate and deform two of her bodily orifices, her nose and her ears, then watch her bleed to death in her bedroom. When Joe details his planned maiming of the widow, his accomplice cries out, "My God, that's-"; the reader may supply the rest (pp. 198-99). Overt rape, of course, was hardly suitable stuff for a nineteenth-century boy's book, but it can be interpreted as a significant element in the novel's thematic development. Like the violation of Horse Williams's grave, Injun Joe's planned rape-like assault on the kindly and charitable Widow Douglas is a symbolic violation of the innocent world of St. Petersburg. By thwarting the assault, the arch-innocent Huck Finn rescues the widow from death and ignominy and preserves the town's honor. Like the "resurrection" from Jackson's Island, Huck's rescue of the widow apparently occurs on a Sunday morning (p. 201).

Chronologically overlapping Huck's adventure are Tom's and Becky's adventures in McDougal's Cave and their eventual escape—an episode possibly inspired by an 1873 news story about some children lost in the Hannibal cave.[17] If the boys' return from Jackson's Island is resurrection as comic spectacle, the episode of the cave—the book's climactic adventure—is resurrection as suspenseful melodrama. The young couple, after being separated from their picnic party, become lost in the cave's vast and trackless caverns, exhaust their candles, and apparently spend three days and nights—Saturday through Monday—in total darkness. The children's descent into the cave becomes a descent into the nether world of sheer terror and the shadow of death. In one of the most romantic passages in all of Mark Twain's fiction, Tom and Becky wander into the uncharted interior of the cave and draw close in their innocent attachment—an episode that would later have its counterpart in Mark Twain's affectionate sketches of Adam and Eve, those idealized versions of Sam and Livy Clemens. But the cave episode involves no fall from Paradise: only a resurrection from the cave and from what the St. Petersburg folk fear to be the deaths of the young pair.

As the children descend among the galleries of "fantastic pillars" of stalactites and stalagmites, they become lost, disoriented, and disheartened. So frenzied is Becky's weeping "that Tom was appalled with the idea that she might die, or lose her reason." In despair, Becky dozes off into a happy dream, but her waking laugh is "stricken dead upon her lips." Her strong premonition of death is conveyed in the conventional terms of sentimental romance: "I've seen such a beautiful country in my dream. I reckon we are going there." Then, in a ritual that is ambiguously connubial or funereal, the pair wander until they find a spring of water—a token of holiness. There in the timeless world of darkness (although the pair speculate that is may be Sunday—"Sabbath morning"—in the outside world), Tom unwraps a bit of "wedding-cake" that Becky had saved from the children's picnic. As Mark Twain unfolds this sentimental/romantic game of death, he has Becky remark: "I saved it from the pic-nic for us to dream on, Tom, the way grown-up people do with wedding cake—but it'll be our—." There by the underground spring, without hope of rescue, the young pair await their deaths. They watch fascinated as their brief candle—the last "bit of candle"—melts in its niche in the rock and leaves them in total darkness; so that, metaphorically at least, they have carried out their funeral services and have died. But Mark Twain never intended to pursue the quintessential romantic theme of the deaths of children to its tragic conclusion; the book is, after all, a comedy, and soon Tom, although "sick with the bodings of coming doom," is busily exploring the cave again, looking for an exit. And on the third day, he perceives a "speck" of daylight and is able to save himself and Becky (pp. 209-18).

Apparently Mark Twain was careful not to stage Tom's and Becky's "resurrection" on a Sunday. But when the two children return home the church bells peal and the "frantic half-clad" cheering and joyous townspeople (p. 217) fill the town's main street to surround and acclaim the young pair. In his second adventure of return from the dead, Tom is again a hero basking in the adulation he receives and embroidering his tale of derring-do to admiring listeners. And to top off Tom's triumph, he and Huck become rich and Judge Thatcher, bestowing the mantle of bourgeois respectability on him, predicts that one day Tom may become a lawyer or a soldier—a conforming member of the established society. So that what began as a descent into the dark world of terror and death ends as a joyous game; and the elevation to the bourgeoisie that young Sam Clemens had fancied for himself is here bestowed on young Tom.[18]

And by way of eerie counterpoint to Tom's death game, the body of Injun Joe, whom Tom had glimpsed very much alive in the cave near the buried treasure, so close that Joe could have stabbed him (he had kept the terrible secret from Becky), is later discovered by some townsfolk near the mouth of the cave. Joe had died of thirst and starvation. Throughout the novel Joe is portrayed as a cartoon-like villain whose shadow hovers over Tom to cast the thrill of terror over all his joyous game play. But Mark Twain appears to have been uncomfortable with this last bit of melodrama concerning Joe's demise, and he embellishes Joe's death with some purple prose more appropriate to the lecture circuit and with a misplaced sexist sermonette on the soft-hearted "sappy women" (p. 221) who dabble in politics and show sympathy for rascals like Joe. But soon after these awkward digressions the jolly game of death is resumed as the whole town celebrates Joe's death, joining in a chorus of jubilation and fun that may suggest a streak of sadism beneath their apparent respectability.

So end the games of death in The Adventures of Tom Sawyer. Never again in Mark Twain's major writings will death games be played with such elan, joy, and light-heartedness. Surely, The Adventures of Huckleberry Finn opens with some innocent killing games organized by Tom Sawyer. In the novel, Huck is "resurrected" from his father's bondage into a free and lonesome soul who witnesses over a dozen deaths, most of them violent and in some of which he may be partially complicit.[19] Yet Huck's world being a "real" world, the deaths are tragic and shocking; death is no longer a childish game. Surely, Hank Morgan, in A Connecticut Yankee in King Arthur's Court, is "resurrected" into the Boss and saved from certain death by predicting the spectacular "miracle" of the solar eclipse. Hank—who has a streak of Tom Sawyer in him—relishes the game of dispatching hostile knights, during his random encounters with them, with guns and bombs and with a deadly gamesmanship that does not trouble his conscience. But the novel turns grim and bitter and ends at the Sand Belt with the tragic slaughter of thousands of knights by electrocution, machine-gunning, and miasmal infection—results of the grandiose last stand planned by an obsessive Hank Morgan in his campaign to root out feudalism. Surely, Young Satan, in the Mysterious Stranger manuscripts, is literally able to be consumed by fire and to resurrect himself in the most spectacular fashion. For this superb creature without a conscience or a "moral sense," it is all part of a pleasant game, he explains, done with a Tom-Sawyerish exuberance and with a zeal for showing off (indeed he compares his own showmanship to that of P.T. Barnum):

> "I'm only a youth, and it's natural. I love shows and spectacles, and stunning dramatics, and I love to astonish people, and show off, and to be and do all the gaudy things a boy loves to be and do; and whenever I'm here [on earth] and have got matters worked up to where there is a good prospect to the fore, I shut down the works and have a time!"[20]

As we know, Young Satan casually and sportively makes and unmakes human lives and creates spectres of live humans as if to show that the forces that rule the universe are uncaring and that the individual life (or death) has little significance in the scheme of things. Satan's games are those of a demonic god and are used to illustrate the dark determinist philosophy of Mark Twain's later years. (Some other late writings also toy grimly with the games of death.) But The Adventures of Tom Sawyer in its innocence and joy reflects a happy Mark Twain and his idealized dream world of youth in which the games of death - despite some lurking shadows—may still be played as an innocent form of pure adventure. As such, it is a major triumph.

NOTES

1. On the structure of *The Adventures of Tom Sawyer*, see Hamlin Hill, "The Composition and Structure of Tom Sawyer," *American Literature* 32 (1961): 379-92. On the St. Petersburg folk, see Lyall Powers, "Mark Twain and the Future of Picaresque," in *Mark Twain: A Sumptuous Variety*, ed. Robert Giddings (London and Totowa, NJ: Vision and Barnes & Noble, 1985), pp. 159-60.

2. *The Adventures of Tom Sawyer; Tom Sawyer Abroad; Tom Sawyer, Detective*, ed. John C. Gerber, Paul Baender, and Terry Firkins (Berkeley and Los Angeles: Univ. of California Press, 1980), p. 50. The editors place the novel's action within the historical area of Hannibal and identify specific loci (p. 3). Other page references are made in the text.

3. *The Adventures of Tom Sawyer*, p. 483 (notes). According to Dixon Wecter, there is no record of such a grave robbery in Hannibal. For Mark Twain's familiarity with Dickens, see Howard G. Baetzhold, *Mark Twain & John Bull: The British Connection* (Bloomington and London: Indiana Univ. Press, 1970); Alan Gribben, *Mark Twain's Library—A Reconstruction* (Boston: G. K. Hall & Co., 1980), 1:185-92. See also Andrew Sanders, *Charles Dickens, Resurrectionist* (New York: St. Martin's Press, 1982).

4. James H. Lampton, younger half-brother of Clemens's mother, attended McDowell's Medical College in St. Louis. Its preceptor was said to be "a skillful though eccentric physician who encouraged his students to steal corpses." In 1868 Clemens noted cryptically: "Jim Lampton and the dead man in Dr. McDowell's College." See *Mark Twain's Notebooks and Journals*, ed. Frederic Anderson and Michael B. Frank (Berkeley and Los Angeles: Univ.

of California Press, 1975), 1:136. An earlier Dr. McDowell — Dr. E.D. McDowell — preserved a girl's cadaver in *McDowell's Cave* (the novel's McDougal's Cave), which he owned. See Harry B. Wonham, "McDougal's Cave," in *The Mark Twain Encyclopedia*, eds. J. R. LeMaster and James D. Wilson (New York and London: Garland Publishing Co., 1993), p. 478. The two Drs. McDowell may have formed a mnemonic link in Mark Twain's mind, connecting the cemetery episode and that of Tom and Becky lost in McDougal's Cave.

5. Norman Adams, *Dead and Buried?: The Horrible History of Bodysnatching* (Aberdeen: Impulse Publications, 1972), p. 5.

6. A notable history of the phenomenon, from which many of these details are taken, is Martin Kaufman and Leslie L. Hanawalt, "Body Snatching in the Midwest," *Michigan History* 55 (1971): 23-40.

7. Howard G. Baetzhold, *Mark Twain and John Bull: The British Connection*, pp. 298-99. In the unpublished manuscript of The Adventures of Huckleberry Finn, Jim is frightened "while warming a cadaver for a medical student." See Tom Quirk, *Coming to Grips with Huckleberry Finn: Essays on a Book, a Boy, and a Man* (Columbia and London: Univ. of Missouri Press, 1993), pp. 5-6.

8. *The Gilded Age: A Tale of To-Day* (Hartford: American Publishing Co., 1874), pp. 147-48. For the authorship of the chapter, see Bryant Morey French, *Mark Twain and "The Gilded Age"* (Dallas: Southern Methodist Univ. Press, 1965), p. 61.

9. Kaufman and Hanawalt, "Body Snatching in The Midwest," p. 38.

10. On Mark Twain's penchant for "corpse humor," see Guy Cardwell, *The Man Who Was Mark Twain: Images and Ideologies* (New Haven and London: Yale Univ. Press, 1991), pp. 164-68; for a good example, see Contributions to "The Galaxy"—1866-1871, by Mark Twain, ed. Bruce R. McElderry, Jr. (Gainesville: Scholars' Facsimiles and Reprints, 1961), p. 95.

11. Frank Baldanza, *Mark Twain: An Introduction and Interpretation* (New York: Holt, Rinehart, and Winston, 1961), p. 109.

12. Gribben, 1:48.

13. Everett Emerson, *The Authentic Mark Twain: A Literary Biography of Samuel L. Clemens* (Philadelphia: Univ. of Pennsylvania Press, 1984), p. 82.

14. Forrest G. Robinson, *In Bad Faith: The Dynamics of Deception in Mark Twain's America* (Cambridge and London: Harvard Univ. Press, 1986), p. 112.

15. Mark Twain conceived a series of "amended obituaries" to be written by his literary friends and published in *Harper's Weekly* in 1902-1903 as a sort of ante mortem tribute to himself. He halted the project when Mrs. Clemens became seriously ill. See William R. Macnaughton, *Mark Twain's Last Days as a Writer* (Columbia and London: Univ. of Missouri Press, 1979), pp. 186-87.

16. *Mark Twain's Satires & Burlesques*, ed. Franklin R. Rogers (Berkeley and Los Angeles: Univ. of California Press, 1968), pp. 238, 241, 257, 274, 288-89.

17. Emerson, p. 81.

18. On Sam Clemens's transition to bourgeois respectability, see Jeffrey Steinbrink, *Getting to Be Mark Twain* (Berkeley and Los Angeles: Univ. of California Press, 1990).

19. Arthur G. Pettit, *Mark Twain & The South* (Lexington: The Univ. Press of Kentucky, 1974), p. 84.

20. *Mysterious Stranger Manuscripts*, ed. William M. Gibson (Berkeley and Los Angeles: Univ. of California Press, 1969), p. 386.

12

Huck the Thief

—Eric Carl Link

Fortunately, Tom got shot. It may be lovely to live on a raft, but only when you can live high, hogging watermelons without having to "chaw" over a lot of Tom's "gold-leaf distinctions." Had the grand evasion gone as planned, had Tom, Huck, and Jim made it to the raft safely, the beauty and simplicity of raft life would have been diminished by Tom's insistence that they leave off "borrowing" the occasional chicken or cantaloupe from local farms. Tom can't even purloin a few candles without leaving five cents on the table for pay. Lighting out for the territory ahead of the rest may be a bittersweet ending to a bittersweet novel, but it beats having to share a raft on the southern Mississippi with Tom.

In his 1966 article "Thief and Theft in Huckleberry Finn," Robert Vales demonstrates that thievery is a major theme in Huckleberry Finn, appearing in virtually every major episode. Vales argues that the theft motif helps unify the book, as well as justify the much-maligned "evasion" ending. Vales's observations are astute, for the predominance of thievery in the novel does serve to bind many of the episodes of the novel together around a recurring plot device. Theft, however, serves as much more than a simple, if ingenious, plot device or character trait. In fact, Huck's role as a thief in The Adventures of Huckleberry Finn provides a means of observing his growth and change. As the narrative progresses, the succession of thefts performed by Huck—from the imaginary "julery" and "ingots" stolen by Tom's harmless band of robbers, to the very real act of slave-stealing on the Phelps's farm—chart Huck's growing moral depth and awareness. What one witnesses in Huck is a willingness to engage in increasingly serious acts of thievery, coupled with an expanding awareness of the moral implications connected to these same acts.

With the promise of relentless robbery and murder, Tom's band of robbers seems a likely candidate for adventure and general mayhem. But, in the series of fanciful raids led by Tom, the theft is imaginary. The highlight of Tom and Huck's brief career as highwaymen is an aborted raid on a Sunday School picnic; they nearly made away with some doughnuts and jam, a rag doll, and a hymn-book, but, as Huck tells us, the "teacher charged in and made us drop everything and cut" (15). With these essentially innocuous boyhood pranks, neither Huck nor Tom faces any significant moral dilemmas. There is no moral content to an imaginary theft of invisible diamonds; there is no need to reconcile deed with conscience. With little at stake, either materially or morally, Tom's hapless band of robbers soon dissolves.

The early exploits of the band of robbers was but a prelude to greater thefts to come. With his flight from Pap and St. Petersburg, Huck leaves Tom and the band of robbers far behind, and, at the same time, Huck leaves behind a bit of his boyhood. As he takes to the raft with Jim, Huck not only drifts south, into the somber heart of the Southern slave system, but psychologically, Huck also begins to drift into the somber territory of moral awareness. The change is simple at first, expressing itself in a need to justify his acts of petty theft and assuage his conscience. For example, soon after fleeing Jackson's Island, Huck explains how he found food: "Every night, now, I used to slip ashore, towards ten o'clock, at some little village, and buy ten or fifteen cents' worth of meal or bacon or other stuff to eat; and sometimes I lifted a chicken that warn't roosting comfortable, and took him along" (79). To leave the explanation here would indicate that Huck's conscience bothered him little, if any. Instead, however, Huck explains why it was okay for him to steal chickens: "Pap always said, take a chicken when you get a chance, because if you don't want him yourself you can easy find somebody that does, and a good deed ain't ever forgot. I never see pap when he didn't want the chicken himself, but that is what he used to say, anyway" (79). The tone in this passage suggests that Huck knows that there is something disingenuous about his father's altruism. In the passage that follows, however, Huck reveals that his conscience was actually bothering him about his acts of petty theft:

> Mornings, before daylight, I slipped into corn fields and borrowed a watermelon, or a mushmelon, or a punkin, or some new corn, or things of that kind. Pap always said it warn't no harm to borrow things, if you was meaning to pay them back, sometime; but the widow said it warn't anything but a soft name for stealing, and no decent body would do it. Jim said he reckoned the widow was partly right and pap was partly right; so the best way would be for us to pick out two or three things from the list and say we wouldn't borrow them any more—then he reckoned it wouldn't be no harm to borrow the others. So we talked it over all one night, drifting along down the river, trying to make up our minds whether to drop the watermelons, or the camelopes, or the mushmelons, or what. But towards daylight

> we got it all settled satisfactory, and concluded to drop crabapples and p'simmons. We warn't feeling just right, before that, but it was all comfortable now. (79-80)

By ruling out crabapples and p'simmons (an act, curiously, that shows the same disingenuous spirit as Pap's chicken-borrowing theory) Huck is able to rationalize his thievery and assuage his slightly bothered conscience. The chief difference between the band of robbers and chicken-lifting lies in the consequences involved: with the imaginary thefts of Tom's band there were no consequences, hence no moral implications; with the theft of chickens and melons come certain consequences, such as the farmer's loss of product (and, more importantly, the Widow Douglas's disapproval); thus, Huck is bothered by the moral implications of his theft. Around this same time Huck and Jim happen upon the wreck of the Walter Scott. A potential goldmine, Huck can't pass by the wreck without first giving it a good "rummaging" in search of the captain's five-cent "seegars" (81). Huck wasn't the only one interested in giving the Walter Scott a good rummaging, however. As he hides in the stateroom, Huck gets another lesson in "morals" as he listens to two of the three roughs on the ship discuss the fate of the third. After giving the ship a thorough rustling, suggests one, they will "shove for the shore and hide the truck." Then they will wait the ship to break up and wash down the river, drowning the captive Jim Turner. "He'll be drowned," argues the robber, "and won't have nobody to blame for it but his own self. I reckon that's a considerable sight better'n killin' of him. I'm unfavorable to killin' a man as long as you can git around it; it ain't good sense, it ain't good morals. Ain't I right?" (84). The reasoning in this argument could have come straight out of Pap's own ethics manual: as long as they feel they aren't the immediate cause of Jim Turner's death, then Bill and Jake feel absolved of guilt. Upon hearing this plan, Huck swiftly decides to cut their boat loose, trapping all three on the ship, then to report them to the local Sheriff.

Both Huck and the robbers desire the same thing: to give the sinking ship a good rummaging. But while the robbers try to figure out how to commit murder without having to feel guilty about it afterwards, Huck, after he and Jim escape from the Walter Scott in the robbers' boat, needs to alleviate the feelings of guilt he feels after leaving the robbers stranded. "Now was the first time that I begun to worry about the men," Huck tells us; "I reckon I hadn't had time to, before. I begun to think how dreadful it was, even for murderers, to be in such a fix. I says to myself, there ain't no telling but I might come to be a murderer myself, yet, and then how would I like it?" (87). And, after convincing the ferryman to go rescue the robbers, Huck tells us that "I was feeling ruther comfortable, on accounts of taking all this trouble for that gang, for not many would a done it. I wished the widow knowed about it. I judged she would be proud of me for helping these rapscallions, because rapscallions and dead beats is the kind the widow and good people takes the most interest in" (91). The unfortunate irony is that Huck does become a murderer of sorts: by stealing their canoe Huck does—presumably—condemn the robbers to death, for the Walter Scott soon breaks up and sinks. When the sinking ship floated by Huck, he could "see in a minute there warn't much chance for anybody being alive in her." This leaves Huck a "little bit heavy-hearted about the gang, but not much, for I reckoned if they could stand it, I could" (91). The key difference between the Walter Scott robbers and Huck is that Huck shows genuine concern for the safety of the robbers, while their concern lies only in rationalizing their way out of guilt over the proposed killing. In a strange twist of events, although Huck seems to have condemned the robbers to death by stealing their canoe, what he learns from the robbers is how not to be murderous himself by showing a genuine concern for the well-being of others.

How "not to be murderous" was only one of several lessons for Huck. In another lesson, Huck learns not to take advantage of the innocent. In the latter half of Huck Finn, Huck's thievery takes on new heights. No longer dealing solely with chickens and mushmelons and five-cent "seegars" in a Captain's stateroom, Huck decides to steal six thousand dollars. The "Royal Nonesuch" and other cons pulled by the King and the Duke were one thing, but claiming to be the English relatives of the deceased Peter Wilks seemed to Huck an all-time low. It was, Huck remarks, "enough to make a body ashamed of the human race" (210). Stealing the bag of money from the King and the Duke entailed serious consequences: for the Wilks, their livelihood was at stake; for Huck, the threat of harm at the hands of the King and the Duke was a real one. Moreover, should the King and the Duke seek retaliation in some manner, Jim would be in danger. Stealing the Wilks's money back from the King and the Duke was fraught with risk, and this translated into moral wrangling for Huck. At first, the risk of unwelcome entanglements with the King and the Duke kept Huck in line, but as Huck becomes more impressed with the kindness and goodness of the Wilks sisters his desire to help them outweighs his instinct to self-preservation. Huck remarks: the sisters "all jest laid their selves out to make me feel at home and know I was amongst friends. I felt so ornery and low down and mean, that I says to myself, My mind's made up; I'll hive that money for them or bust" (225). Because there was no easy way to let the sisters in on the scam without alerting the King and the Duke, Huck comes to the conclusion that "I got to steal that money, somehow; and I got to steal it some way that they won't suspicion that I done it" (226). Huck steals the money, hiding it in Peter Wilk's coffin, and plays the guilt off on the Wilks's slaves, who had already been sold, and thus were clear of revenge at the hands of the King and the Duke. Ultimately, Huck steals the money because he has come to terms with the gravity of stealing money—and a hefty pile of it, too—from the innocent and well-meaning Wilks family. Thus, by observing the immoral actions of the King and the Duke, Huck's own moral nature grows stronger.

Imaginary "julery," chickens and watermelons, loot aboard the Walter Scott, the Wilks's inheritance—these pale in comparison to Huck's final act of thievery. Huck's decision to steal Jim from captivity on the Phelps's farm threatened the severest consequences, thus requiring the strictest moral conviction, and producing the greatest moral growth. Stealing a slave was so serious because it undermined the whole Southern plantation system. Stealing a slave not only affected the owner's pocketbook—a slave such as Jim would be worth eight hundred dollars or more—it also asserted that slaves were worth stealing, not because they were a commodity (abolitionists did not steal for the purpose of resale), not because they were humans with an inherent right to freedom. Moreover, slave stealing, as Huck is only too aware, automatically aligned the stealer with the North and the abolitionist program, blatant affronts to the Southern slave-holding community. Huck doesn't have to think nearly as hard about stealing the six thousand dollars as he does about stealing Jim. Stealing chickens and cigars does not necessarily lead to hellfire. But stealing Jim requires a firm commitment, and an acceptance of the consequences, which, for Huck, means accepting damnation.

No easy decision, Huck's growing awareness of the consequences of his actions can be seen in a comparison of Huck's resolve in chapter thirty-one to steal Jim out of slavery with Huck's reaction earlier in the novel to Jim's plan—once free—to hire an "Ab'litionist" to steal his own children out of slavery if he can't purchase them outfight (124). When Huck hears of Jim's plan, he remarks:

> It most froze me to hear such talk. He wouldn't ever dared to talk such talk in his life before. Just

> see what a difference it made in him the minute he judged he was about free . . . Here was this nigger which I had as good as helped to run away, coining right out flat-footed and saying he would steal his children—children that belonged to a man I didn't even know; a man that hadn't ever done me no harm. I was sorry to hear Jim say that, it was such a lowering of him. (124-25)

Here Huck's conscience bothers him so much at the thought that Jim might steal someone else's property that he decides to "paddle ashore at the first light, and tell." Huck doesn't carry this plan through, however, because Jim impresses upon Huck that he is "de only fren' ole Jim's got now" and the "on'y white genlman dat ever kep' his promise to ole Jim" (125). In this case, Jim's pleas keep Huck from relieving his conscience by handing Jim over to the authorities. The lesson begun here deepens and magnifies in chapter thirty-one, where Huck, remembering the earlier occasion on the raft when he came perilously close to turning Jim in, allows the loyalty of friendship to outweigh his social and religious convictions. He decides to "work and steal Jim out of slavery again; and if I could think up anything worse, I would do that, too; because as long as I was in, and in for good, I might as well go the whole hog" (271). This decision brings both the novel and Huck's growing moral awareness to a climax; the succession of greater and more serious acts of thievery themselves charting Huck's moral growth.

Huck fully understands the seriousness of his decision. This awareness is not only illustrated in his resolute decision to "go to hell," it is also illustrated in Huck's astonishment at Tom's decision to help him steal Jim out of slavery.

> "I know what you'll say. You'll say it's dirty low-down business; but what if it is?—I'm low-down;

> and I'm agoing to steal him, and I want you to keep mum and not let on. Will you?"
>
> His eye lit up, and he says:
>
> "I'll help you steal him!"
>
> Well, I let go all holts, then, like I was shot. It was the most astonishing speech I ever heard—and I'm bound to say Tom Sawyer fell, considerable, in my estimation. Only I couldn't believe it. Tom Sawyer a nigger stealer! (284; c.f. page 292)

The reintroduction of Tom Sawyer into the novel in chapter thirty-three has been cause for chagrin by many readers of Mark Twain's text. The intellectual, moral, and social strides taken by Huck during his journey down the river seem to disintegrate under the influence of Tom's domineering personality. Contemporary debate over the "evasion" ending originated with Leo Marx's response to the defenses of the ending set forth by T.S. Eliot and Lionel Trilling. A fine introduction to more recent (circa 1980s) criticism of the evasion ending is that of Gary Henrickson, who surveys dozens of critical responses to the ending of the novel, developing the argument that as Twain critics continue to invent ever more ingenious defenses of the evasion ending, Twain scholars are turning up more evidence that suggests Twain's genius was not suited for devising such complex narrative structures (for an extensive treatment of the issue post-Marx, but pre-1980s, see James M. Cox Mark Twain: The Fate of Humor). In fact, when confronted with the vast body of Twain scholarship in the past fifty years, one need exaggerate only a bit to assert that since the 1940s it has been difficult to find a sustained examination of Huckleberry Finn that does not engage debate over the relative merits of the evasion ending.Although certain criticisms of the "evasion" ending seem justified it is too long, the burlesque too exaggerated and drawn out—it seems somewhat unjust to fault Twain, and the ending of the novel, merely for the reintroduction of Tom into the narrative, or even for Huck's seeming intellectual and moral reversals. Structurally and thematically, the reintroduction of Tom into the narrative during the "evasion" sequence not only lends to the narrative a certain roundness or wholeness—what Lionel Trilling referred to as "a certain formal aptness" (cf. John Gerber's treatment of the symmetry of the novel, and Richard Adams's and Frank Baldanza's arguments for the unity of the novel based on the principle of repetition and variation)—it also allows Twain to highlight Huck's moral growth. The real interest in the evasion ending is in the clash of Tom the Thief with Huck the Thief. Tom acts as a yardstick with which to measure Huck's moral and intellectual development. During the days of Tom's band of robbers, Huck, Tom, and the other boys engaged in harmless, imaginary acts of theft with no moral content. A summer and a trip down the Mississippi River later, Tom and Huck once again engage, in tandem, in an act of thievery. Although they both seek the same objective—to "steal" Jim—this act of thievery has drastically different moral implications for the two would-be thieves. For Tom, stealing Jim is of no more consequence than the exploits of the band of robbers; knowing that Jim has already been legally freed by Miss Watson, "stealing" Jim is just another boyhood game with no moral weight and no possible repercussions to consider. Tom has not changed: he is the same boy he was at the beginning of the novel. For Huck, the situation is entirely different. Not knowing that Jim has already been freed, Huck views his act of theft as a real and punishable offense that could lead to jail or a lynching on earth, and hellfire in the hereafter. Thus, stealing Jim is of great consequence and possesses a deep moral significance. As for the artistic value of the much maligned evasion ending, it is a testament to Twain's literary craftsmanship that he is able to create a scene in which the same action—stealing Jim—can so vividly illustrate the moral gulf that separates Tom and Huck at the end of the novel.

Aside from illustrating the dynamic nature of Huck's character in the novel (as opposed to Tom's static character) the moral gulf between Tom and Huck during the evasion ending has another dimension. Tom is not amoral or immoral; he simply holds a vastly different moral system than Huck. Huck expresses a moral system based not on absolute principles, but on character and situation. This system stands in opposition to the more dogmatic and rule-based morality of Tom. Much has been made of the Huck-as-realist/Tom-as-romantic contrast, and the conflicting moral systems of the two characters can be seen as stemming from their broadly different philosophical perspectives. Huck holds to an ethic where honest desire and a pragmatic approach to a situation stands for something; his is a very human and subjective ethic. "Honest desire," however, is far too simple a proposition to play any large role in Tom's complex web of authorities and principles. This contrast is writ large throughout the evasion ending, and can be seen clearly in Tom and Huck's debate over what instrument to use to dig a tunnel. According to Tom's "authorities," the proper tool for the job is the highly impractical, if not absurd, case-knife. Huck, the moral pragmatist, prefers the utility of the pick. When Tom decides that case-knives simply won't get the job done, he has to somehow reconcile using a pick with the dictates of his authorities. He remarks: "I'll tell you. It ain't fight, and it ain't moral, and I wouldn't like it to get out—but there ain't only just the one way: we got to dig him out with the picks, and let on it's case-knives" (307). Hearing this, Huck replies: "Now you're talking! . . . your head gets leveler and leveler all the time, Tom Sawyer . . .

> "Picks is the thing, moral or no moral; and as for me, I don't care shucks for the morality of it, nohow.

> When I start in to steal a nigger, or a watermelon, or a Sunday school book, I ain't no ways particular how it's done, so it's done . . . and if a pick's the handiest thing, that's the thing I'm agoing to dig that nigger or that watermelon or that Sunday school book out with; and I don't give a dead rat what the authorities thinks about it, nuther."

"Well," responds Tom, "there's excuse for picks and lettingon, in a case like this; if it warn't so, I wouldn't approve of it, nor I wouldn't stand by and see the rules broke—because right is right, and wrong is wrong, and a body ain't got no business doing wrong when he ain't ignorant and knows better" (307). Tom's inflexible deference to authorities and Huck's more pragmatic reliance on character and situation is also highlighted when Huck wonders why Tom insists that he dress like a servant girl in order to deliver the "nonnamous letter" in the middle of the night. Nobody would see him anyway, notes Huck. Tom responds: "That ain't got nothing to do with it. The thing for us to do, is just to do our duty, and not worry about whether anybody sees us do it or not. Hain't you got no principle at all?" (333).

Within this ongoing contrast between Tom's morals of "principle" and Huck's morals of "situation" seems to be a submerged religious satire. Huck's more earthly and subjective moral system is ridiculed by the dogmatic Tom. Tom bases his moral system on a series of principles derived from a set of texts—gothic, medieval, and historical romances. This corresponds with the Church's reliance on biblical principle. Tom's deference to "authorities" is critiqued through the myriad absurdities Tom foists upon Huck and Jim during the evasion sequence (swallowing sawdust? writing in one's own blood?) Tom's domineering personality and his insistence that they follow the dictates of the "authorities" mirrors the towering presence of the Church, and helps explain why Twain, symbolically, allows

Huck—during the evasion ending—to be swallowed up by Tom's vision and personality. One need not—as critics like Leo Marx do—read Huck as reverting back to an earlier moral state: Jim would still be freed, simply not in an efficient, reasonable manner. Instead, one can read the Huck/Tom relationship at the end of the text as Twain's critique of the Church's role in Western culture. This association of Tom's "authorities" and the nineteenth-century Church is suggested by Huck when Tom condemns him for stealing a watermelon. A thief, according to Tom, is a "mean ornery person." But, if the thief is stealing because he is "representing a prisoner," then he has a right to steal (according to the examples established by textual authority, of course). The watermelon, says Tom, was not stolen for the benefit of the prisoner; thus, taking the melon was an act of immoral thievery. Hearing this, Huck remarks:

> Tom said that what he meant was, we could steal anything we needed. Well, I says, I needed the watermelon. But he said I didn't need it to get out of prison with, there's where the difference was. He said if I'd a wanted it to hide a knife in, and smuggle it to Jim to kill the seneskal with, it would a been all right. So I let it go at that, thoughI couldn't see no advantage in my representing a prisoner, if I got to set down and chaw over a lot of gold-leaf distinctions like that, every time I see a chance to hog a watermelon. (303)

Rather than have to muddle through a series of "gold-leaf distinctions," Huck prefers a moral system based on honest desire and a pragmatic approach to individual situations. If a tunnel can be dug most efficiently with a pick, then dig it with a pick, regardless of the dictates of authority. Perhaps Twain is not so much critiquing biblical principle itself as he is targeting the type of obtuse, legalistic interpretation of biblical principle metaphorically engaged in by Tom. Rather than focus on the larger principles underlying the specific situations described in his textual authorities, Tom legalistically adheres to the idiosyncratic particulars of the situations described by the authorities. If a prisoner in a castle tower writes a journal in blood, then all prisoners must keep a journal in their own blood, no matter that the prisoner in the story didn't have access to any other writing implement. This legalistic focus often results in a very real cruelty (for treatments of the cruelty theme in Huck Finn, see John Gerber and Henry Nash Smith). Historically, one can see it in the horrors of the Inquisition and other dark moments in religious history; in Twain's text one can see it in Tom's cruel treatment of Jim during the evasion ending. "Human beings can be awful cruel to one another" notes Huck as he watches the tarred and feathered King and Duke "astraddle of a rail" (290). Knowing Jim was legally free, and nevertheless subjecting him to days of living with rats, spiders, and snakes, eating sawdust, writing in his own blood, and so forth, goes beyond mere boys-will-be-boys pranks. One laments that Huck allows Tom to put Jim through this nonsense, but Huck, at least, believed it was all anterior to a higher purpose: stealing a slave out of captivity. Tom, knowing Jim had been freed by Miss Watson, was simply using Jim for sport. Tom's attitude toward Jim is no different than it was back in the days of the band of robbers. In chapter two, when Huck and Tom are sneaking away from the Widow's house late at night, Tom can't pass up an opportunity to have a little fun at Jim's expense. After Tom and Huck have stolen several candles (Tom, we recall, leaves five cents on the Widow's table for pay), Tom decides to play a prank on Jim: "I was in a sweat to get away; but nothing would do Tom but he must crawl to where Jim was, on his hands and knees, and play something on him" (7). On this early occasion the prank is harmless enough: he hangs Jim's hat on the bough of a tree. Jim uses this episode to construct a tale of witchery. At the end of the book, with Jim held captive in the darkness of the Phelps's shack—a darkness both real and figurative, for Jim had no idea Miss Watson had freed him—Tom's "pranks" take a decidedly cruel turn.

Tom's brand of "principled" or "legalistic" morality is ultimately doomed to backfire. for in its attempt to set idealistic goals it fails to account for the simple realities of individual situations. This failing is underscored in a passage at the beginning of chapter forty-one. Huck has gone to fetch a doctor to attend to Tom, wounded in the calf by a bullet during the attempt to free Jim. Thinking himself an abolitionist now, Huck is loath to reveal the reason Tom lies wounded, so he constructs another of his many stories:

> I told him [the Doctor] me and my brother was over on Spanish island hunting, yesterday afternoon, and camped on a piece of a raft we found, and about midnight he must a kicked his gun in his dreams, for it went off and shot him in the leg . . .
>
> "Who is your folks?" he says.
>
> "The Phelpses, down yonder."
>
> "Oh", he says. And after a minute he says: "How'd you say he got shot?"
>
> "He had a dream," I says, "and it shot him."
>
> "Singular dream," he says. (343)

Tom's unrealistic, narrow, idealistic morality of authorities and "gold-leaf" distinctions is the stuff of dreams, and, for Twain, these idealistic dreams will eventually turn upon the dreamer. Ironically, it is Huck's moral nature that proves superior to the tarnished morality of Tom and most of the other characters in the narrative. Early in the novel, Huck, frustrated in his attempts to make sense of Miss Watson's religious platitudes, seeks counsel from the Widow Douglas, who explains that what one could get from praying was "spiritual gifts." What this meant was that Huck must "help other people, and do everything I could for other people, and look out for them all the time, and never think about myself" (13). Curiously, although he dismisses the advice at the time because of its apparent impracticality, Huck, of all the major characters in the novel, comes closest to keeping this golden rule advice. Huck's famous declaration in chapter thirty-one that he would "go to hell" if it meant stealing Jim out of slavery was not the first time Huck had determined to forego the rewards of Heaven for a more earthly alternative. It was the second. The first time occurs in the novel's opening chapter. Miss Watson, having scolded Huck for putting his feet on the furniture and sitting improperly, threatens Huck with fears of hellfire:

> Then she told me all about the bad place, and I said I wished I was there. She got mad, then, but I didn't mean no harm. All I wanted was to go somewheres; all I wanted was a change, I warn't particular . . .
>
> Now she had got a start, and she went on and told me all about the good place. She said all a body would have to do there was to go around all day long with a harp and sing, forever and ever. So I didn't think much of it. But I never said so. I asked her if she reckoned Tom Sawyer would go there, and she said, not by a considerable sight. I was glad about that, because I wanted him and me to be together. (3-4)

In this passage, Huck elects to go to hell without any particular regard for what such a decision implies. In chapter thirty-one, Huck makes the same decision, only this time he does so in complete awareness of the gravity of such a choice. These dual decisions lend a certain symmetry to the novel as they illustrate Huck's deepening moral awareness. So too does the contrast of Huck and Tom in the opening and closing frames of the novel. In fact, re-introducing Tom into the narrative during the evasion ending brings full-circle a pattern of contrast established early in the work. Throughout the novel, Huck's acts of thievery are set against comparable acts of thievery by others. The cycle begins with Tom's band of robbers. Then, early in the novel, Huck's thievery is set against the exploits of Pap and the Walter Scott ruffians. Later, Huck's more "moral" thievery is set in contrast to the deceitful and immoral chicanery of the King and the Duke. Finally, on the Phelps's farm, with his greatest triumph of thievery, Huck is again teamed with Tom, whose "dream" shoots him.

Late in the novel, Tom deduces Jim's location on the Phelps's farm when he sees a man bringing food to the "hut down by the ash-hopper." Huck had seen the man deliver the food—which included a slice of watermelon—but had not drawn the inference that the food was for Jim; the food, thought Huck, could easily have been intended for a dog. When Tom tells Huck of his discovery, Huck replies: "Well, it does beat all, that I never thought about a dog not eating watermelon. It shows how a body can see and don't see, at the same time" (291). If ever Twain dropped a clue to interpreting his novel, this is it, for the idea of "seeing and not seeing" at the same time is the key to many of the novel's mysteries. It helps set the circus scene, in which Huck watches as a bumbling drunk gradually sheds a series of costumes, transforming himself into a skilled acrobat, into context. It also is the key to understanding the complexity of Jim's character: Huck sees Jim, but does not see him—does not see through the minstrel mask worn by the beleaguered runaway slave (cf. Forrest Robinson's treatment of Jim). It may also be a clue to Huck's own character, as Twain asks us to see beyond Huck's surface roguishness at the moral development his acts of thievery indicate.

REFERENCES

Adams, Richard P. "The Unity and Coherence of Huckleberry Finn." *Tulane Studies in English* 6 (1956), 87-103; rpt. in Barry A. Marks, ed. *Mark Twain's Huckleberry Finn*. Boston: D.C. Heath, 1959. 82-94.

Baldanza, Frank. "The Structure of Huckleberry Finn." *American Literature* 27 (1995), 347-55; rpt. in Barry A. Marks, ed. *Mark Twain's Huckleberry Finn*. Boston: D.C. Heath, 1959. 75-81.

Cox, James M. *Mark Twain: The Fate of Humor*. Princeton: Princeton University Press, 1966.

Eliot, T.S. (Introduction). *The Adventures of Huckleberry Finn*. New York: Chanticleer, 1950.

Gerber, John. *Mark Twain*. Boston: Twayne, 1988.

Henrickson, Gary. P. "Biographers' Twain, Critics' Twain, Which of the Twain Wrote the `Evasion'?" *Southern Literary Journal* 26:1 (Fall 1993), 14-29.

Marx, Leo. "Mr. Eliot, Mr. Trilling, and Huckleberry Finn." *American Scholar* 12 (1953), 423-40.

Robinson, Forrest G. "The Characterization of Jim in Huckleberry Finn." *Nineteenth Century Literature* 43:3 (1988), 361-91.

Smith, Henry Nash. *Mark Twain: The Development of a Writer*. Cambridge: Belknap, 1962.

Trilling, Lionel. (Introduction). *The Adventures of Huckleberry Finn*. New York: Rinehart, 1948.

Twain, Mark. *The Adventures of Huckleberry Finn*. Berkeley: University of California Press, 1985.

Vales, Robert L. "Thief and Theft in Huckleberry Finn." *American Literature* 37 (1966), 420-29.

13

Mark Twain's Cross-Dressing Oeuvre

—Laura Skandera-Trombley

Mark Twain apparently enjoyed nothing better than writing a rollicking transvestite tale. Beginning with his uncompleted short story *"A Medieval Romance"* (begun in 1868) and continuing in his 1894 novel *Pudd'nhead Wilson*, Twain was irresistibly drawn to loving descriptions and painstaking explorations of the contexts and implications of cross-dressing. He left a myriad of texts that testify to his fascination with transvestism; in addition to the short story and novel mentioned above, cross-dressing can be found in such various works as *1,002d Arabian Night* (1883), *Adventures of Huckleberry Finn* (1885), *Personal Recollections of Joan of Arc* (1896), *Following the Equator* (Vol. 2 1897), *Wapping Alice* (1898, 1907), *How Nancy Jackson Married Kate Wilson* (c. 1902) [also known as *Feud Story and the Girl who was Ostensibly a Man*], and *A Horse's Tale* (1907).

In his transvestite tales Twain was identifying and challenging social constructions of gender, distribution of power within a patriarchal society, and socially determined racial categories. An evolution of what Marjorie Garber terms "transvestite effects" can be traced in Twain's transvestite tales from his first genderswitch short story where stereotypical gender roles are presented then problematized, to introducing a female "gender-trickster" figure in *Adventures of Huckleberry Finn* who identifies and controls these constructions; to ultimately creating intersections where gender, race, and class identities meet in *Adventures of Huckleberry Finn* and *Pudd'nhead Wilson.*[1]

While I am not the first to discuss Twain's use of cross-dressing (both Susan Gillman and Garber include substantive explorations), what has not been previously explored is the society being reflected in Twain's writings whose culture and history is being portrayed. Indeed, in utilizing the element of cross-dressing in short stories and novels (such as *A Medieval Romance* and *Personal Recollections of Joan of Arc*), where gender themes are foremost, Twain may well have been paying tribute to upper-class, EuropeanAmerican female reformers and suffragettes.[2] In addition, in novels where racial themes are paramount, such as *Adventures of Huckleberry Finn* and *Pudd'nhead Wilson*, he was openly recognizing oral and written contributions made by African-American women in the form of slave narratives.

In his first transvestite text, *"Medieval Romance,"* Twain introduced a theme that would resurface in a more developed form in *"1,002d Arabian Night."* In both stories, the sex of the heroine necessitates cross-dressing in order for inheritance and dynastic structures to remain intact. Yet, in inventing the transvestite heroine, Twain was consciously subverting these systems. While the patriarchal order superficially remains intact at the end of these stories, a sexual revolution has been effected by transvestites who transform the monarchy and sultanate into matriarchies. What takes place here is that the figure of the transvestite restructures the existing society.

In *"Medieval Romance,"* the main character Conrad has been raised as a male by her father, who is determined that the throne will belong to his side of the family, not his brother Ulrich's. When Conrad is twenty-eight years old, her father relates the story of her birth and the reasons for her male gender. Appalled, Conrad remonstrates, "Oh, my father! Is it for this my life hath been a lie? Was it that I might cheat my unoffending cousin of her rights? Spare me, father, spare your child!" (*The Complete Short Stories of Mark Twain 56*).

With Conrad, Twain introduced his first gender-trickster transvestite character, although Conrad does not realize she is tricking anyone until her father informs her that her identity has been a deception in order to win the monarchy. However, despite her father's attempts to fool his brother, by the end of the tale Conrad and her father are out-tricked by Ulrich's daughter Constance. Constance has been seduced by one of her Uncle's henchmen, and she has given birth out of wedlock. It is decided that she must stand trial. Conrad, speaking from the throne, informs Constance that she must name the father of her child. Constance, enraged because Conrad has earlier rejected her advances, names Conrad. Conrad and her father, overcome by the accusation, both swoon. Apparently this plot twist complicated the story to such an extent that after this revelation Twain broke off the narrative and printed a disclaimer in the *Buffalo Express* explaining, "I have got my hero (or heroine) into such a particularly close place that I do not see how I am ever going to get him (or her) out of it again, and therefore I will wash my hands of the whole business" (*The Complete Short Stories of Mark Twain 56*). Twain's language, "hero (or heroine)" and "him (or her)," is a good example of what Garber means by the transvestite's causing a "failure of definitional distinction."

Twain's next depiction of transvestism would come eight years after *A Medieval Romance,* in the 1876 portion of *Adventures of Huckleberry Finn*, a novel where all of the main characters (Huckleberry, Jim, and Tom) don female dress at different junctures. The two scenes of cross-dressing contained in the first section of the manuscript (chapters 1-18) are of particular interest here. Early in the novel, there occurs an odd incident which Huckleberry Finn matter of factly recounts: a body had been found in the river. This in itself is not particularly unusual; what is noteworthy about this drowning is the victim's apparel:

> Well, about this time [Pap] was found in the river drowned, about twelve mile above town, so people said . . . They judged it was him, anyway . . . They said he was floating on his back in the water. They took him and buried him on the bank. But I warn't comfortable long, because I happen to think of something. I knowed mighty well that a drownded man don't float on his back, but on his face. So I knowed then, that this warn't pap, but a woman dressed up in a man's clothes. (15)[3]

If Huck is correct (and he is regarding Pap), then the reader must contend with the possibility of a female cross-dresser who may have met with foul play. Without any other immediate reference, the aside is easily overlooked when Huck continues his story. Yet this mention, while brief, is crucial and contains two questions begging to be asked: is the drowned woman simply a southern transvestite, or could Twain have been testing his reader's knowledge of African-American antebellum history? There does exist an historical explanation for the identity of the drowning victim: she may have been an African-American woman fleeing North to escape enslavement who in her flight had either accidently drowned or been murdered.

If we pursue the possibility that the drowned woman might have been African-American, this incident would signal the beginning of Twain's conflating gender identification with racial categories.[4] Indeed in this quick aside, Twain seems to be developing a paradigm where gender and race meet. Garber explains that,

> the apparently spontaneous or unexpected or supplementary presence of a transvestite figure in a text . . . that does not seem, thematically, to be primarily concerned with gender difference or blurred gender indicates a category crisis elsewhere, an irresolvable conflict or epistemological crux that destabilizes comfortable binarity, and displaces the resulting discomfort onto a figure that already inhabits, indeed incarnates, the margin. (17)

Huck's inability to determine the sex of the dead person, and the historical possibilities for explaining his/her presence, certainly indicate a "category crisis elsewhere"—indeed, the "irresolvable conflict" within *Adventures of Huckleberry Finn* is that of slavery.

A connection can be made between this episode and African-American women's slave narratives where cross-dressing was a familiar component. Tales of escape from the South were well known, and hundreds of formerly enslaved African-Americans told their stories on the anti-slavery lecture circuit in the Northeast. According to Henry Louis Gates, Jr., "over one hundred [African-Americans] wrote book-length 'slave narratives,' before the end of the Civil War" (ix). Between the years of 1703 and 1944, these accounts were so numerous it has been estimated that "six thousand and six ex-slaves had narrated the stories of their captivity, through interviews, essays, and books" (*The Classic Slave Narratives ix*).

Among the published narratives were two that received a great deal of attention. William and Ellen Craft's *Running a Thousand Miles for Freedom*, published in London in 1860, is by any measure a remarkable story. Ellen Craft, who was fair-skinned, disguised herself as a European-American southern planter, and her husband assumed the role of her/his slave. Travelling together, they managed to escape to the North and later fled to England. By the time William Still's *The Underground Rail Road* was published in 1883, the Crafts were so renowned that in addition to telling the story of their escape, Still included an account of their post-slavery life (Freedman xv).

Another slave narrative featuring a cross-dressed woman was published in 1861 by Harriet Jacobs under the pseudonym Linda Brent. Gates calls Jacobs's *Incidents in the Life of a Slave Girl* "the major black woman's autobiography of the mid-nineteenth century" (*The Classic Slave Narratives xvi*). Could Twain have known of Harriet Jacobs? It seems almost impossible that he would not. Contained within his personal library were histories of slavery by Charles Ball and Still as well as Lydia Maria Child's *Anti-Slavery Catechism* (Gribben 43, 141, 666).[5] In addition, after making her escape from the South in 1849, Jacobs moved to Rochester where she joined abolitionists and began working in an anti-slavery reading room and office located above Frederick Douglass 's newspaper, *The North Star* (Yellin xvi). The Langdons were well acquainted with Douglass; Jervis Langdon served as a conductor on the Underground Railroad and had aided Douglass during his escape from slavery (*Mark Twain's Letters. 1867-68 2*: 244). In subsequent year, Douglass was often a guest in the Langdon home. Twain met and spoke with Douglass in December 1869 and later wrote a letter to President Garfield endorsing Douglass for a federal job (*Mark Twain's Letters. 1869 3*: 428). It seems logical that considering the Langdons's times to the Underground Railroad and abolitionist societies and both the Langdons and Twain's personal relationships with Douglass, that they knew of Jacobs's *Incidents*.

This initial transvestite allusion in *Adventures of Huckleberry Finn*, read in isolation from other scenes of transvestism, quickly becomes buried as Huck races along in his narrative. Buried, that is, until the next incident of cross-dressing. Huck, attempting to "find out what was going on," clumsily disguises himself as a girl and inquires at the dwelling of Mrs. Judith Loftus to see if she has any news about the search for him and Jim (47). Loftus informs Huck that she thinks Jim is still in the area—over on Jackson Island. She then proceeds to tell Huck, in precise terms, her husband's plan for the evening. A frightened Huckleberry takes up needle and thread and, after watching him fumble, Mrs. Loftus asks him to throw and catch. Sharp-eyed Mrs. Loftus soon suspects that Huck is not a girl, and after she observes him awkwardly trying to thread a needle, she cleverly devises a series of tests to prove her suspicions: she has Huck throw a lump of lead at a rat and then drops a piece of lead in his skirted lap to see how he catches it—Huck gives scripted "masculine" responses to each of the tests, meaning that his throw is accurate and he clamps his legs together instead of widening them.

After the threading, throwing, and catching is completed, Mrs. Loftus's suspicions have been proven correct: Huck is indeed a boy. Loftus then asks Huckleberry to tell her the real reason he is there: "You just tell me your secret, and trust me. I'll keep it; and what's more, I'll help you. So'll my old man, if you want him to" (52). Mrs. Loftus asks Huck another series of questions to determine if he is from the country or the city and concludes that at least he has not lied to her about his country origin. After his perceptive hostess completes her questions, she then allows Huck to choose his new fake name, George Peters, and cautions him to remember it: "Don't forget and tell me it's Elexander before you go, and then get out by saying it's George-Elexander when I catch you" (53). Before she allows Huck to take his leave, Loftus says "Now trot along to your uncle, Sarah Mary Williams George Elexander Peters [here Loftus verbally acknowledges that Huck's gender identity is still a fabrication], and if you get into trouble you send word to Mrs. Judith Loftus, which is me, and I'll do what I can to get you out of it" (53).

Myra Jehlen poses two important questions in her discussion of the Loftus episode in her essay *"Gender"*: "What is the role in all this of the feminine disguise"; and "Why and to what effect does Huck pass through the crisis of rejecting his born identity dressed as a girl?" (267) What Twain may have been doing in having Huck don female garb is to assist him in gaining insight into Jim's dilemma. Before Huck can understand Jim's plight, he must experience what it means to be powerless. Twain cannot make Huck African-American, but he can make him a girl (granted Huck isn't exactly a privileged member of the Southern elite, although compared to enslaved African-Americans and women he certainly enjoys more personal freedoms).

Dressed as a girl, Huck, under the guidance of Loftus, learns that being female means, among other things, restricted movement and a required lack of intellectual and physical prowess. What is particularly fascinating about Loftus is that, unlike Twain's preceding and subsequent gender-trickster characters, she reveals her methodology for tricking (thus giving her secrets to and, in conjunction, sharing her power with Huck). In other words, working within Gates's definition of the trickster and signifying language, Loftus, a straightdressed gender-trickster, is explaining the art of signifying to the transvestite Huck (*Figures in Black*236-41). The gender-tricksters who appear in Twain's other works act out their roles, either male or female—cross-dressed or not-but never openly discuss and deconstruct the act as Loftus does.

When Loftus tells Huck that missing rats is what girls do, she is giving him a lesson on gender roles and expectations. Loftus is teaching Huck how the game is played, and once the rules are understood by Huck, the implication is not only that he can play but that he can win. Who was once powerless is now empowered. As Mrs. Loftus informs him, "You do a girl tolerable poor, but you might fool men, maybe" (53).

If there are any fools here, Twain seems to be saying, they are those who do not realize that such women as Mrs. Loftus are gender-tricksters who can manipulate and thus subvert socially prescribed gender roles. Huck learns from Loftus the powerlessness associated with female gender; Jim will instruct him about the powerlessness inherent in slavery. Huck, and by implication the reader, will eventually realize that racial hatred is, like gender, a sociocultural construct, not a biological certitude.

There is a close connection between Huck's willingness to cross gender lines and his later act of questioning and rejecting racial categories. These two discourses, race and gender, contain overlapping margins whose intersections surface in the figure of the transvestite. Throughout the novel, Huckleberry (as does Jim) adopts and abandons different male and female disguises as well as rejecting activities considered purely male or female. At the end of the novel, Twain has Jim and Tom share Huck's experience of cross-dressing when the two don Aunt Sally's clothes and flee. With such constancy of crossdressing it may be possible to reinterpret Huck's flight as a response to the death of the father leading to a quest for contact with the feminine.

During the summer of 1883 when Twain was completing work on *Adventures of Huckleberry Finn,* he was also writing *"1,002d Arabian Night"* (*Mark Twain's Satires and Burlesques 88*). While it is true, as (Gillman recognizes, that Twain creates "a hero-heroine pair whose behavior reverses stereotypical masculine and feminine characteristics—but always the sexes are distinguished in terms of traditional traits," unlike *"A Medieval Romance,"* Twain completes the narrative and introduces as the narrator of the tale a third female gender-trickster protagonist (108).

Scherezade, attempting to delay her execution by King Shahriyar, tells him tale *"Number One Thousand and Two."* Her story concerns two babies whose genders are switched at birth. She chronicles the infants' lives and how they eventually marry and have twins. When the cross-dressed pair show their son and daughter to their celebrating subjects, the people wonderingly comment: "To think that the father, and not the mother, should be the mother of the babes! Now of a truth are all things possible with God . . ." (*Mark Twain's Satires and Burlesques 91*; 132). The pair's unconsciousness of possessing each others' supposed "correct" gender is similar to Conrad's apparent unawareness of being raised male in *"Medieval Romance."*

Scherezade keeps extending her story (and her literal deadline), and the King finally dies. It is important to recognize that while Scherezade acts out the part of the acquiescent and submissive female (each time the king interrupts her narrative she meekly replies "I hear and obey"), by the conclusion she has managed to manipulate her prescribed feminine role until she ultimately triumphs in the misogynist King's demise (*Mark Twain's Satires and Burlesques 93*).

The intersections of gender and race manifested in cross-dressing introduced in *Adventures of Huckleberry*

Finn have their fullest rendering nine years later in *Pudd'nhead Wilson*, where various uses of cross-dressing traceable in Twain's earlier works merge in and become inextricable from the narrative. When the reader is first introduced to the world of Dawson's Landing, everything appears to be in order and everyone is carefully controlled: women are firmly deposited in their "sphere," African-Americans know their "place," and the upper class treats the lower strata of society with benign neglect. However, upon closer examination, none of this reflects the reality of the town and its population. As the narrative proceeds, little is as it initially appears to be and all is marked by the figure of the cross-dresser.

Garber argues that category crises "can and do mark displacements from the axis of class as well as from race onto the axis of gender" (17). It is exactly these crises/intersections that form the narrative of *Puddn'head Wilson*. The person upon whom the plot hinges, namely Valet de Chambre, is descended from the recently deceased Colonel Cecil Burleigh Essex, a member of the F.F.V. (First Families of Virginia). Roxana, far from trying to hide her liaison, is outspoken regarding her illicit connection with the upper class: "He was de highest quality in dis whole town—Ol Virginny stock, Fust Famblies, he was" (43). Even before Roxana switches babies, Twain calls her own racial identity into question: "To all intents and purposes Roxy was as white as anybody, but the one-sixteenth of her which was black out-voted the other fifteen" (8). Twain also provides the "percentage" of African-American blood in her son: "Her child was thirty-one parts white, and he, too, was a slave, and by a fiction of law and custom a negro" (9).[6] In addition, Roxana does not remain in her "place," rather at age thirty-five when she is freed she leaves Dawson's Landing to work on a river boat and carefully invests her money so that she may enjoy a worry-free retirement—only to later lose her savings in a bank failure.

Frederick Anderson notes that the way Twain explored what he terms "multiple identity" can be observed in a summary of the roles taken by Chambre and Roxana. Anderson first describes Chambre's instances of cross-dressing: "There are, in sequence, that of a white man with a beard, a young white woman, an old white woman (whose clothes Tom borrows from his Negro mother), a young Negro woman wearing a veil, and finally 'a disguise proper for a tramp'" (294-95).[7] In adopting these various disguises, Anderson contends, Chambre makes "multiple interchanges of sex, race, and social position" even though he must simultaneously maintain "the role of a respectable member of the family of the town's leading citizen, and a corrupt and dissolute gambler in St. Louis. When he learns of his Negro heritage he must assume the further role of a Negro passing as white" (295). Chambre's blurring of social classes, racial categories, and gender roles is indicative of an epistemological crisis in the novel that Twain would deliberately leave unresolved.

Of course, Roxana also acts out a transvestite role, necessitated by her escape from enslavement in the deep South. As Anderson points out, Roxana must "disguise herself further by blackening her face in order to make her skin color conform to her Negro speech" (295). When the history of this crossdressing duo is traced it becomes evident that Chambre's male power, position in society, and racial superiority decrease each time he assumes female garb, while Roxana's transvestism has the inverse effect. When Roxana enters her son's room during a rainy night in St. Louis, Chambre sees what he thinks is a man's back. The unknown man proceeds to turn around and a frightened Chambre tries to order him away, but he is silenced—for the first time in the text. In the course of their conversation, Roxana deduces that Chambre is lying about the bill for her capture, hatches a plan for Chambre to buy back her freedom, and makes him walk with her to the wharf while she keeps a knife ready to plunge into him at the slightest provocation. The Roxana in this scene is quite a departure from the helpless young mother who, earlier in the narrative, contemplated suicide as her only recourse. Like Huck, she has had a lesson in power—and uses it to her advantage.

Much of the material Twain uses in *Pudd'nhead Wilson* can be found in the slavery narratives of Roxana's real-life counterparts, Ellen Craft and Harriet Jacobs. Just two pages into the Craft's narrative, they challenge the existence of a definable black and white binary: "slavery in America is not at all confined to persons of any particular complexion; there are a very large number of slaves as white as any one . . ." (2-3). This strategy is echoed by Twain when he reveals Roxana and Chambre's blood "percentages" at the beginning of chapter two.

But it is in Jacobs's *Incidents* that the most parallels can be made. Like Roxana, the unmarried Jacobs enters into a sexual liaison with an upper-class European-American male. While both suffer feelings of guilt, it is less for themselves than for the legacy they have brought upon their children. As Jacobs explains, "I will not try to screen myself behind the plea of compulsion from a master; for it was not so. Neither can I plead ignorance or thoughtlessness . . . I knew what I did, and I did it with deliberate calculation" (xxx). Both Jacobs and Roxana have bills posted for their capture, both cross-dress, and both must darken their faces with charcoal in order to pass as African-American.

Gillman recognizes that Chambre and Roxana, in darkening their faces and cross-dressing, "conflate" gender and racial categories. According to Gillman, this combining, "explicitly pursued by Twain after *Pudd'nhead Wilson* . . . comes through partially even here: if 'male' and 'female' are as readily interchanged as 'black' and 'white,' then gender difference may prove to be as culturally constituted"

(79). To echo Twain, such distinctions would eventually he recognized as "a fiction of law and custom." Yet, the question that Twain poses in *Pudd'nhead Wilson* and tries in part to answer is: what does one do with this fiction, and how does it fit into preconceived narrative structures? While acknowledging the possibility of conflation, Gillman cautions that if a pattern of association is established between the two categories, "we must ourselves be careful . . . not to blur distinctions" (102). But this is exactly what Twain is trying to do and what Garber identifies: "*Pudd'nhead Wilson* is in fact an exemplary instance of the category crisis, the slippage from one borderline to another, in this case race to gender, or gender to race, marked by the appearance of the transvestite" (289).

This "slippage" of borderlines, how to conceive of this blurring of distinctions and how to understand these intersections, is not restricted to nineteenth-century prose but is also clearly a contemporary issue. Twain did not wait until after *Pudd'nhead Wilson* to explore the social and cultural constitutions of race and gender; actually he began this investigation in his earliest tale of gender switching, and his examination continued into the last years of his life.[8] Gillman is correct in that both gender and racial differences were highly important topics to Twain; however, Twain's investigations of gender constructs using the figure of the transvestite preceded his focus on race. In creating cross-dressing characters Chambre and Roxana, Twain shatters such binaries as what it means to be African-American and European-American, master and slave, and male and female. By the end of the story when Tom is sold down the river, former ways of knowing, have by necessity, been abandoned, and an epistemological crisis looms as no new systems have been constructed to replace the old.

By the end of the story, this intersection of race and gender as evidenced by the figure of the transvestite has so disrupted the world that was Dawson's Landing that there will be no hope of ever restoring it. Within *Pudd'nhead Wilson* there are several related category crises: the first is, again, slavery; the second is reconstruction (it is worth taking into account that Twain wrote *Pudd'nhead Wilson* thirty-two years after emancipation in the aftermath of the failure of Reconstruction), and the third is the difficulty in trying to narrate the reality of the African-American female experience.

In Twain's writing after *Pudd'nhead Wilson*, cross-dressing was a frequent occurrence. Twain's historical transvestite novel, *Personal Recollections of Joan of Arc*, features a young woman whose objective is transgressing defined social boundaries. Joan's transvestism results in some of the most injurious accusations leveled against her at her trial. Among the sixty-six articles with which she is charged are "discard[ing] the decencies and proprieties of her sex" and "irreverently assuming the dress of a man and the vocation of a soldier" (377). When Joan makes her first appearance in court, she approaches the bench in male apparel: "A wide collar of this same black stuff lay in radiating folds upon her shoulders and breast; the sleeves of her doublet were full, down to the elbows, and tight thence to her manacled wrists; below the doublet, tight black hose down to the chains on her ankles" (352).

When Joan is asked by the court whether she would remove her male attire if she were allowed communion, Joan replies: "When one receives the sacrament, the manner of his dress is a small thing and of no value in the eyes of Our Lord" (378). After this response, the court charges Joan with being "stubborn" (379). In conjunction with her transvestism, she is castigated for performing a traditional male role in choosing combat and "deserting the industries proper to her sex" (379). Joan finally loses patience with the court's attempts to "resex" her and responds: "Peace!

Without the permission of God I will not lay it off [her male clothing] though you cut off my head" (380).

In two incomplete short stories written within one year of *Personal Recollections of Joan of Arc* Twain continues his experiments with gender sans transvestism. In "John Brown and Mary Taylor," no cross-dressing occurs, although there is a crossing-over of gender characteristics. John Brown's distinguishing traits are shyness and passivity, and he is described as "good, gentle, bashful, timid" (*Mark Twain's Short Stories*381). Mary Taylor, on the other hand, is an active, thoughtful, problem- solver and leader of a band of women.

The story commences with Brown, a fussily dressed Presbyterian Sundayschool superintendent, driving his carriage to Mary Taylor's home to propose marriage. Four miles into his journey, a gust of wind flips off his straw boater and it flies into a creek. Unwilling to present himself to his intended less than completely outfitted, Brown strips and wades into the stream. When he emerges from the water, he discovers that his buggy has disappeared. He chases and catches his horse and dresses himself from the upper body down—but before he can don his pants he spies four women approaching him and he quickly covers himself with his new white, embroidered, linen lap-robe. Coming down the lane are Mary, her mother, and two elderly friends. Mary asks John to drive the aged sisters home and then return. The highly embarrassed Brown, who has remained silent throughout the exchange with the women except to say he is unwell, is relieved upon hearing Mary's plan but he quickly becomes alarmed when she reaches out her hand for the lap-robe. At that point, Twain ends the story and then mischievously adds that it is "the reader's privilege to determine for himself how the thing came out" (387).

In "Hellfire Hotchkiss," like in "1,002d Arabian Night," Twain presents a second female-male couple with switched genders (although neither crossdress). Rachel, nicknamed "Hellfire," is a fearless heroine who possesses superior athletic ability and rescues a frightened, weeping Oscar "Thug" Carpenter from drowning. In a scene reminiscent of the drowned woman episode in *Adventures of Huckleberry Finn*, Rachel casts aside her bonnet and shawl and leaps into the icy Mississippi with a whiskey flask tucked inside her "bosom" (*Mark Twain's Satires and Burlesques*189). Hellfire, though, unlike the unfortunate drowned woman, does not succumb to the currents of the river. Instead, after arriving at the emergency scene astride her "great black horse" she swims to the ice floe, makes Thug strap on a life preserver, and pulls him to shore.

Despite initial approbation from the townspeople who witnessed her selfless heroics, Hellfire is later informed by her Aunt Betsy that gossips are maligning her "masculine" ways. After agreeing to cease riding astraddle and going hunting, boating and skating with male companions, Rachel laments: "Oh, everything seems to be made wrong, nothing seems to [be] the way it ought to be" (*Mark Twain's Satires and Burlesques*199). Here is a marked tonal shift to Twain's later gender-switch stories. Instead of the humor and eventual success of the gender-trickster in " 1,002d Arabian Night," in "Hellfire Hotchkiss" there is a sense of society closing in and crushing those who tempt to transgress rigid gender bifurcations.

In 1904 Twain completed a short story involving a couple with exchanged genders, namely the extraordinary "The $30,000 Bequest" (*Mark Twain Collected Tales*597-626). Twain's prior gender-switch tales, "John Brown and Mary Taylor" and Hellfire Hotchkiss" practically serve as drafts of this later, completed piece. "The $30,000 Bequest" features two main characters: "Saladin Foster" nicknamed "Sally" and "Electra Foster" nicknamed "Aleck." Sally is a devoted husband and father who daydreams about spending a thirty thousand dollar bequest to be left to him by a distant male relative on the occasion of his death. Aleck is a loving wife and mother as well as a talented money manager and investor.

The story consists of the two fantasizing about investing and spending their future bequest until Aleck has managed to parlay the initial thirty thousand dollars into an imaginary three hundred million. All is lost, though, in the imaginary Wall Street crash and both Sally and Aleck are plunged into despair. After their fantasy bankruptcy, the story ends with the pair discovering that the relative left no estate at his death and the town was forced to pay for his burial. The discovery that there will be no forthcoming money shatters the make-believe world the two have constructed together and the tale concludes with their deaths.

The remainder of Twain's transvestite writings, *Following the Equator*, *"Wapping Alice," "How Nancy Jackson Married Kate Wilson,"* and *"A Horse's Tale"* all contain cross-dressing themes and subject matter traceable to earlier works. Twain's difficulties with *"Wapping Alice"* (also never completed), especially in his wavering in deciding whether *"Wapping Alice"* is male or female, is reminiscent of his inability to complete the narrative in *"A Medieval Romance." Following the Equator* returns to the twin issues of race and gender, and Twain again treads upon familiar ground when he describes his young Singhalese man-servant in ways that denote him as belonging to an indeterminate world. Gillman observes that in describing the young man, Twain draws a connection between race and sex: "a world between: between black and white, masculine and feminine" (99). Such indeterminacy has already been expressed most poignantly by a bitter Tom Driscoll when he replies to Roxana: "Bofe of us is imitation white—dat's what we is—en pow'full good imitation, too—Yah-yah-yah!—we don't 'mount to noth'n as imitation niggers" (35).

"How Nancy Jackson Married Kate Wilson" bears certain similarities to *"A Medieval Romance"* and the Loftus scene in *Adventures of Huckleberry Finn*. This story contains two gender-tricksters who act against each other. Nancy Jackson has been involved in a murder and is forced by Thomas Furlong, the witness, to don male dress, move away from home, and forever after be known as Robert Finlay. After securing Nancy's promise to do as he tells her, Furlong, in a take-off of the Loftus scene, tells Nancy to put on the clothes of a lynched African-American man and to burn her dress: "I'll trim your head and make a young fellow of you. Every day you'll practice, and I'll help you; and by and by when you're letter perfect and can walk and act like a male person and the lynch-fever has blown over, I'll take you out of this region some night and see you safe over the border and on your way" (How Nancy Jackson Married Kate Wilson103).

While Furlong is giving lessons on gender-tricking to Nancy, Kate Wilson is failing in love with a young male stranger who will soon desert her. Panicked because she is pregnant and abandoned by the young man, Kate decides to make her father's new hired hand, "Robert Finlay," fall in love with her. She asks Robert to kiss her and is furious when he does not respond. Kate then informs her parents that Robert is the father of her unborn child and they are forced to wed. As in *"Medieval Romance,"* the cross-dressed female trickster is ultimately outfoxed by the female tricking within her feminine gender.

Twain's last transvestite tale, "A Horse's Tale," written during the fall of 1905, owes much to Twain's youngest daughter, Jean Clemens, and to *Personal Recollections Joan of Arc*.[9] The heroine of the story, nine-year-old Cathy Allison, is sent to live with her uncle, General Allison, after the death of her parents in Europe. Cathy travels to the western territory from Rouen, France (the site of Joan's trial and execution), and immediately becomes the fort's darling. She is made an officer and routinely inspects her soldiers and returns salutes while dressed in medieval military garb similar to the description of Joan's clothes.

After all this exchanging of clothing, it seems fair to ask if Twain himself ever transgressed into cross-dressing. Quite often so it appears. An avid participant in charades and family drama productions, Twain would readily outfit himself to meet the demands of the moment. Sandra Gilbert and Susan Gubar assert that "for the most part . . . men of letters tended to wear clothes that emphasized some version of masculinity, as if to suggest that the right garments reflect the right relationship not only between the sexes but between anatomy and destiny" (327). This was not the case with Twain. Perhaps in part due to his wife and her family's influence or perhaps because of his own evolving views on race and gender, Twain proved to be willing to explore what other authors feared. Indeed his life might be viewed as a series of categorical crises: impoverished/wealthy, Confederate/Yankee, westerner/easterner, humorous short story writer/serious novelist and social commentator. Twain's personal involvement in cross-dressing quite possibly reflects his willingness to engage the issue fictionally, and his apparent eagerness to don female dress may have allowed him to escape (albeit briefly) and thereby challenge stifling constructions of masculinity. In his life and his writing, Twain extravagantly proved Garber's thesis that "transvestism is a space of possibility structuring and confounding culture."

The most touching artifact of Twain's transvestism is a photograph taken circa 1890 of the author and his eldest daughter, Susy. In the picture the two are posing on the porch of a rustic cabin holding hands high above their heads. Susy is dressed as a princess with a cape, and her father is wearing a woman's dress over rolled-up long underwear with a bonnet on his head and a hot water bottle hanging from his neck. Looking as though he was photographed in the midst of a merry jig, Twain, trickster himself, never stopped dancing between the accepted and the taboo.

NOTES

1. In coining the term "gender-trickster," I am indebted to Henry Louis Gates, Jr.'s discussion of African-American trickster figures and signifying language in *Figures in Black* 236-41. Also useful is Lawrence Levine's chapter on signifying language in *Black Cultures and Black Consciousness* (New York: Oxford UP, 1978) 103, 121-23.

   By gender-trickster, I mean several different categories: characters who successfully cross-dress are gender-tricksters, while those characters whose attempts to crossdress fail (as when Huckleberry dons a dress) are not. Gender-tricksters need not necessarily be cross-dressed. These are characters who either recognize gender as a construction and openly identify it as such (Judith Loftus is the best example), or characters who are clearly manipulating stereotypical gender characteristics without identifying they are doing so Kate Jackson is such an example).

   Marjorie Garber divides her discussion of cross-dressing into two sections entitled Transvestite Logic and Transvestite Effects. According to Garber, "transvestite logic" occurs when "transvestism creates culture," and "transvestite effects" when .culture creates transvestites." Garber argues that "one of the most consistent and effective functions of the transvestite in culture is to indicate the place of . . . 'category crisis,' disrupting and calling attention to cultural, social, or aesthetic dissonances . . ." This "category crisis" indicates a "failure of definitional distinction"; in other words, "a borderline that becomes permeable, that permits of border crossing from one . . . category to another": such as male/female, master/slave, black/white, and at various points between the binaries. Therefore, the figure of the cross-dresser becomes a sign for "development [and] progress" (16). The crux of Garber's argument is that "transvestism is a space of possibility structuring and confounding culture" (17).

2. For a detailed history of the Langdon family's political and social activism, including acts of public cross-dressing, see chapters 4 and 5 in Laura Skandera-Trombley's *Mark Twain in the Company of Women* (Philadelphia: U of Pennsylvania P, 1994).

3. Albert Bigelow Paine records how as a young boy Twain, accompanied by several friends, found the body of a drowned slave in a swamp, *Mark Twain: A Biography* (New York: Harper, 1912) 64.

4. Gillman argues that "conflating categories of gender identification with racial categories" first takes place in *Pudd'nhead Wilson* and would be continued in *Following the Equator* (79). I contend that Twain's combining of gender and race first began with this hint in *Adventures of Huckleberry Finn* and would be pursued in the above two works.

5. The three works as listed in Gribben: Charles Ball, *Slavery in the United States: A Narrative of the Life and Adventures of Charles Ball, a Black Man, who Lived Forty Years in Maryland, South Carolina and Georgia, as a Slave*, Forty Years in Maryland, South Carolina and Georgia, as a Slave (1837) 43; Lydia Maria Child , *Anti-Slavery Catechism* (Newburyport, 1836) 141. [Bound as a volume with W.E. Channing's *Letter on Slavery*, along with five other pamphlets.]; William Still, *The Underground Rail Road: A Record of Facts, Authentic Narratives, Letters, &c., Narrating the Hardships, Hair-breadth escapes, and Death Struggles of the Slaves in Their Efforts Freedom, by Themselves and Others, or Witnessed by the Author* (1883) 666.

   Sholom S. Kahn, in a recent *Mark Twain Circular* article, Mark Twain's 'Original Jacobs's: A Probable Explanation, contends that the title of chapter fifty in *Life on the Mississippi*, The Original Jacobs, is attributable to Linda

Brent's work: "I want to propose that in the title he gave to Chapter 50 of *LOM*, Clemens was alluding to Jacobs's *Incidents in the Life of a Slave Girl Written by Herself* . . ." (8 Jan-Mar 1994): 4-6. In addition, Kahn reasons that it is likely that Twain had Brent's narrative in mind when he composed "A True Story" (4).

6. The conception and formulation of race is still a problematic issue in American law. Michael Omi and Howard Winant, in a chapter entitled Racial Formation, in *Racial Formation in the United States* (New York: Routledge, 1994) include the following example of how the law classifies and quantifies racial identity:

   In 1982-83, Susie Guillory Phipps unsuccessfully sued the Louisiana Bureau of Vital Records to change her racial classification from black to white. The descendant of an 18th-century white planter and a black slave, Phipps was designated 'black' on her birth certificate in accordance with a 1970 state law which declared anyone with at least 1/32nd 'Negro blood' to be black. In the end, Phipps lost. The court upheld the state's right to classify and quantify racial identity . . . Phipps's problematic racial identity, and her effort to resolve it through state action, is in many ways a parable of America's unsolved racial dilemma. It illustrates the difficulties of defining race and assigning individuals or groups to racial categories. It shows how the racial legacies of the past—slavery and bigotry—continue to shape the present. (53)

7. I agree with Anderson; nonetheless it should be noted that what Anderson terms as examples of "multiple identity" are those places in the text where the transvestite forces various displacements of the kind Garber identifies.

8. Gillman argues that while Twain "unequivocally condemned racial stereotypes . . . his writing circles more hesitantly around the whole problem of gender difference, sometimes affirming, sometimes denying that such a clear-cut system of difference does in fact exist. In short, Twain shows himself to be more aware of the invidiousness of racial than sexual stereotypes" (102).

9. In April 1905, *Harper's Weekly*, published a short story by Jean Clemens, "A Word for the Horses," describing the mistreatment of horses by riders using checkreins and martingales. Twain was apparently encouraged by Jean to write a short story exposing Spanish cruelties to bulls and horses used in bullfighting. Twain's "A Horse's Tale" was first published in *Harper's Magazine* in August and September of 1906 and again in 1907 in book form [Everett Emerson, *The Authentic Mark Twain: A Literary, Biography of Samuel L. Clemens* (Philadelphia: U of Pennsylvania P, 1984) 260-61.]

REFERENCES

Anderson, Frederick. Mark Twain and the Writing of Pudd'nhead Wilson. *Pudd'nhead Wilson and Those Extraordinary Twins*. Ed. Sidney Berger. NewYork: Norton, 1980.

Craft, William and Ellen Craft. *Running a Thousand Miles for Freedom*. New York: Amo, 1969.

Freedman, Florence. *Introduction. Running a Thousand Miles for Freedom*. New York: Arno, 1969.

Garber, Marjorie. *Vested Interests: Cross-Dressing and Cultural Anxiety*. New York: Routledge, 1992.

Gates, Henry Louis Jr., ed. *Classic Slave Narratives*. New York: Penguin, 1987.

—. *Figures in Black: Words, Signs, and the "Racial" Self*. New York: Oxford UP, 1987.

Gilbert, Sandra, and Susan Gubar. *No Man's Land: The Place of the Woman Writer in the Twentieth Century*. Vol 2: Sexchanges. New Haven: Yale UP, 1989.

Gillman, Susan. *Dark Twins: Imposture and Identity in Mark Twain's America*. Chicago: U of Chicago P, 1989.

Gribben, Alan. *Mark Twain's Library: A Reconstruction*. 2 vols. Boston: G.K. Hall, 1980.

Jacobs, Harriet. *Incidents in the Life of a Slave Girl. Ed. Jean Fagan Yellin*. Cambridge: Harvard UP, 1987.

Jehlen, Myra. Gender. *Critical Terms for Literary Study*. Ed. Frank Lentricchia and Thomas McLaughlin. Chicago: U of Chicago P, 1990.

Twain, Mark. *Adventures of Huckleberry Finn*. Ed. Sculley Bradley. New York: Norton, 1977.

—. "How Nancy Jackson Married Kate Wilson." Ed. Robert Sattelmeyer. *The Missouri Review 10* (1987): 97-112.

—. *Mark Twain Collected Tales, Sketches, Speeches, and Essays 1891-1910*. New York: Library of America, n.d.

—. *Mark Twain's Letters. 1867-1868*. Ed. Harriet Smith and Richard Bucci. Vol. 2. Berkeley: U of California P, 1990.

—. *Mark Twain's Letters. 1869*. Ed. Victor Fischer and Michael Frank. Vol. 3. Berkeley: U of California P, 1993.

—. *Mark Twain's Satires and Burlesques*. Ed. Franklin R. Rogers. Berkeley: U of California P, 1967.

—. *Mark Twain's Short Stories*. Ed. Justin Kaplan. New York: New American Library, 1985.

—. *Personal Recollections of Joan of Arc*. San Francisco: Ignatius, 1989.

—. *Pudd'nbead Wilson and Those Extraordinary Twins*. Ed. Sidney E. Berger. New York: Norton, 1980.

—. *The Signet Classic Book of Mark Twain's Short Stories*. Ed. Justin Kaplan. New York: Penguin, 1985.

Index

❑❑❑